UPMINSTER
THROUGH TIME

Michael Foley

Michael Foley

AMBERLEY

To Emma Marston, for all your kind remarks.

First published 2016

Amberley Publishing
The Hill, Stroud, Gloucestershire, GL5 4EP
www.amberley-books.com

ISBN 978 1 4456 5995 4 (print)
ISBN 978 1 4456 5996 1 (ebook)

British Library Cataloguing in Publication Data.
A catalogue record for this book is available from the British Library.

Typesetting by Amberley Publishing.
Printed in Great Britain.

Supporters

The publisher and author would like to extend thanks to the following:

Peter Stewart, Havering Museum
Havering Museum is proud to support *Upminster Through Time.*

Acknowledgements

Although every attempt has been made to find the copyright owners of all the illustrations, I would like to apologise to anyone whose copyright has been unintentionally breached.

I would like to thank some of those who have helped me put this book together: John Drury, whose own *History of Upminster and Cranham* was such a help, as well as the advice he gave me and the kind use of a number of his images; Havering Libraries' Local Studies department, for the use of some of their images; and Swan Books, Upminster's independent bookshop, for the use of some of their postcards. I would also like to thank the Upminster and Hornchurch History Group on Facebook for their help in finding the location of one of the cards used in this book.

About the Author

www.michael-foley-history-writer.co.uk

Previous books published by Amberley:
Essex At War Through Time
Martello Towers
Essex Through Time
London Through Time
London's Docklands Through Time
Ilford Through Time
Havering Through Time
London's East End Through Time
Barking and Dagenham Through Time
Essex at War in Old Photographs

Introduction

Upminster began life as a small village which was, in many ways, overshadowed by its near neighbour Hornchurch, with its leather manufacturers and its old priory. In the past, the road that now leads between the two villages was no more than a track crossing the River Ingrebourne, which marked the boundary between the two villages.

As well as the village of Upminster, there were two other nearby villages that had close connections. These were Cranham and Corbets Tey. As Upminster has grown alongside the other two sites, the differences between the three villages has become less obvious and now they are seen as part of a larger Upminster.

Despite it being a smaller village than Hornchurch, Upminster may have had earlier origins than its neighbour, with a church that can be dated back to the seventh century, although much of the present building dates from the thirteenth century. There was obviously some early settlement in the surrounding area because in 1937 a Romford archaeologist, Mr G. T. Carter, found traces of early Stone, Bronze and Iron Age life in a sandpit in Gerpins Lane, close to the border between Upminster and Rainham. This included two Saxon glass drinking horns that are now in the British Museum.

Up until the nineteenth century, the village of Upminster remained as nothing more than a small rural settlement. Upminster has managed to retain its atmosphere as a small pastoral area surrounded by farms and large estates up to the present day. One of the most notable landmarks in the area is the Upminster Windmill which stands by the road between Hornchurch and Upminster and perfectly fits the rural feel of the town. The largest influence on the town's development should have been the arrival of the railway, which came much later than its arrival at nearby Romford. There was a gap of more than forty years between the station opening at Romford and the railway reaching Upminster; although there had been a station at nearby Harold Wood since 1869, it was not until 1885 before the trains began to stop at the new Upminster station.

The planned opening of a new railway line between Upminster and Romford in 1882 led to a dispute between two of the rail companies of the period. Both the Great Eastern Railway and the London, Tilbury & Southend Railway wanted to run lines to Southend. When the LT&SR wanted to build a line to Romford, the GER wanted to also as it would give them further access to the new Tilbury Docks.

The dispute involved local landowners. Col Champion Russell was in support of the new line, perhaps because he was a prospective director of the company. Henry Holmes, once of Harwood Hall and by this time of Grey Towers, was strongly against the plan. He said that it would lower the value of his home since the embankment would block his view, which at the time stretched all the way to the Thames.

Unlike other local areas where the arrival of the railway led to a great expansion in house building, in Upminster it did not happen immediately. It was to be well into the twentieth century before local landowners began to sell their land to builders such as Peter Griggs, who had an influence on building in Ilford and was to be their MP. He then built on part of the Upminster Hall Estate before the First World War.

Although building continued after the First World War, Upminster still retained its rural atmosphere with much of the land to the south of the station being relatively untouched by development. This began to change drastically in the 1930s. Between then and the beginning of the Second World War, Upminster began to expand on a grander scale as other local landowners began to sell their land, and the large estates that once covered the area were broken up. Unfortunately, the growth of house building led to the destruction of many of the larger houses that had stood around the village outskirts in the past.

There were also changes in the boundaries in the local areas as the town grew. In 1934, Upminster became part of the Hornchurch Urban District, which also included areas as far out into Essex as North Ockendon and Great Warley. In 1965, Upminster became part of the London Borough of Havering, which, in 1993, lost part of Great Warley to Essex, with the new border being close to the M25.

Upminster today, along with its neighbours Cranham and Corbets Tey, has retained many of the features that it had in the past. There are still open fields surrounding much of the area and, unlike other nearby towns, there has been little growth of industry. It remains a mainly residential area with a large shopping centre but has its own character; it has manged to retain some independent businesses, including one of the few remaining independent bookshops with a strong connection to thelocal history.

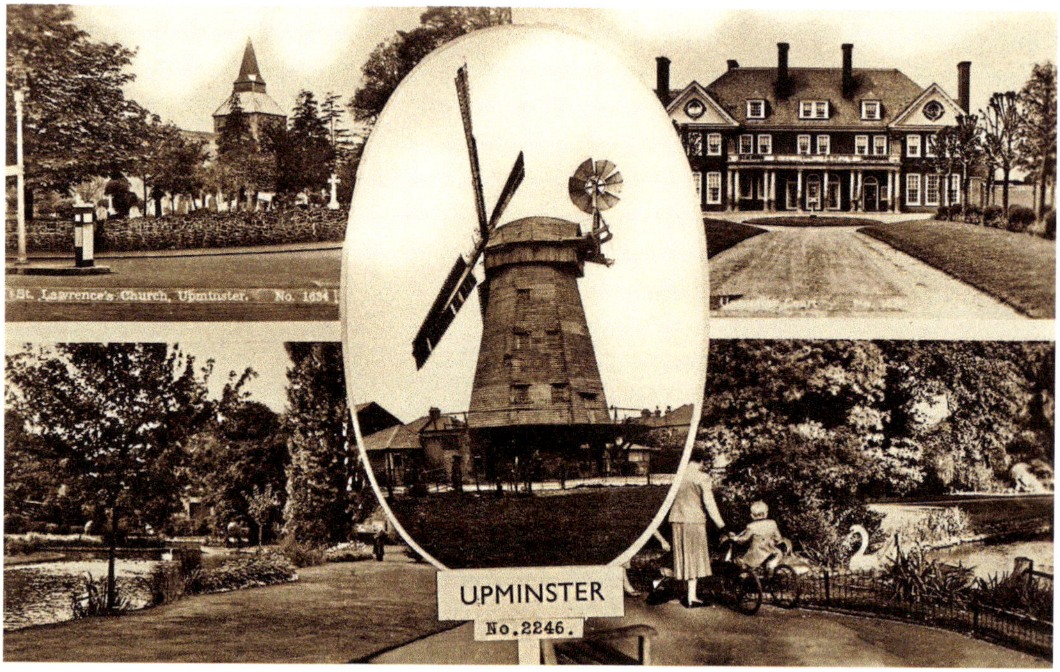

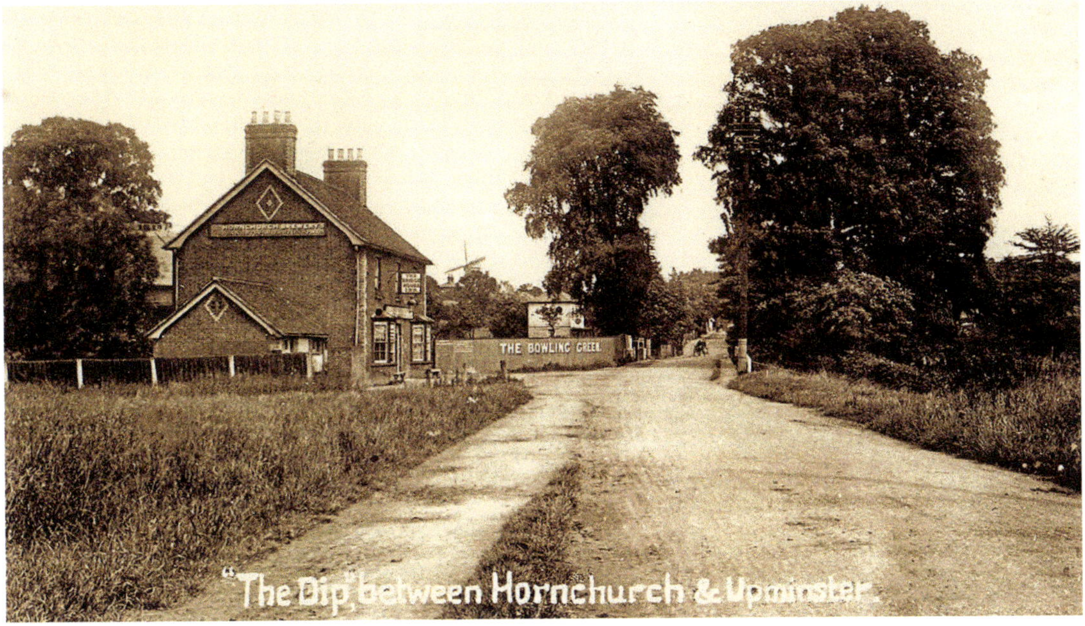

The Road to Hornchurch

The road between Upminster and Hornchurch was once no more than a farm track, but is now a busy road. Hornchurch High Street ends at the Hacton Lane crossroads and becomes Upminster Road until it crosses the Ingrebourne River, which has always been seen as the border between the two towns. It then becomes St Mary's Lane, although part of it was known as Hornchurch Road until 1922. There used to be an old gasometer built in the 1880s next to the Bridge House pub but this was removed in the 1940s. The old cottages on the left used to be the workhouse. The Bridge House still stands, but it is now called the Windmill.

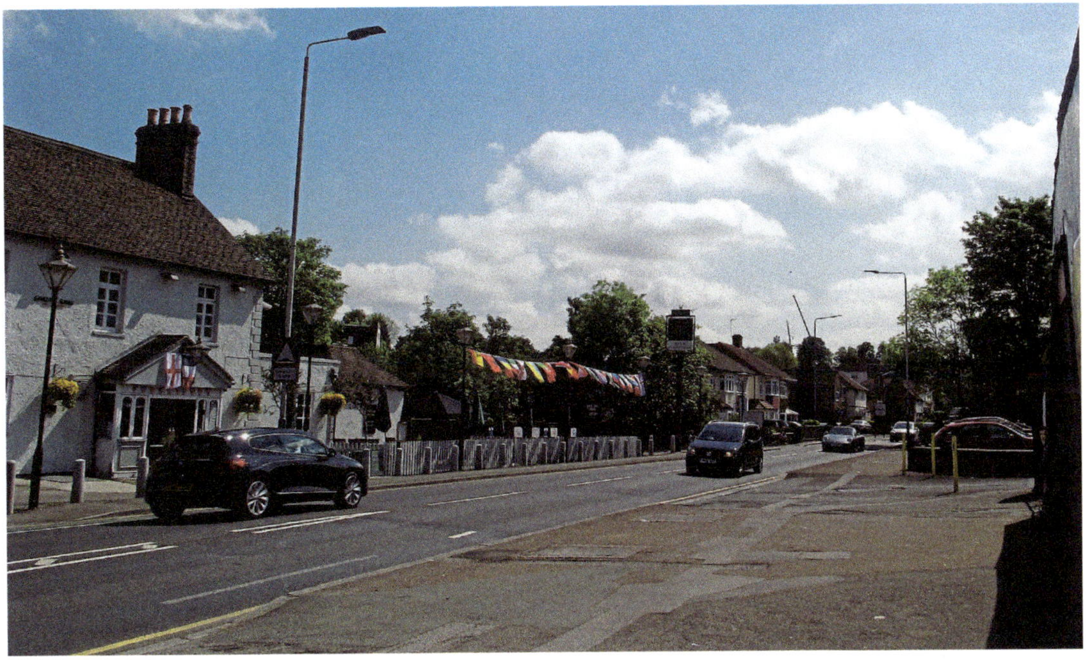

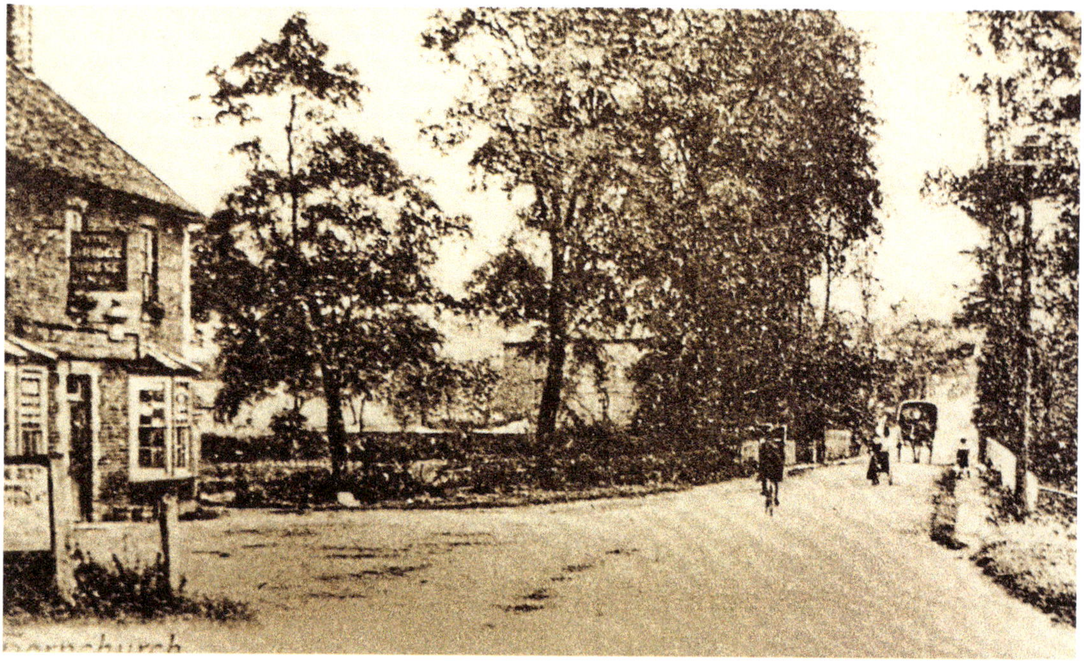

Upminster Hill

Parts of the hill still retain its rural appearance with a number of trees. There have, however, been some changes with several more modern buildings lining the roadway. Some of the older buildings have remained, with the rising ground providing the ideal position for the windmill. There is also the old building, Hill Place, on the right.

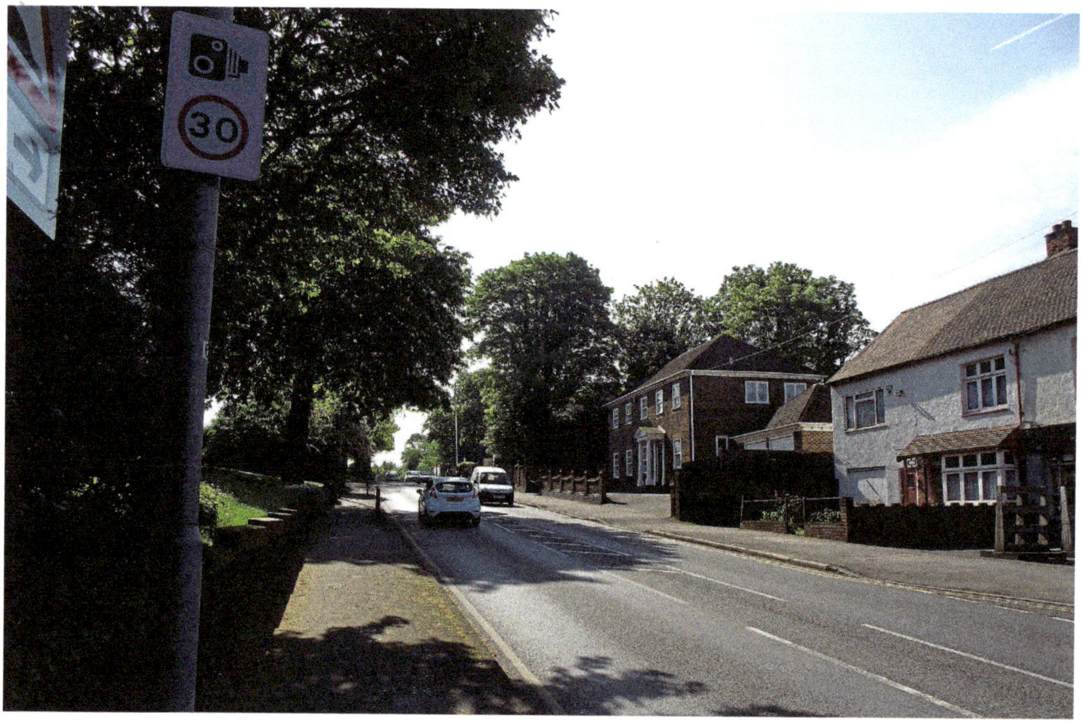

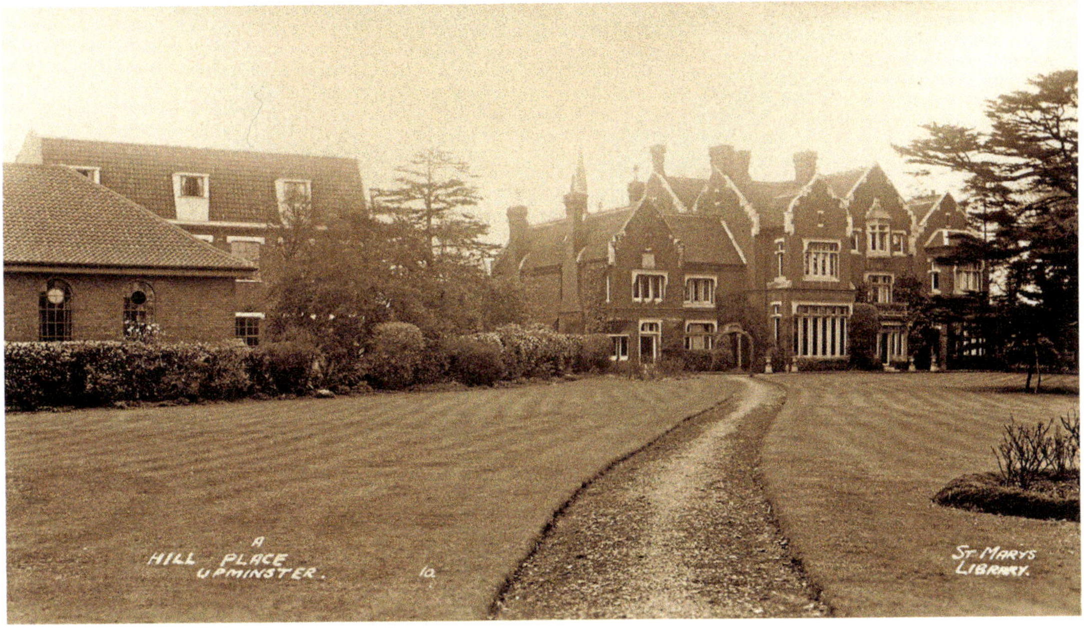

Hill Place

Hill Place dates back to the late eighteenth century and, after changing hands a number of times, the name was changed from Hill House to Hill Place. It was purchased by the Catholic Church in 1927 and became part of the convent school that is still there today. The building is now, at the time of writing, being converted to apartments and houses are being constructed in the grounds. The building was surrounded by large hoardings when the modern image was taken. (With thanks to Havering Libraries Local Studies Dept)

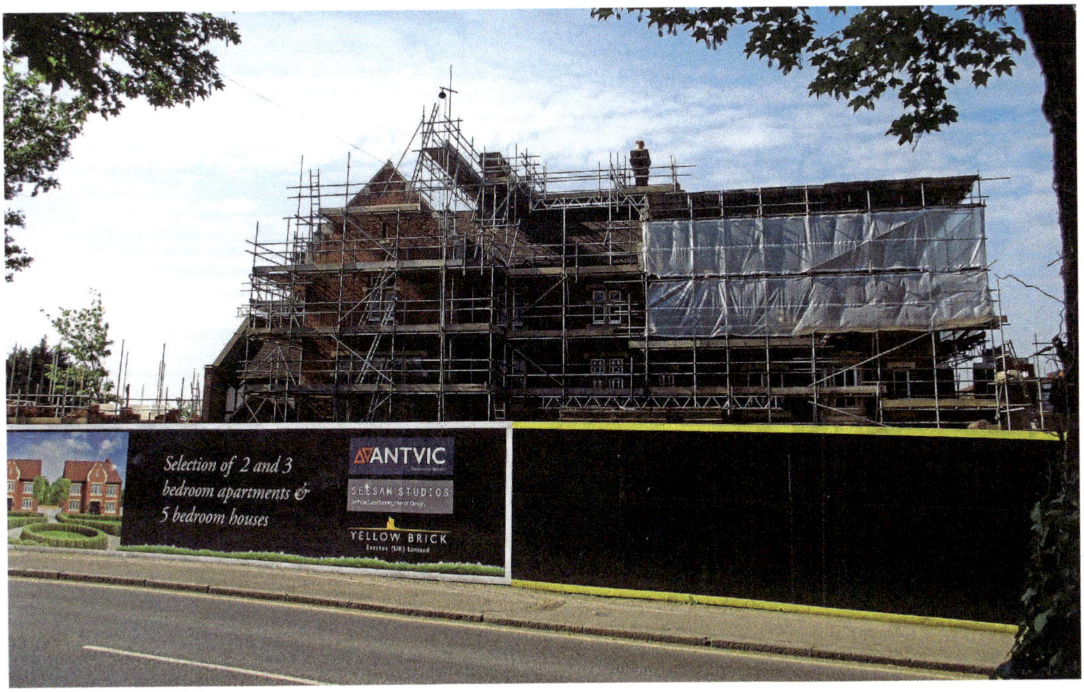

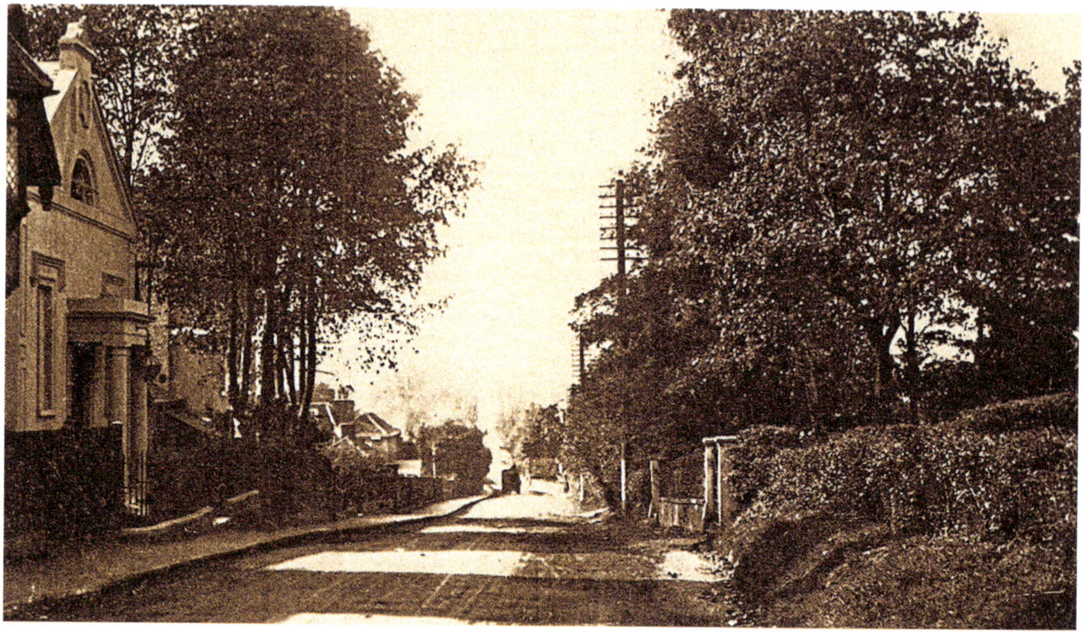

The Old Chapel

The Old Chapel dates back to around 1800 when it was used by Protestant Nonconformists. It was built by Samuel Hammond and was in use for over 100 years until a new Congregational church was built in Station Road in 1910. The building was used by other worshippers up until 1989. The chapel was left unused for many years and fell into a state of disrepair. It has now been refurbished and is used for a number of local history meetings and other public uses. The spire of St Andrew's Church in Hornchurch is visible in the newer photograph.

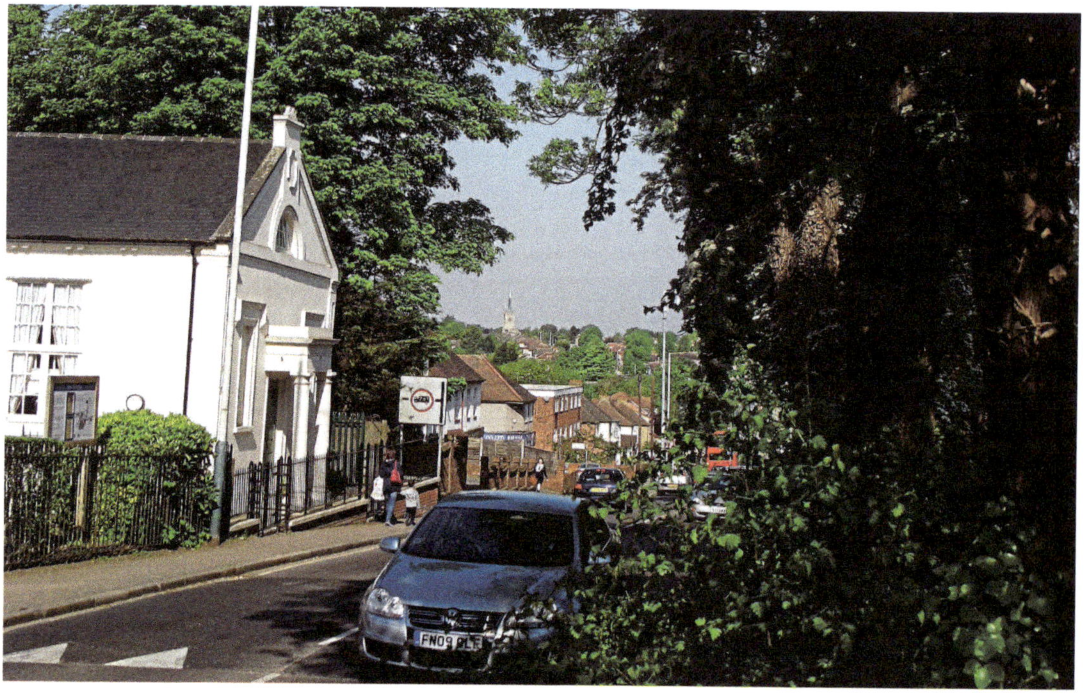

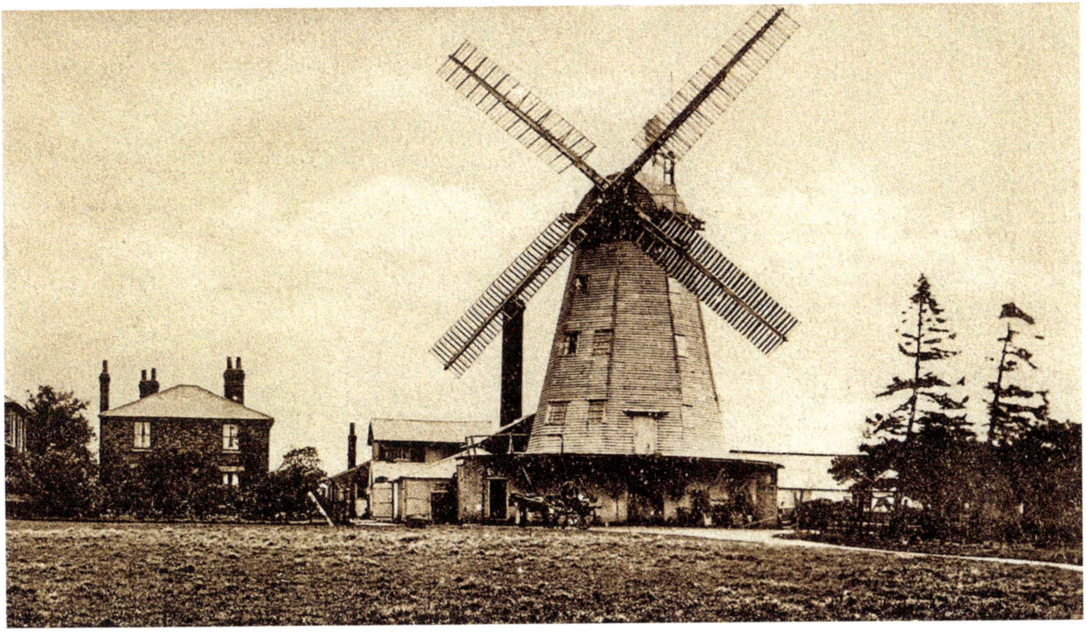

The Windmill I

The Upminster Windmill is a smock mill that was built in 1803 by John Noakes of Hunt's Farm in Corbets Tey on land that was owned by his brother, who also farmed in the area. In 1811, a steam engine was added and the mill worked by both steam and wind for many years. It was owned by a number of men after passing out of the hands of the Noakes family. The construction of an education centre is now underway next to the mill, as can be seen in the modern image.

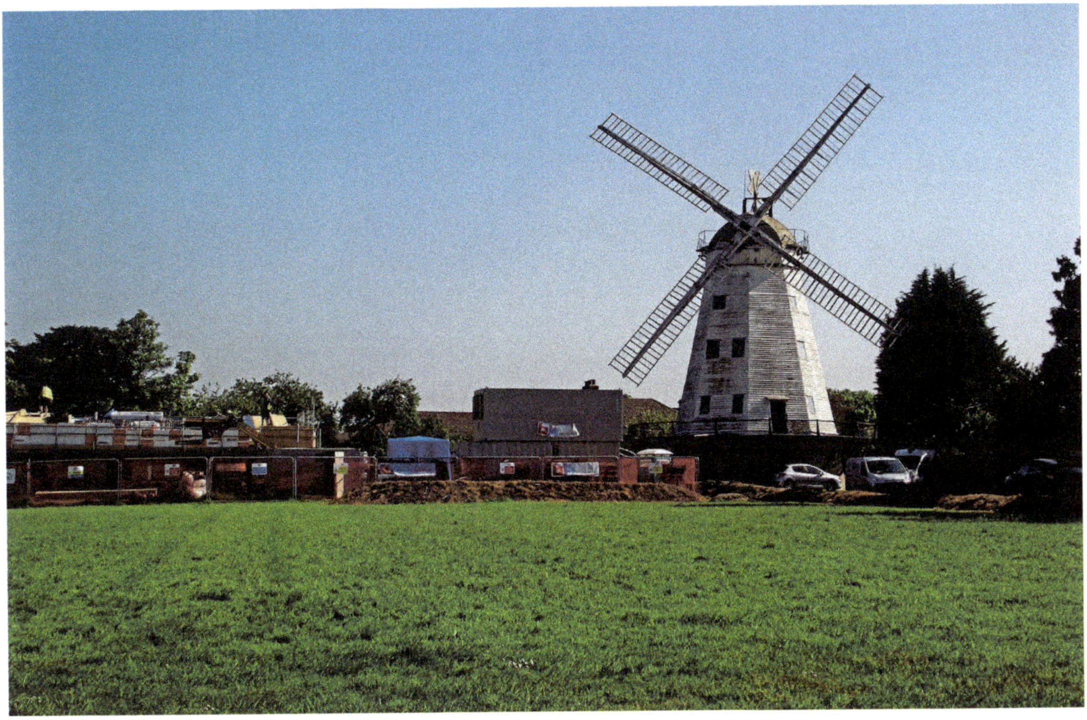

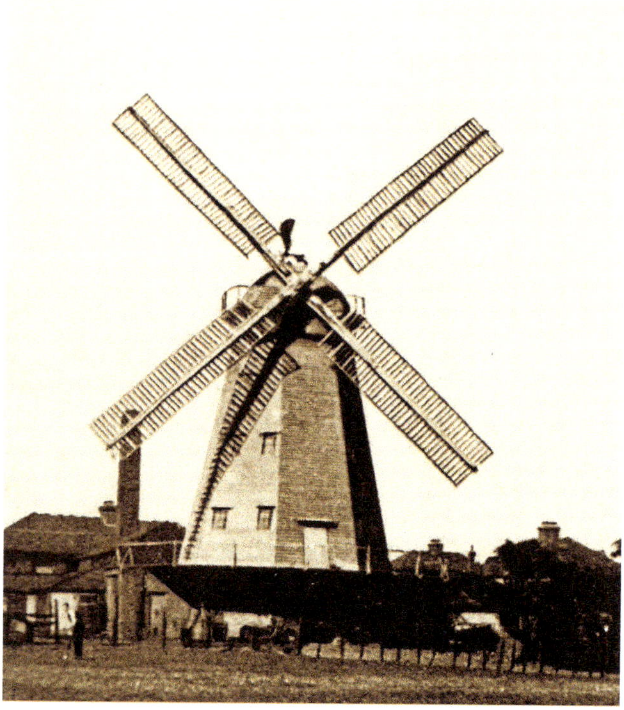

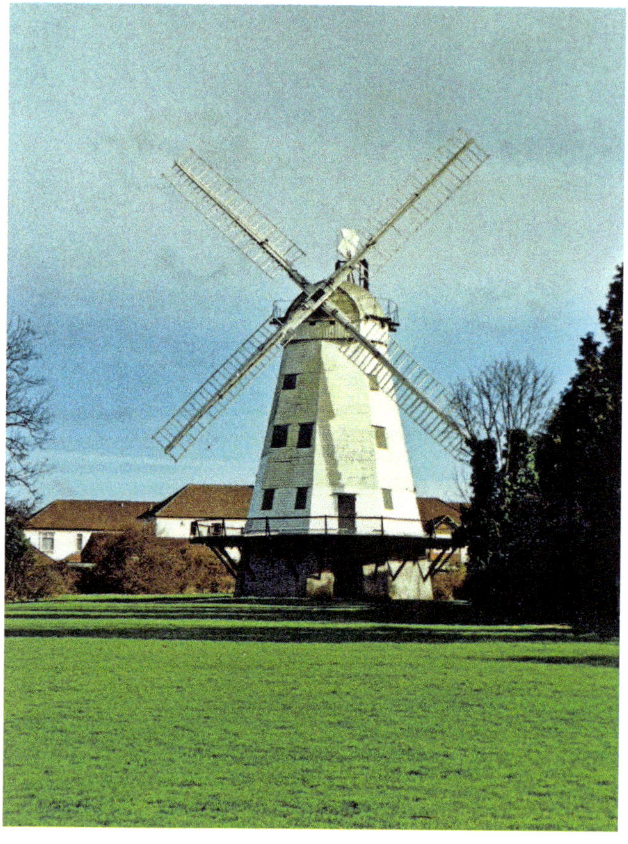

The Windmill II

The windmill was last used commercially in the mid-1930s. Since then, the outbuildings were left to decay and were eventually demolished. It became a listed building in 1955 and is now run by the Upminster Windmill Trust and is open to the public on some weekends. At time of writing, it is currently closed for repairs.

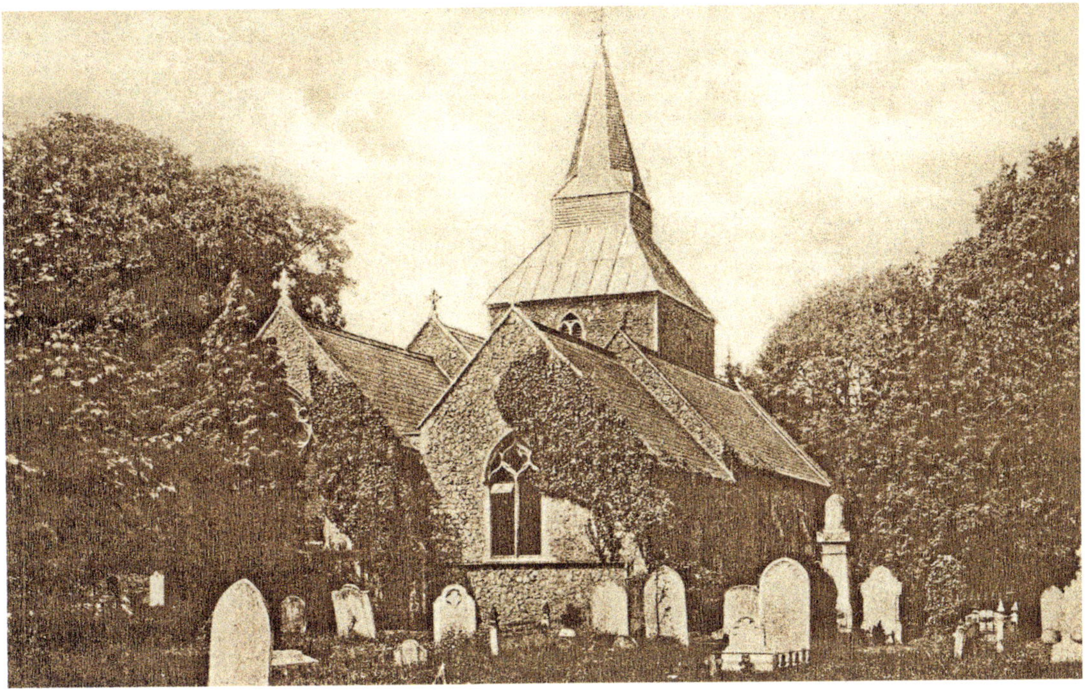

St Laurence Church I

St Laurence Church has a long history and was one of the five churches established in Essex after St Cedd arrived in 653. The church is where the town gets its name from – the upper minster. The congregation must have been very small as, by the time of the Domesday Book in 1086, there were only thirty-one people listed as living in the area. The church was rebuilt in stone in the thirteenth century and in 1400 Alice Perrers, a mistress of Edward lll, was buried there, however there is no memorial for her.

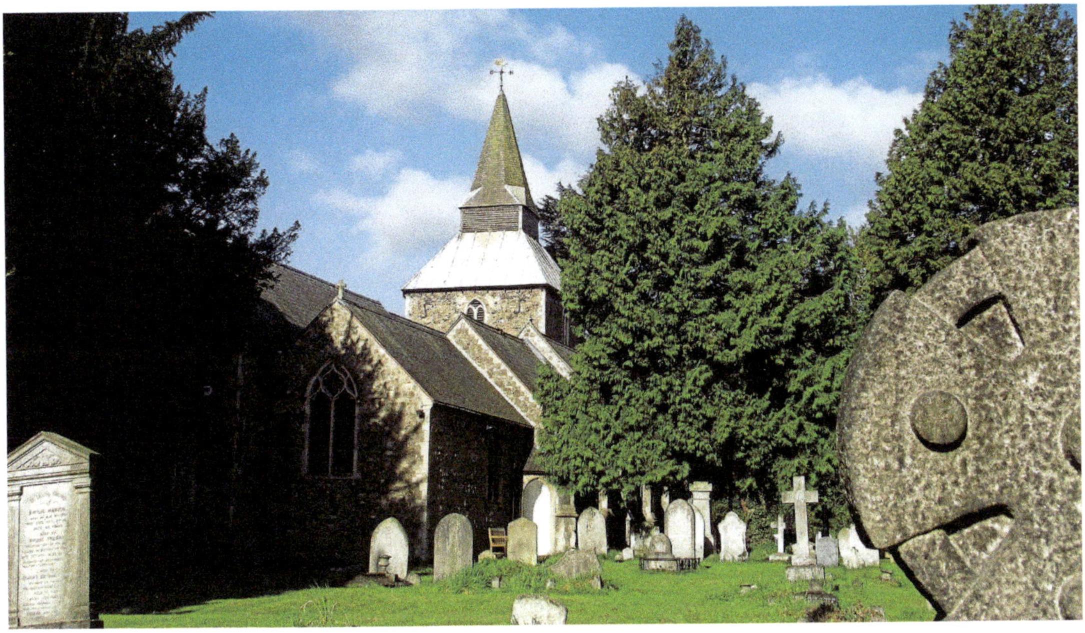

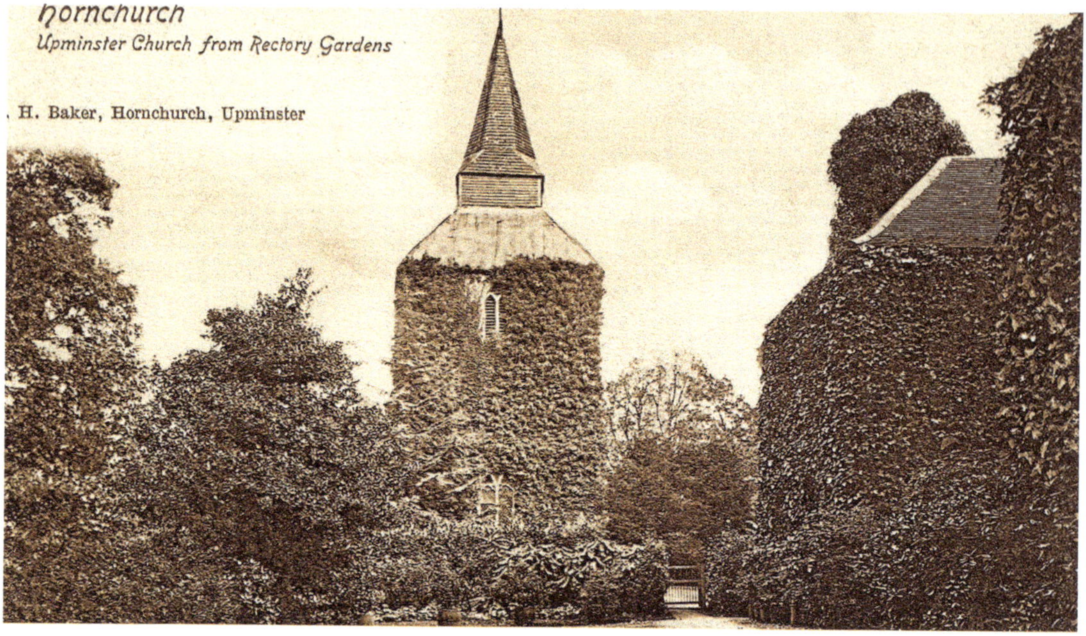

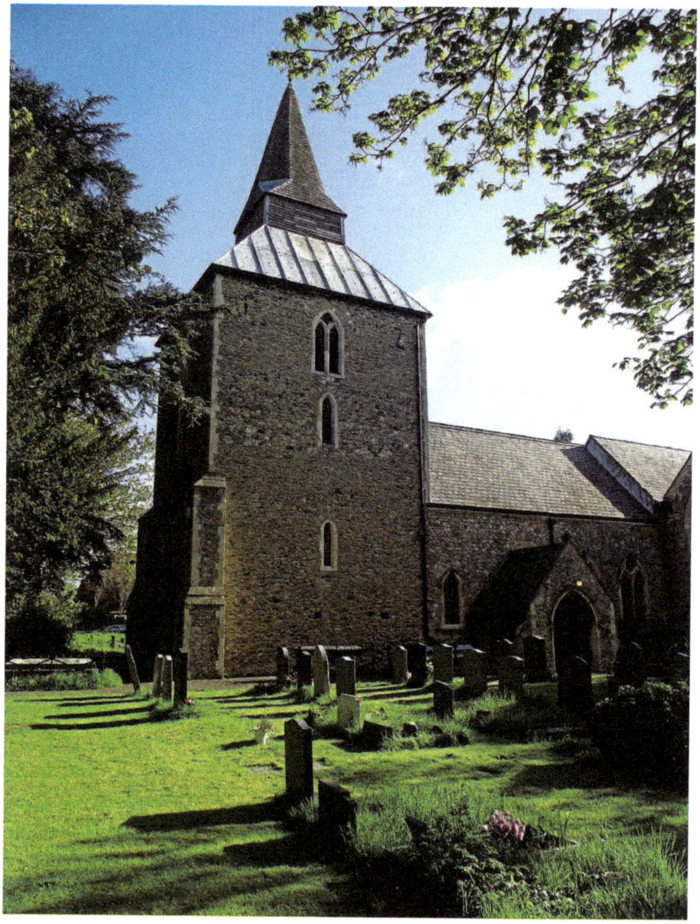

Church II

The church had a famous rector between 1689 and 1735. The Revd William Derham was a well-known writer of his time and a Fellow of the Royal Society. He had a 16-foot-long telescope at the top of the tower at St Laurence and used it to establish the speed of sound. The oldest memorials in the churchyard date from the eighteenth century. The old image was taken from the rectory gardens. That view is now blocked by trees. The old rectory is now used for offices and a new one has been built. The greenery that covered the church tower in the old image has now been removed.

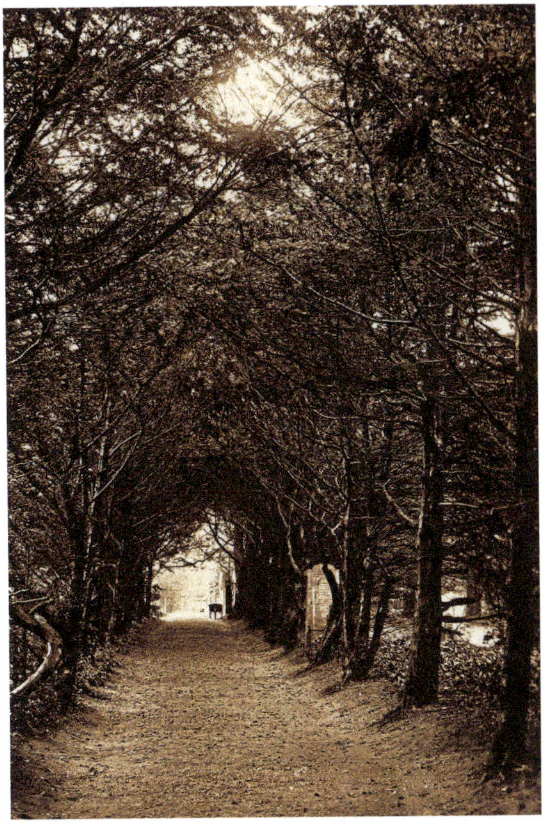

Church Avenue

The old image shows the pathway up to the doors of the church, which is lined with trees screening much of the churchyard from the view of those entering the church. Little has changed between the two images with the trees now having grown even denser.

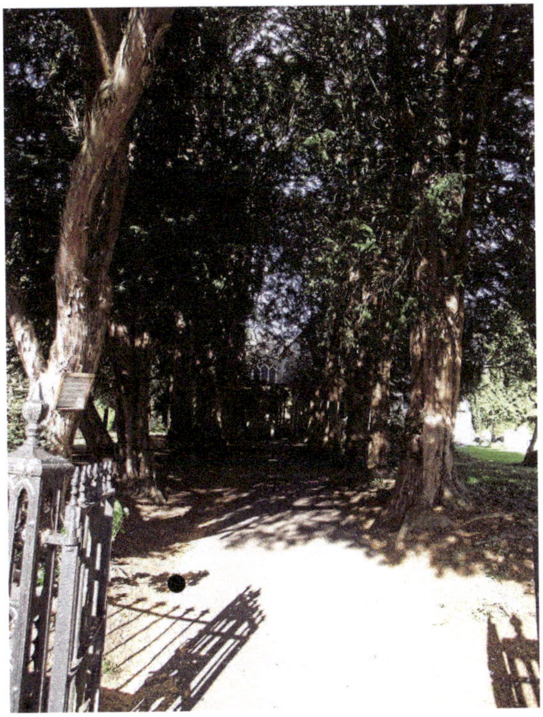

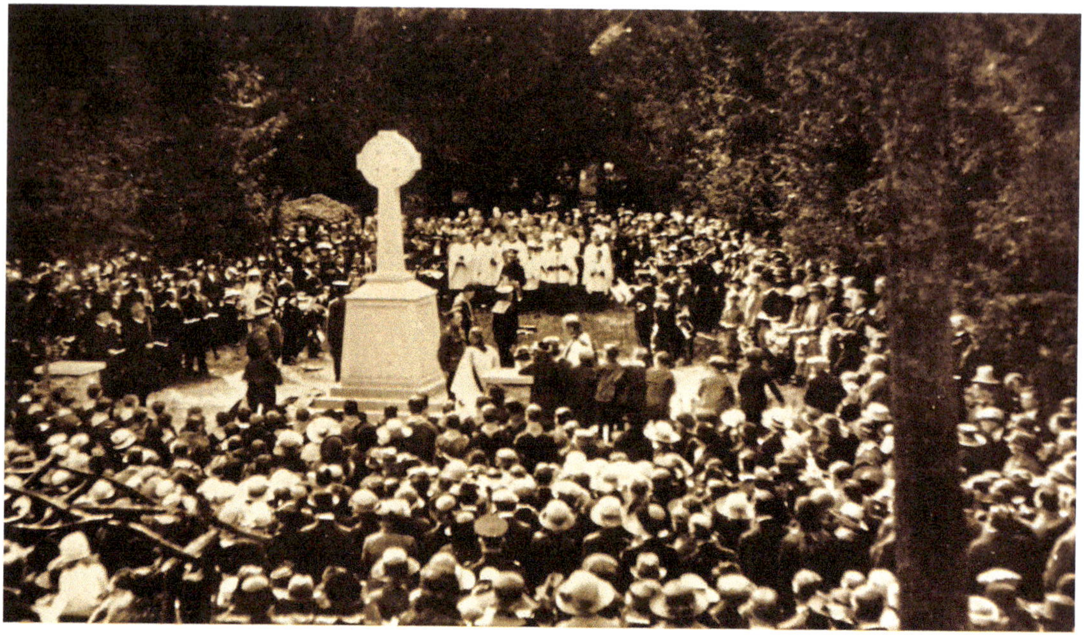

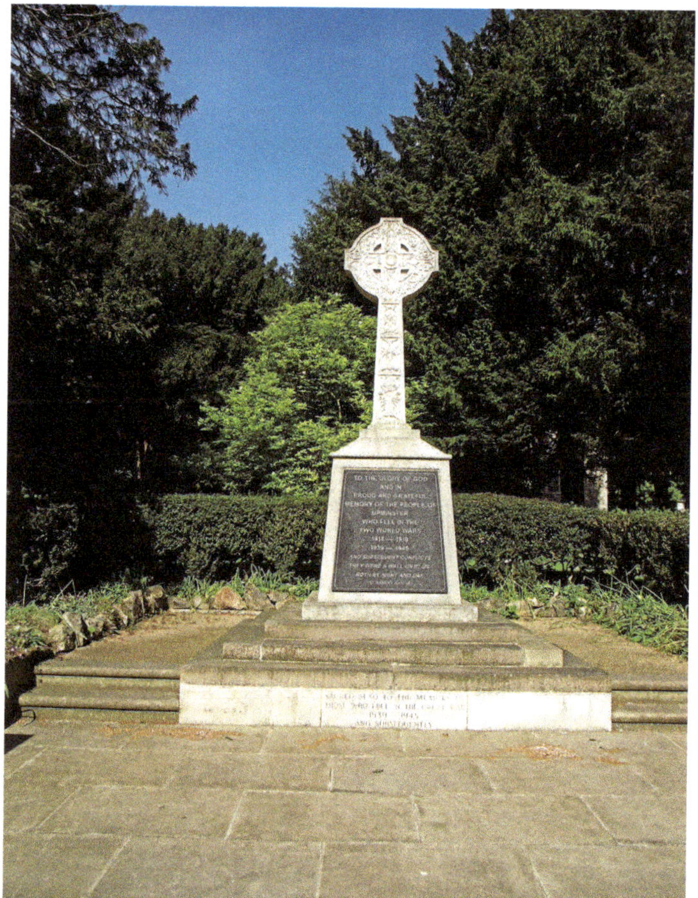

War Memorial

The early post-First World War period was when the majority of towns and villages in the country created war memorials to commemorate local men who died during the conflict. The Upminster memorial took the shape of a Celtic cross, designed by Mr C. Harrup, and was unveiled in May 1921 before a large crowd, many of whom no doubt knew the men whose names appeared on the memorial. (With thanks to Havering Libraries Local Studies Dept)

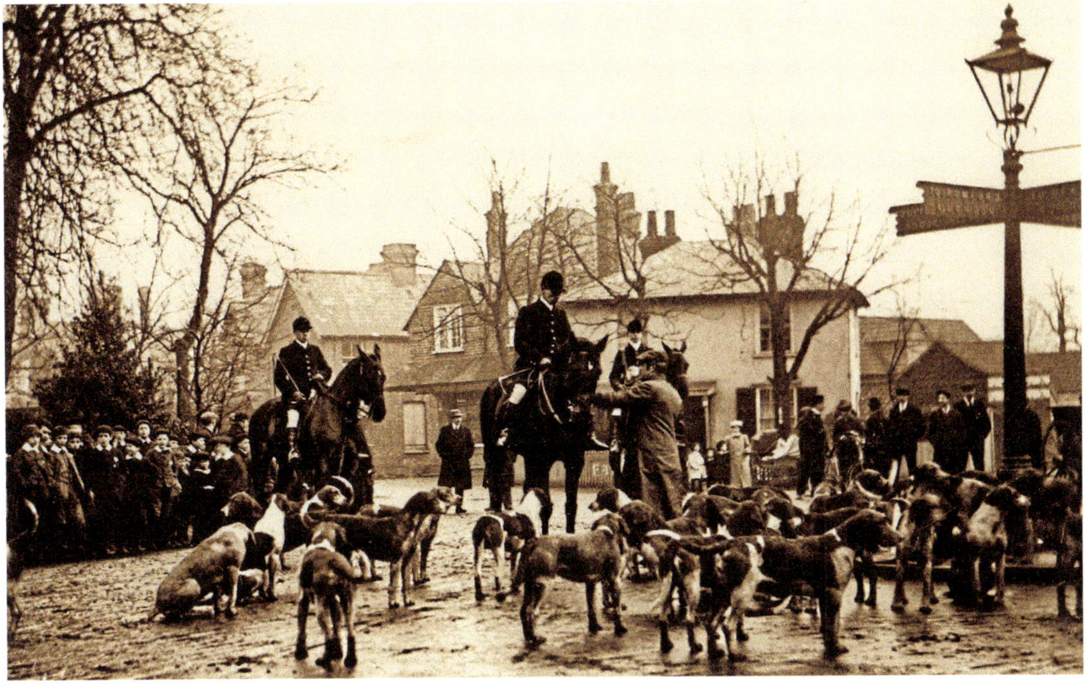

Upminster Hunt

The Upminster Hunt would often meet at the Bell Hotel which stood in the Broadway. The village green was in front of the Bell. There were stocks there until 1814 and the village pond was filled in during the mid-nineteenth century. The building of many new houses in the early twentieth century must have curtailed some of the hunt's activities as the amount of open land began to decline.

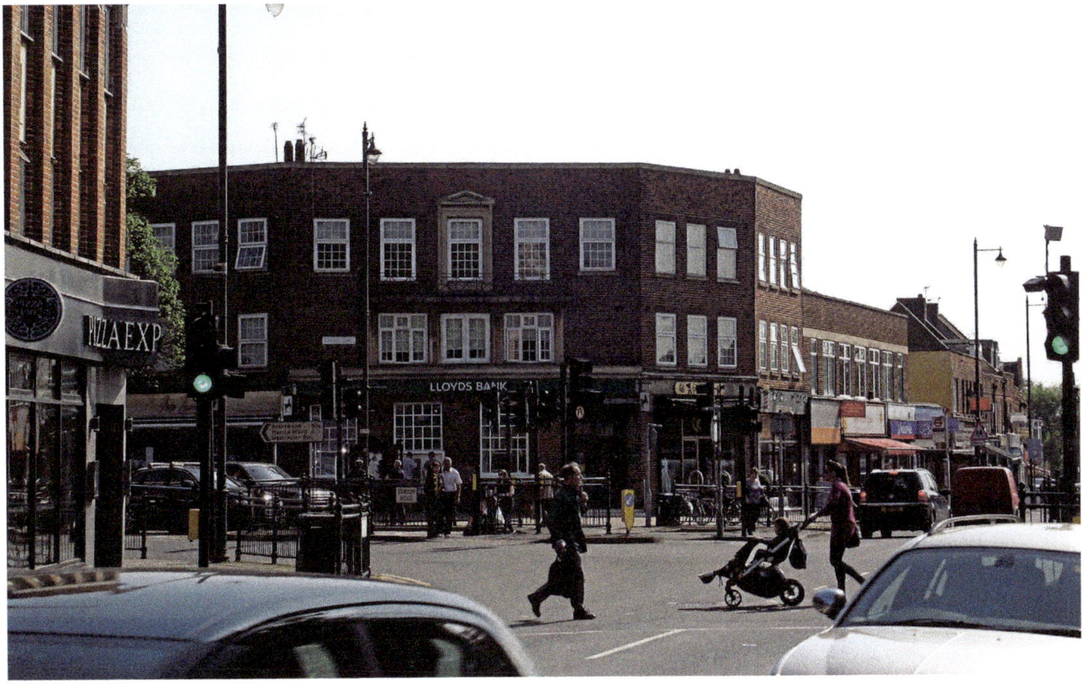

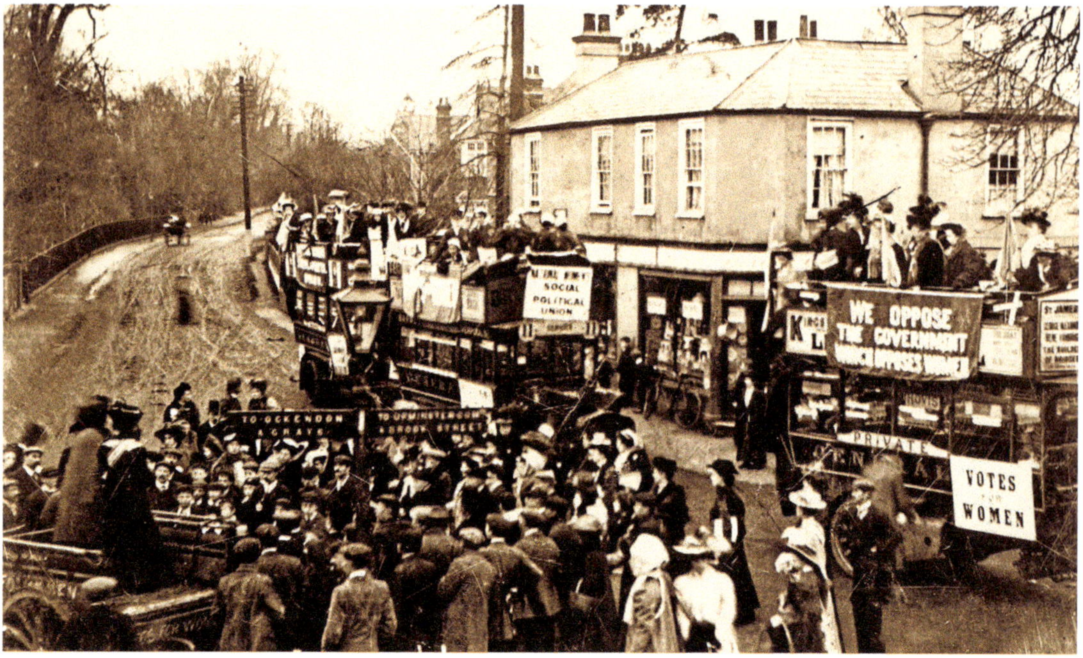

Suffragettes at Upminster

The suffragettes were a women's movement dating from the late nineteenth century to the early twentieth. They were mainly upper-class and middle-class women who were campaigning for the vote with demonstrations, such as the one in the old image. They became more militant in the years before the war and even bombed some churches. During the war, they supported the war effort and, after the conflict ended, some woman were given the vote. There was local connections in that a Miss Henrira Leach Williams lived in Corbets Tey in the cottage. Miss Leach Williams was a suffragette and was arrested during a demonstration in Parliament Square. This was just before she died at her home in January 1911.

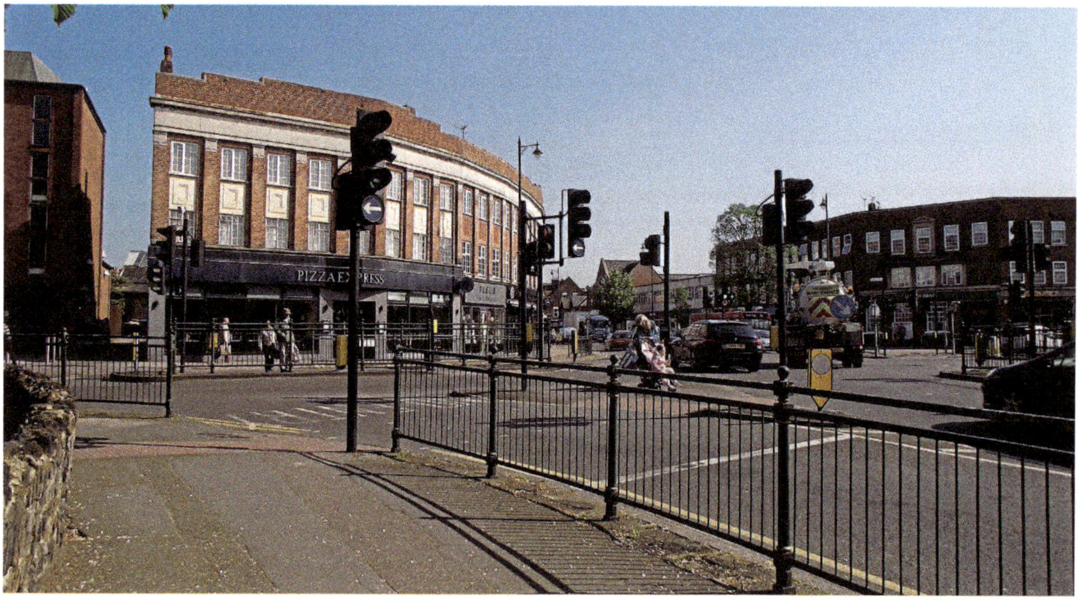

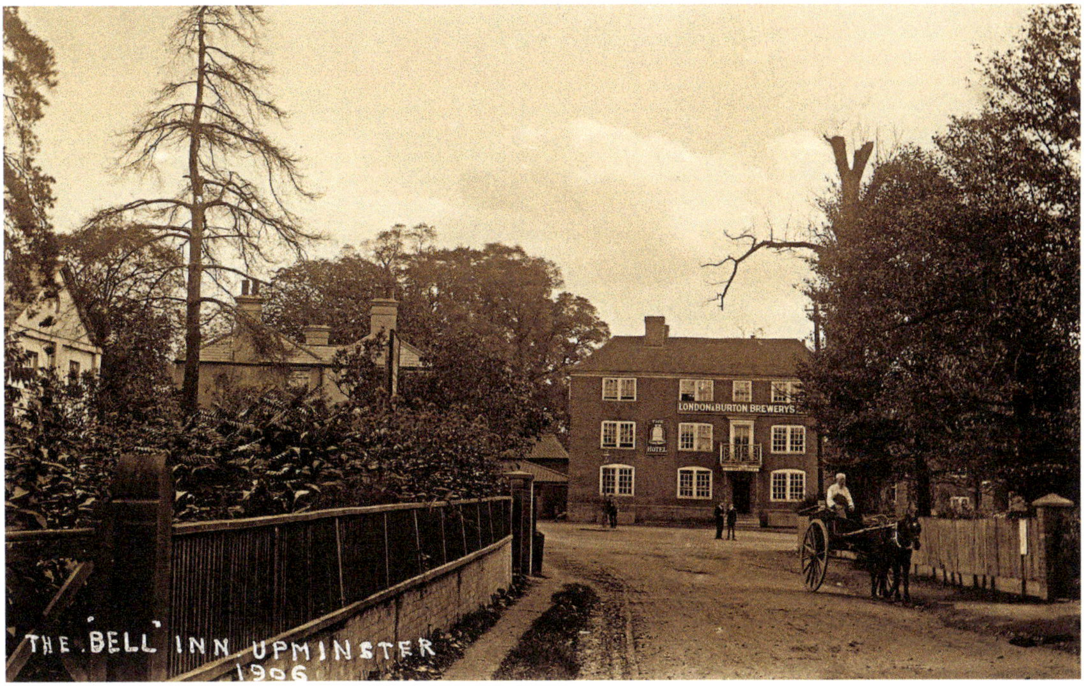

Bell Inn

The original Bell Inn dates back as far as the eighteenth century. It stood on the village green but when the new building was built it was moved closer to the road. The inn gave its name to the area known as Bell Corner. The inn closed and was demolished in the early 1960s. One of the shops that now stands on the site is still known as Bell Corner Jewellers, but this now seems to have shut down. (With thanks to Havering Libraries Local Studies Dept)

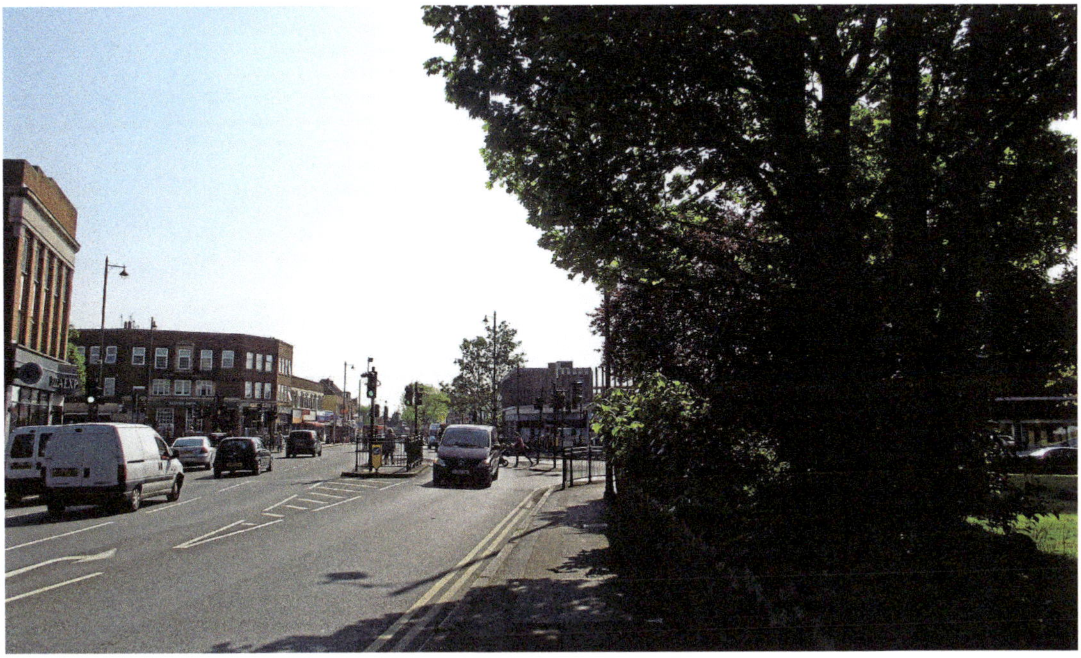

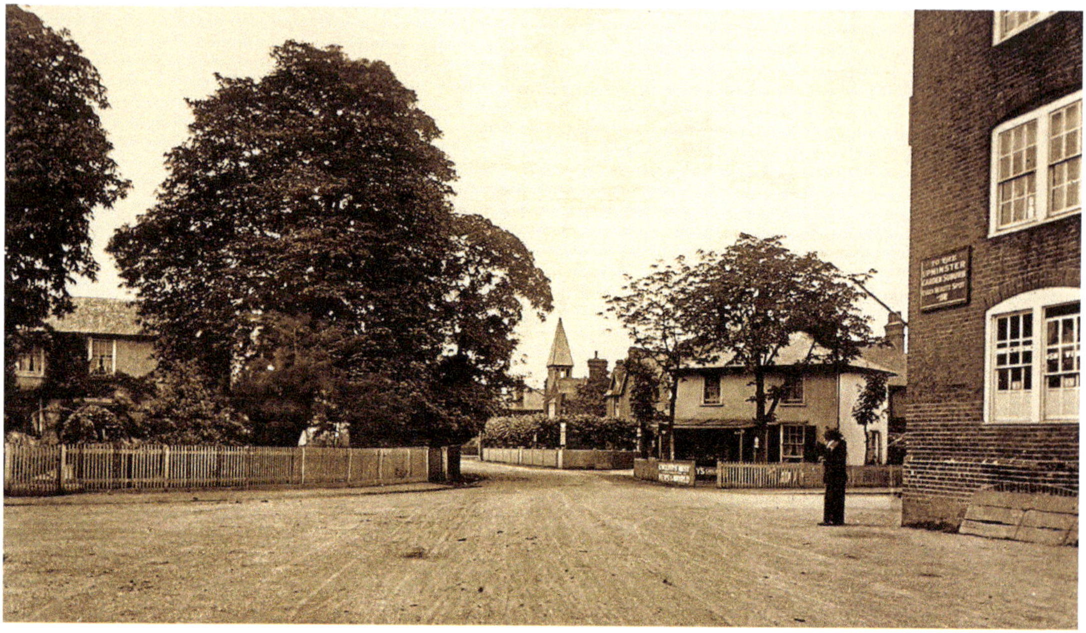

The Cosy Corner

The Cosy Corner shop was built in 1831 as a butcher's shop but passed through various hands and saw use as other types of business. This changed over the years and in 1909 it was obtained by Burgess and became tobacconists with tables outside for refreshments that were also served there. They also published a large number of postcards with views of the local area.

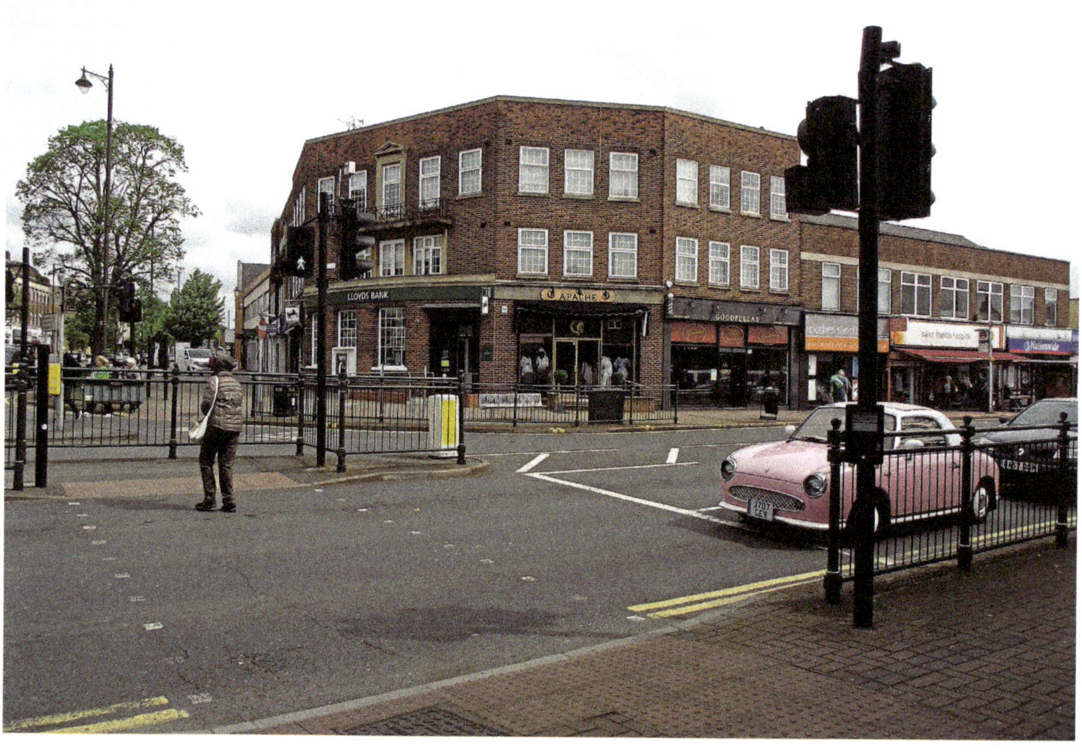

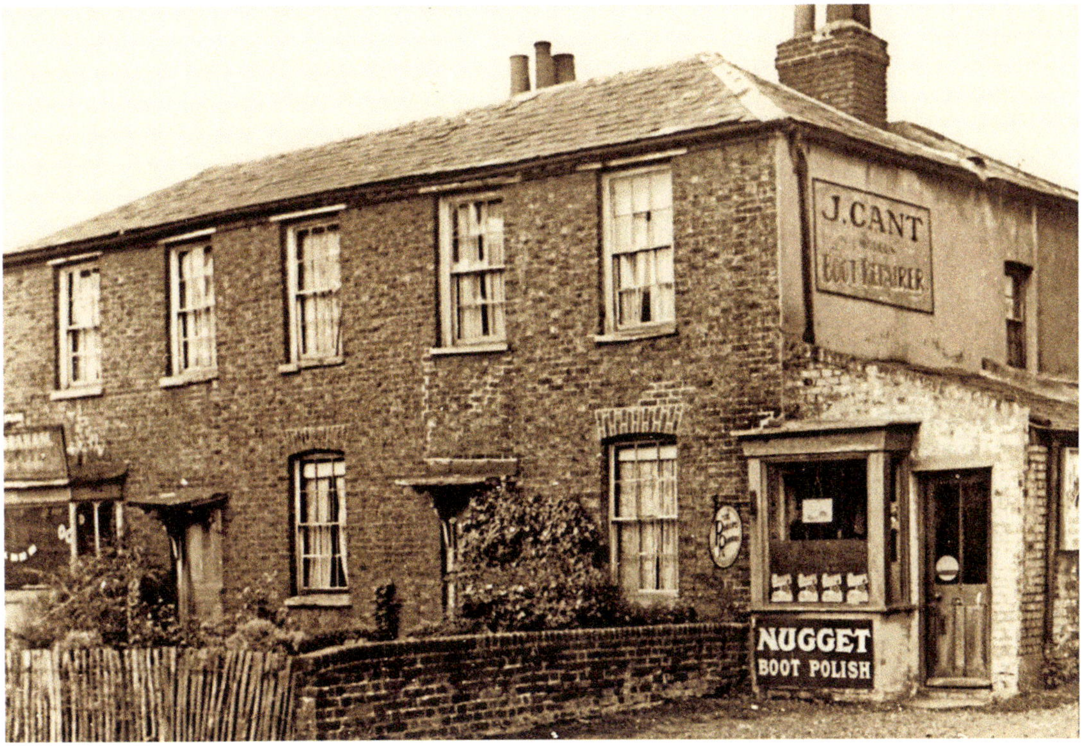

Station Road Cottages I

A row of old cottages stood in Station Road; the one on the northern end was also a business known as Cant's Boot Repairer. There were a number of shops that were based in cottages in the town, including the post office in Corbet's Tey Road before purpose-built shops were constructed. They stood close to where Barclays Bank is now situated.

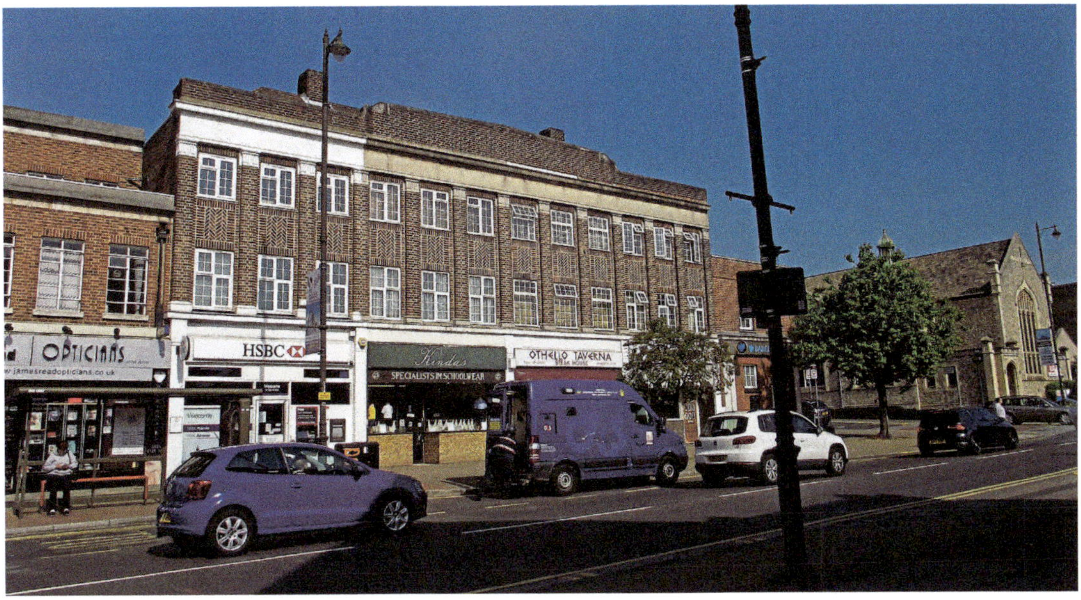

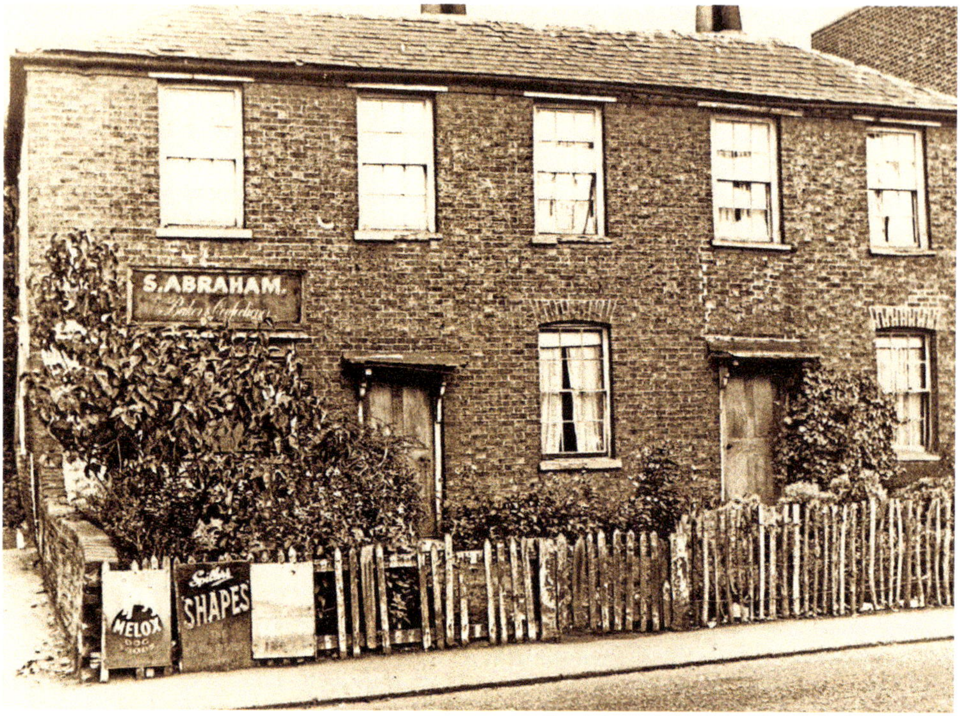

Station Road Cottages II

The cottage at the southern end of the row was occupied by another cottage-based business – Abraham's, the baker's shop. The cottages stood on the left-hand side of the road when facing the station just before Barclays Bank. As with other old buildings in Station Road, they have been replaced with modern shops.

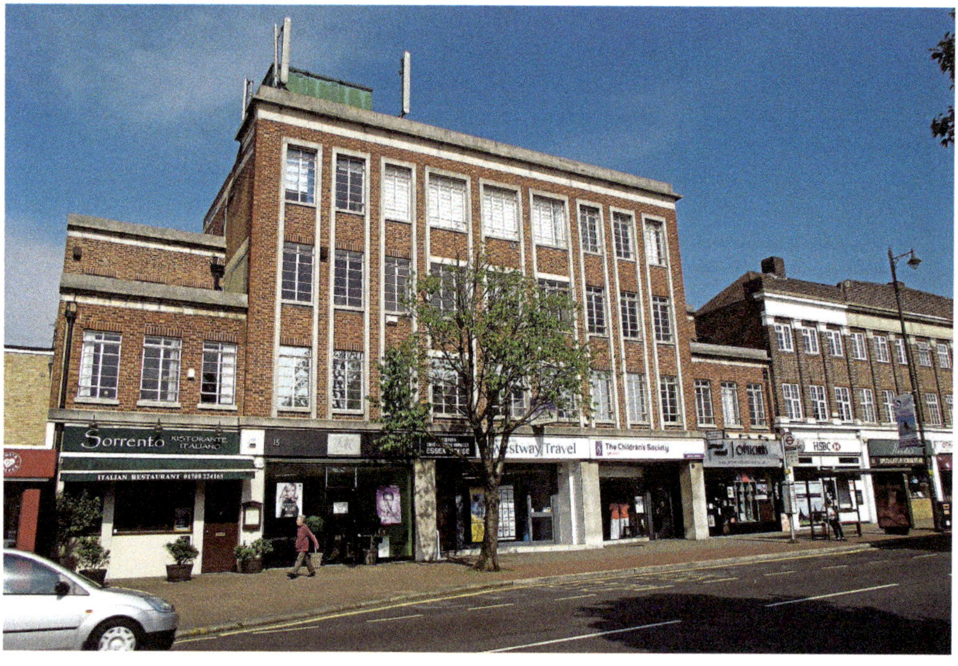

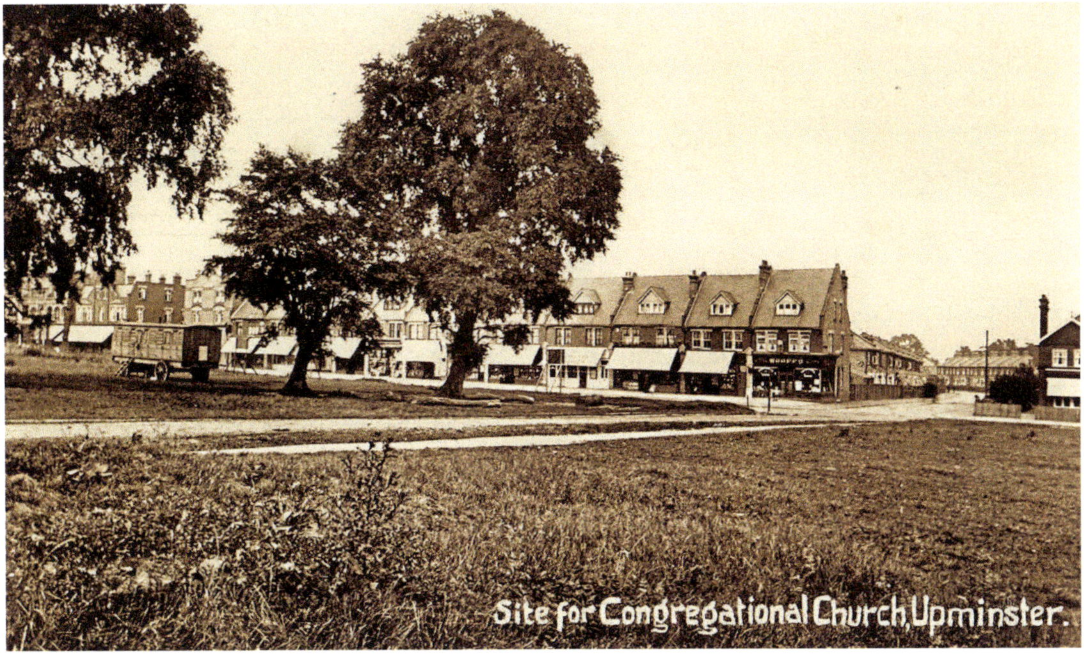

Congregational Church

The Nonconformist church in Upminster has its origins in people's homes until the old chapel in St Mary's Lane was built. This was then sold to another group in 1910 when there were plans to build a new church on the site shown in the old image in Station Road. As the modern image shows, the original shops are still there but the side of Station Road where the church stands is very different today.

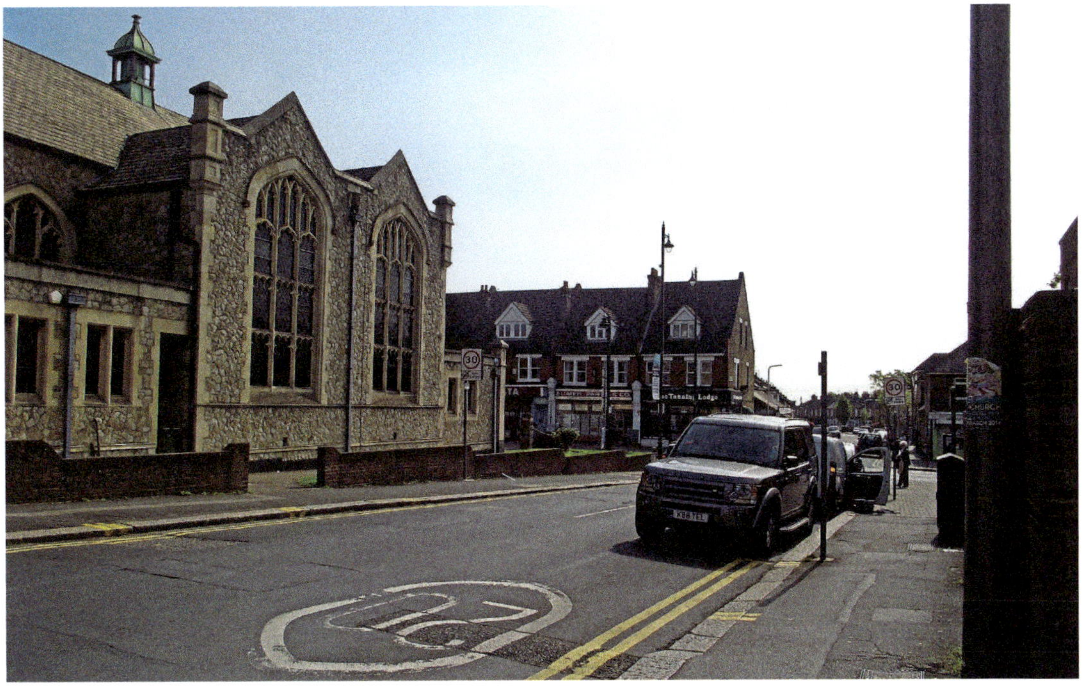

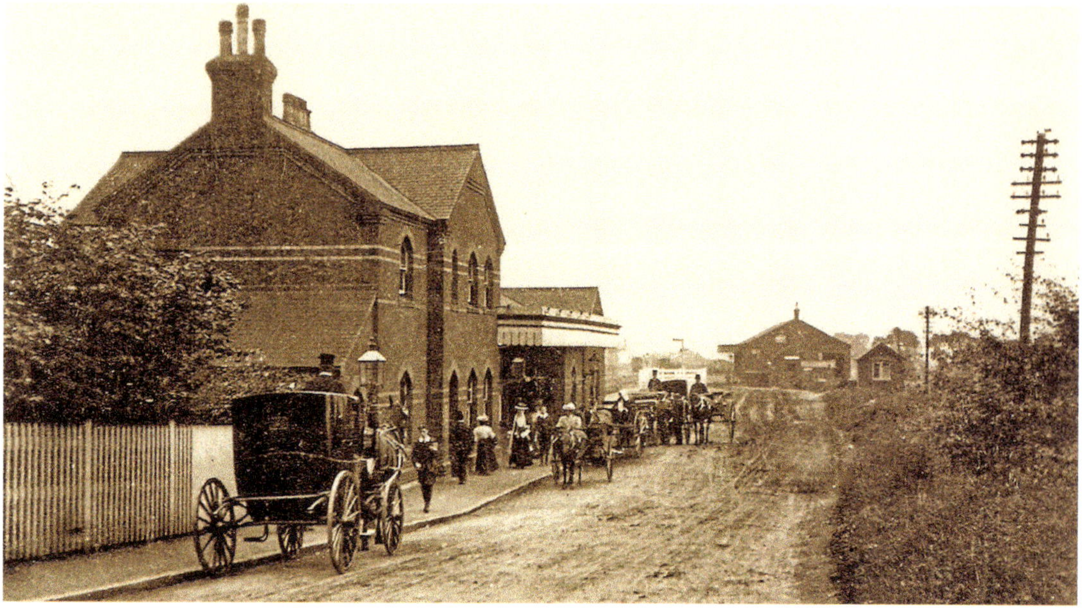

Upminster Station

The station opened in 1885 when the Barking to Pitsea line was opened. Other lines were added later: one to Grays in 1892 and then to Romford in 1893. Upminster lost its line to Barking when the District line was electrified in 1905 as it never reached this far. It wasn't until 1932 that the Upminster line was electrified and joined the District line. The original Victorian station has survived although its interior has changed greatly. The station was extensively expanded in the 1930s when the District line began to run to the station. An extra platform was added to run to Romford and two footbridges were built. There is a very large car park there and the area is also used by buses as a turning point. The rail depot at the station was expanded in the 1960s. The old station building has changed little, although the main entrance is now in Station Road.

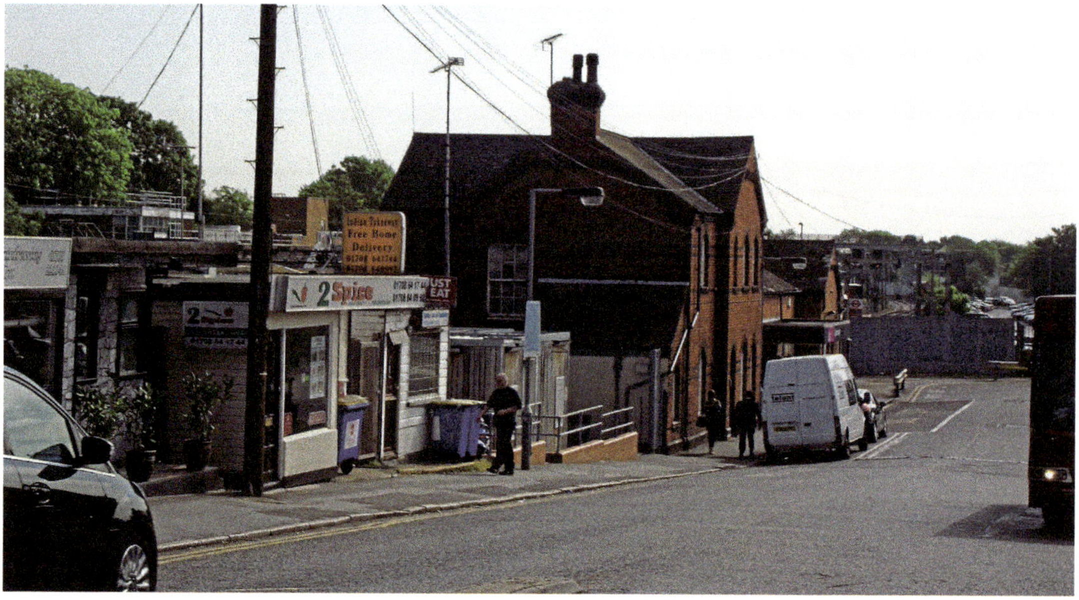

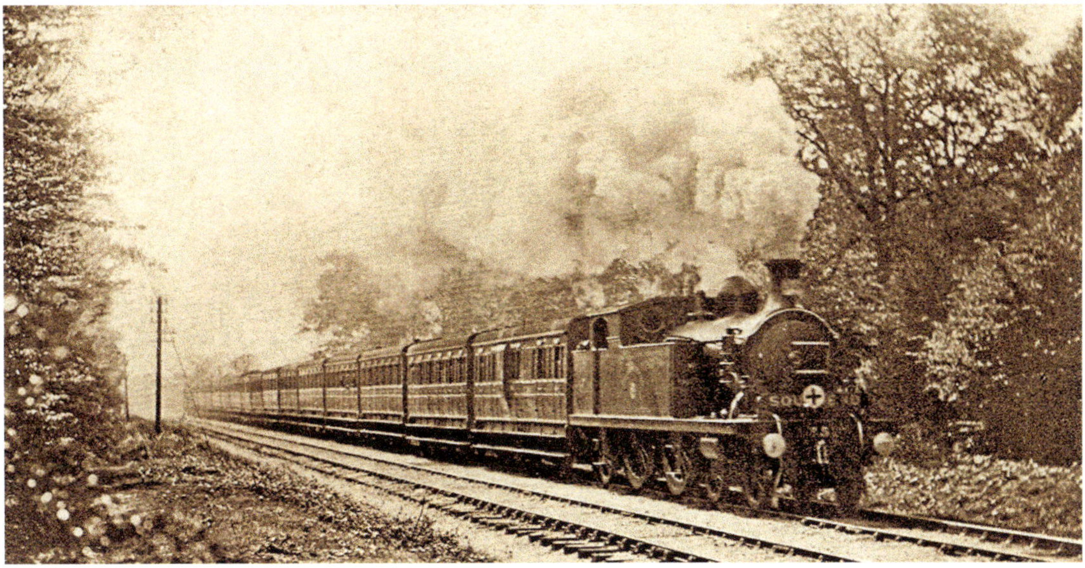

Southend Express

The train in the old image is the *Southend Express* passing at Upminster. It was run by the London, Tilbury & Southend Railway. This was in the days when a number of different railway companies had their own lines. It was much later that these were nationalised and became British Railway. The modern image shows the type of train that typically uses Upminster Station, which is approaching from Hornchurch.

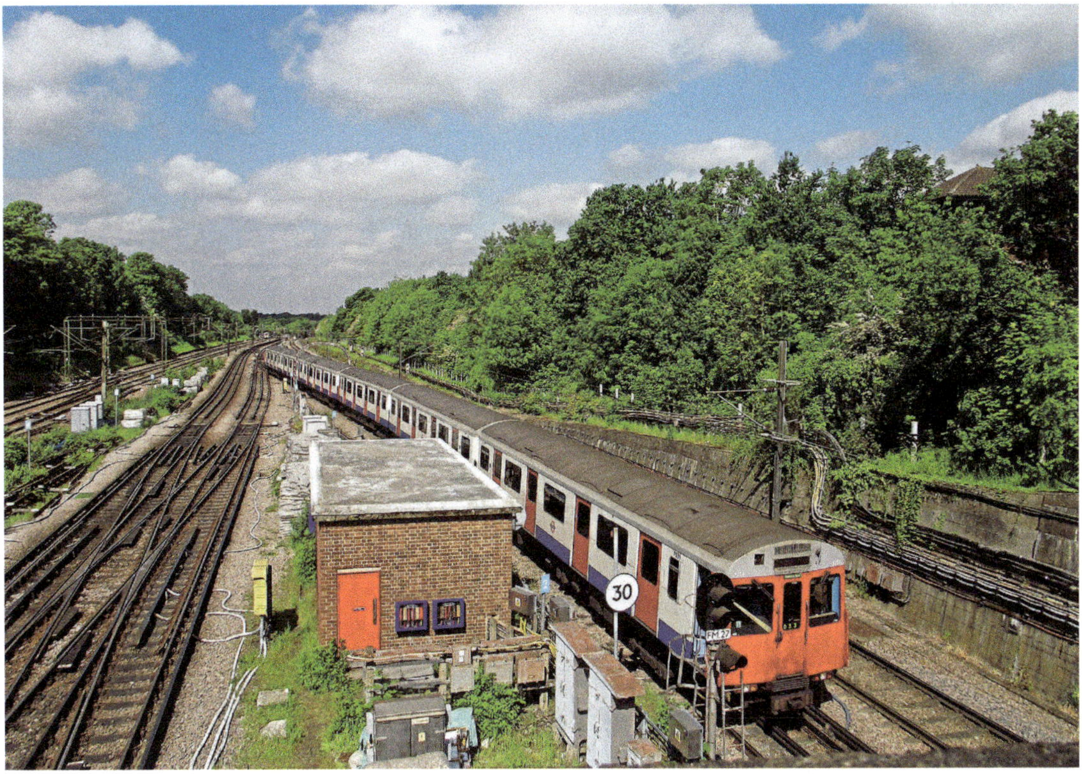

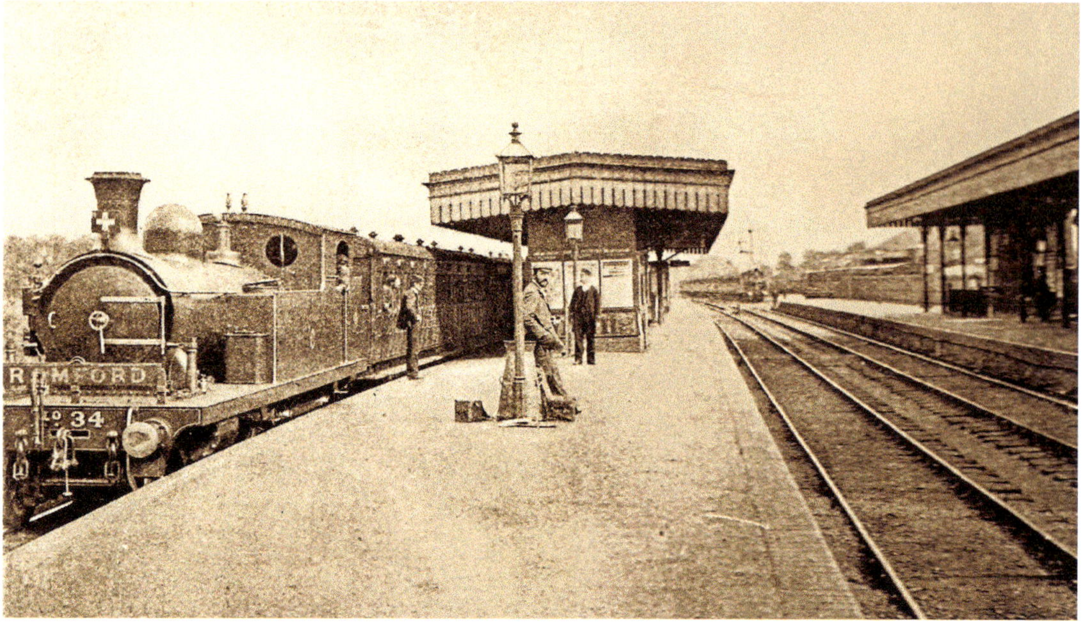

Upminster Station

Although the station has a main entrance in Station Road, there is a further entrance at the side in Station Approach where the original station building stands. The coming of the railway may have made a great difference to Upminster but it also had its problems when crowds of navvies would descend on the area, often living in little more than shanty towns. In February 1906, a metal bar was placed on the line to South Ockendon and it was thought that it may have been due to the dismissal of over 100 navvies. The modern image shows the Romford train pulling into Upminster Station.

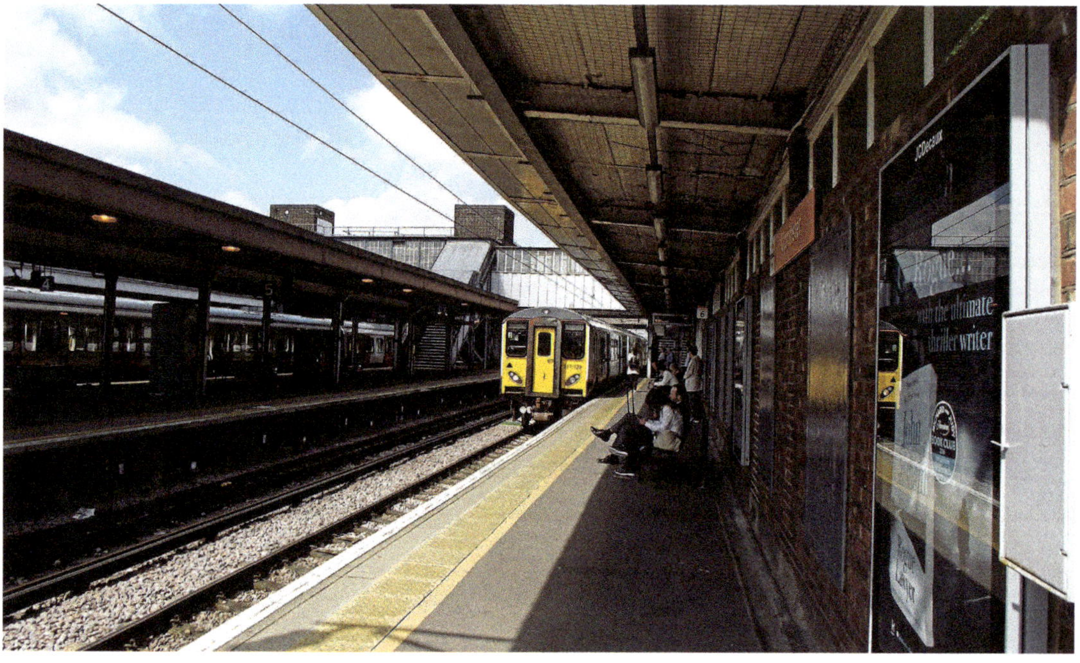

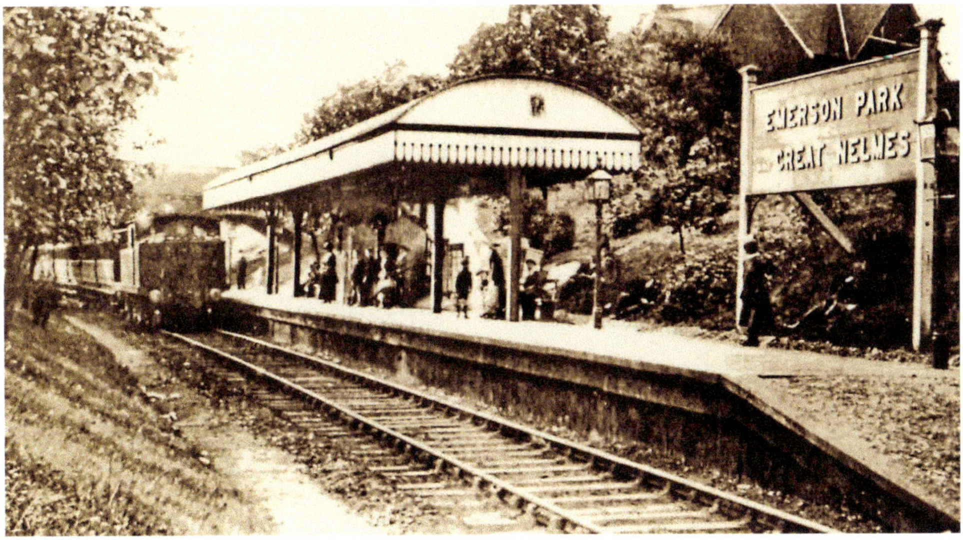

Emerson Park Halt

Although not in Upminster, Emerson Park Halt has been an important part of a railway line that caused much uproar when it was built. It is the only station on the single line between Upminster and Romford and opened in 1909, although the line itself had opened in 1893. The line was a cause of controversy between the Great Eastern Railway and the London Tilbury & Southend Railway, who both wanted to run lines from London to Southend at the end of the nineteenth century. The line between Romford and Upminster was also an attempt by the LT&SR to stop the GER providing transport to the new Tilbury Docks. The dispute resulted in the GER refusing to let the LT&SR use their lines into Romford and they then had to build their own station at Romford and pay the GER rent for the land used. The station stood on the opposite side of the road to Romford GER Station.

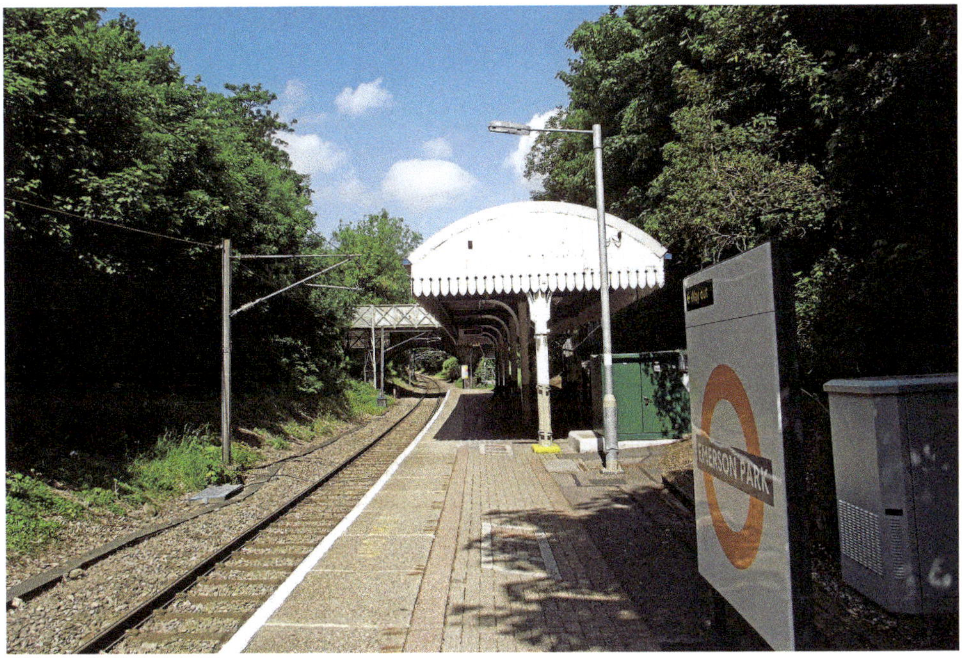

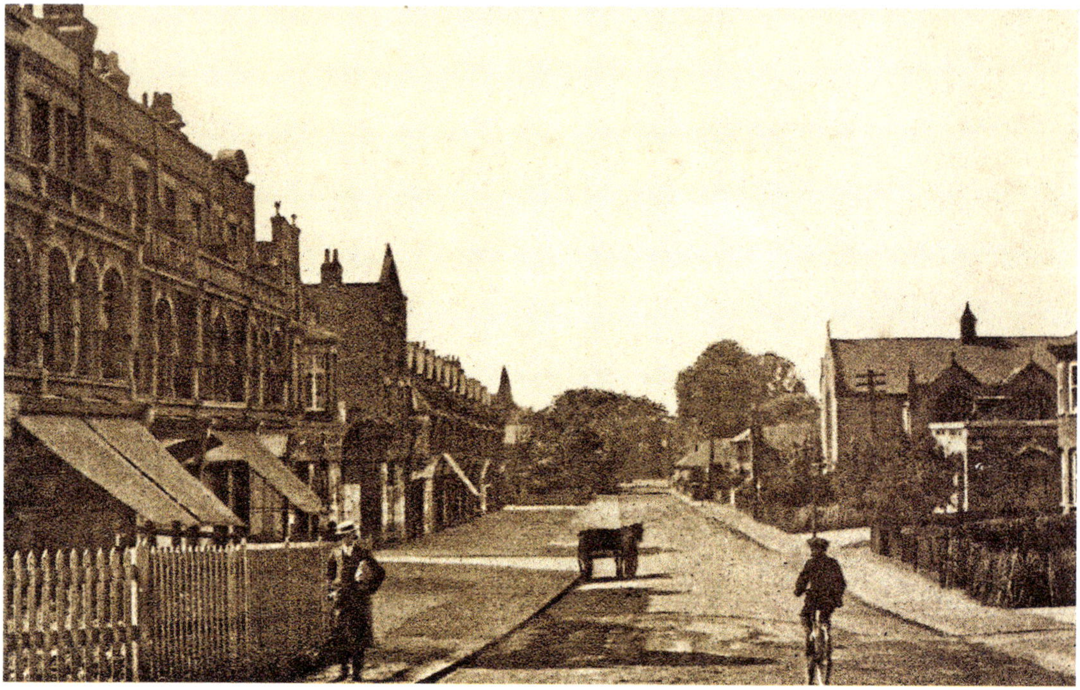

Broadway

According to the old image, this is a photograph of the Broadway; however, it is in fact an image of Station Road from the station. I have had experience of this in other areas where there was once an area known as the Broadway which is often remembered by locals – it is almost impossible to find where exactly the Broadway starts and ends. (With thanks to Swan Books)

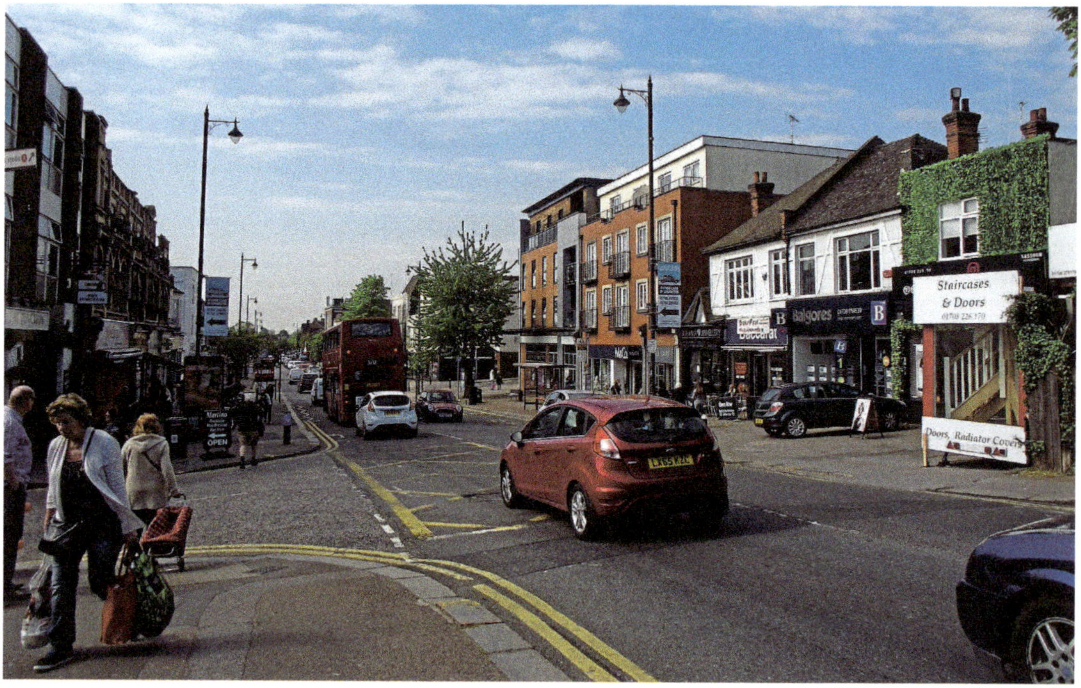

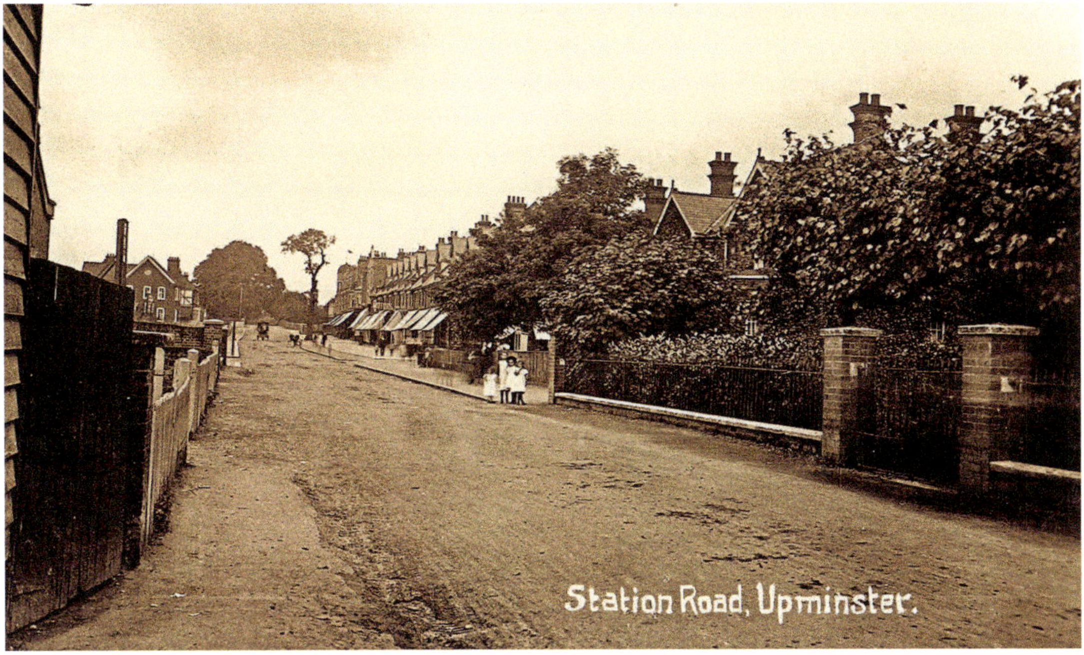

Station Road

Station Road was previously part of Hall Lane until the railway arrived in 1885 when part of it became Station Road. The road has changed dramatically with new buildings replacing old. The National Westminster Bank stands on the site of the old National Boys' School. Roomes store stands on the site of the old doctor's house. The first Roomes shop opened in 1927. Some of the shops on the station side of the road date back as far as 1907 but many of the others are much more modern.

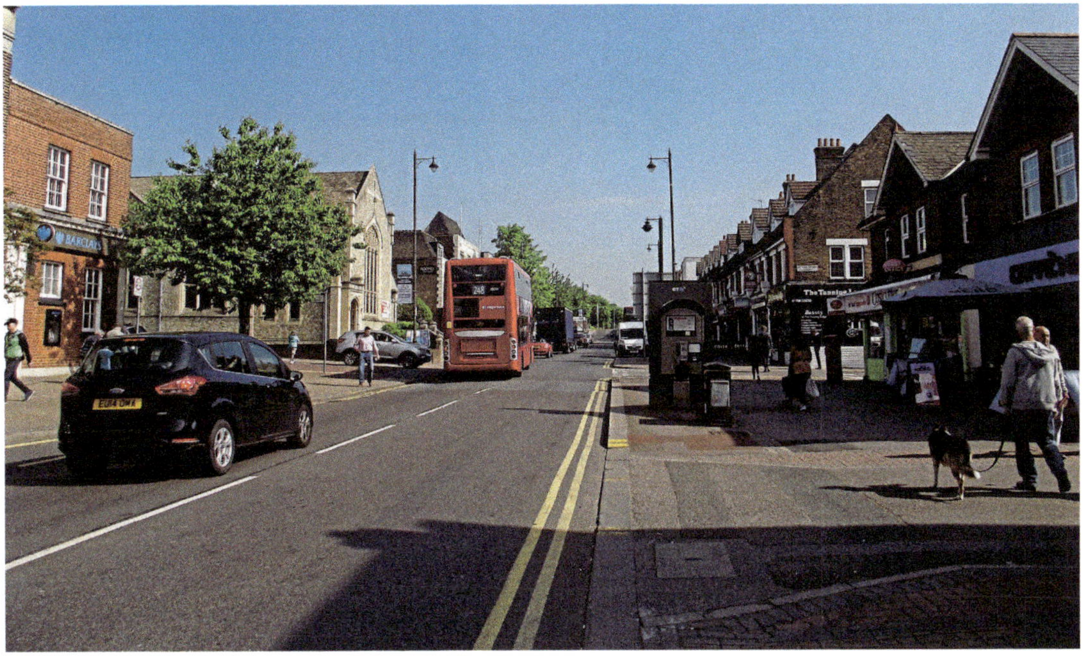

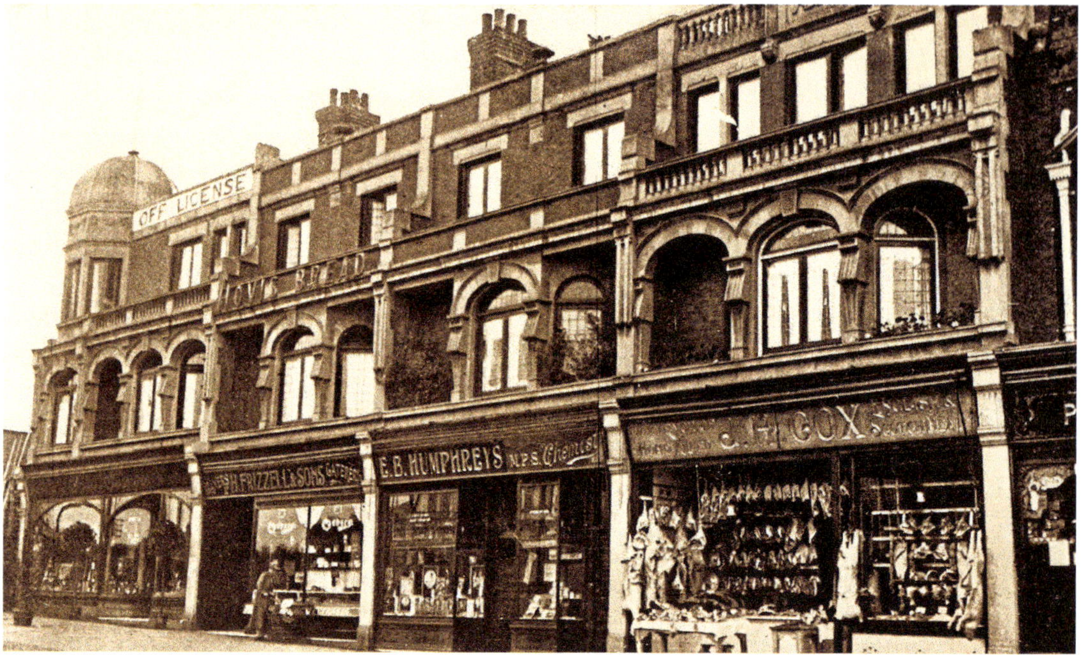

Station Road Shops

Building in Station Road was slow at the beginning of the twentieth century. Although some shops had been built by 1907, few new homes had been built by this time until some of the land was bought by Peter Griggs' building company a few years after the shops were built. In 1955, serious crime came to the area when the post office was robbed by what the police described as expert safe-breakers. Explosives experts from Woolwich Arsenal were called in to examine the scene, which had resulted in the loss of £7,000.

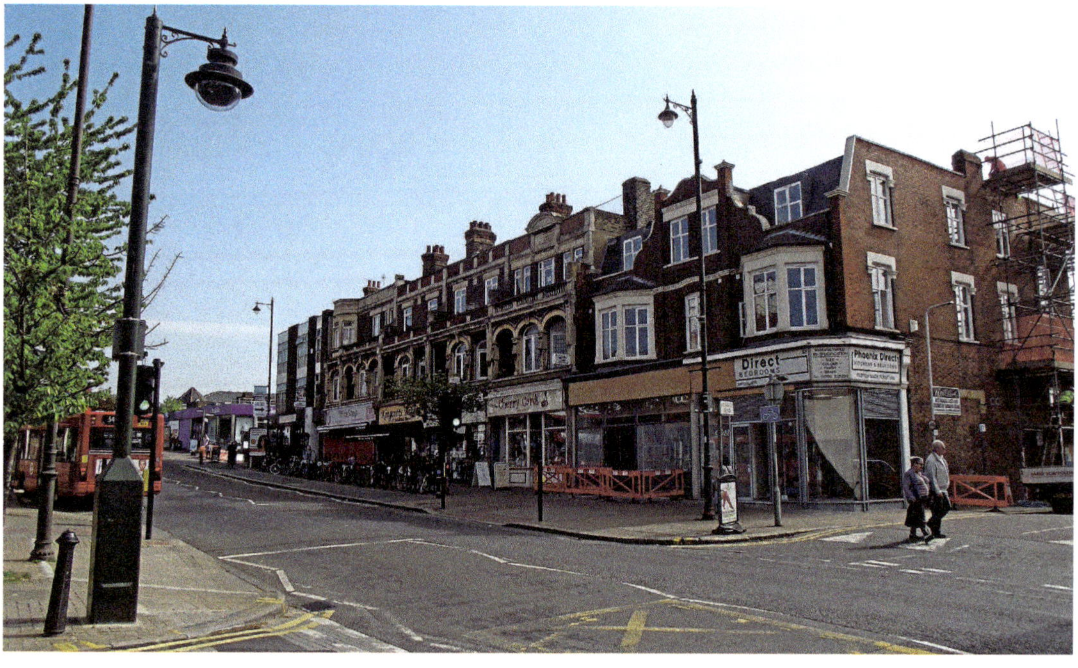

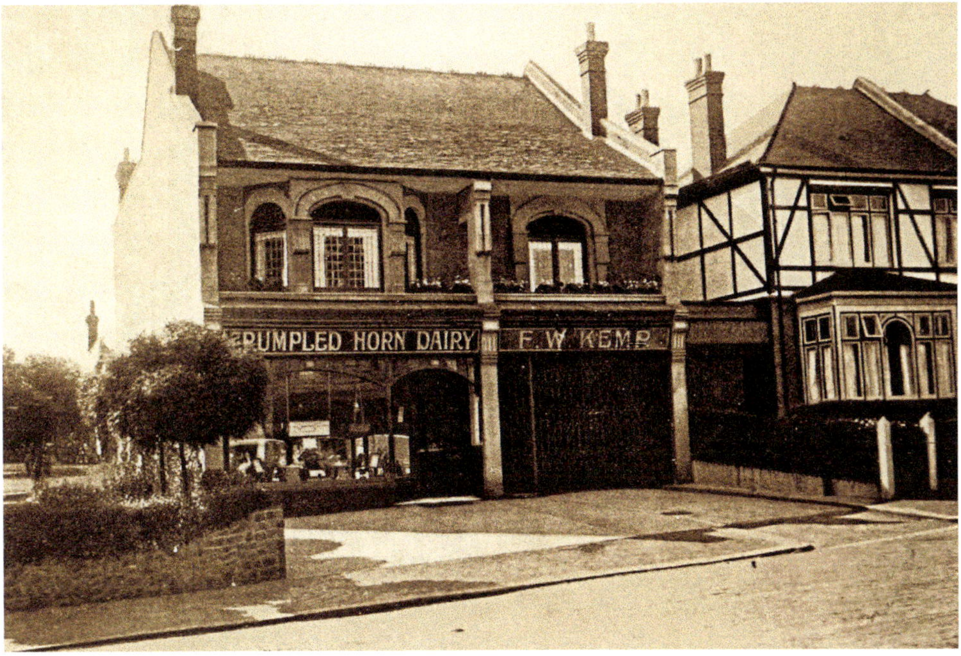

Crumpled Horn Dairy

The Crumpled Horn Dairy had a tea garden at the rear. The inclusion of a photograph of the gardens in an Upminster Estates Office booklet no doubt added to the genteel atmosphere of the area that they were trying to promote. The area of Station Road has retained this type of business with a number of cafés and restaurants today. The dairy building was later used as the post office after the dairy closed. Although the old dairy may no longer be in use, the name has been revived in Upminster as the name of a pub, the Crumpled Horn, in Corbets Tey Road opposite the park, shown in the modern image.

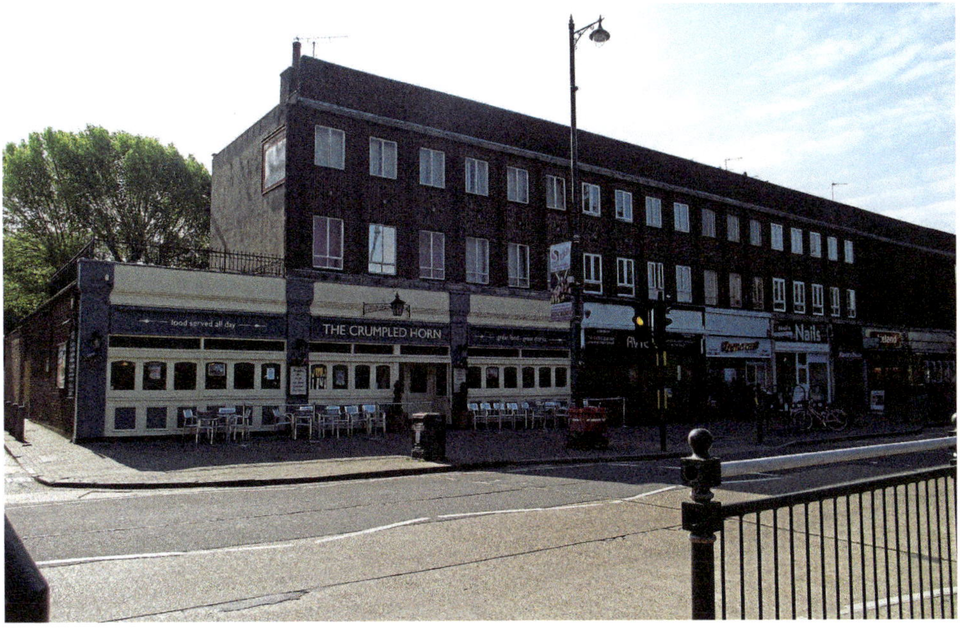

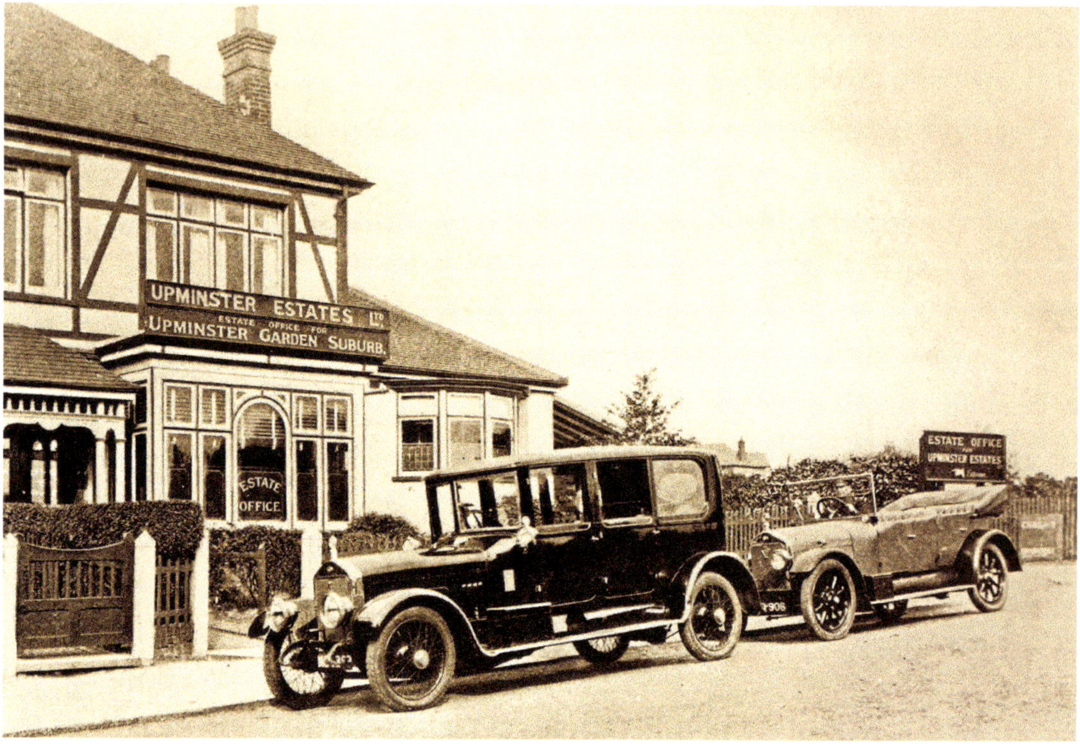

Upminster Estates Office

The Upminster Estates Office was based in a building opposite the station and they were agents for the new houses being built. The company produced a booklet that contained photographs of the new houses and of the area. The booklet also contained a number of poems by Longfellow relating to the countryside. There was information on the cost of a mortgage. You could borrow £600 on a £695 home. So, for a deposit of £95 and a yearly payment of £57.18, you could buy a ninety-nine-year lease. The cost of a freehold property was £825.

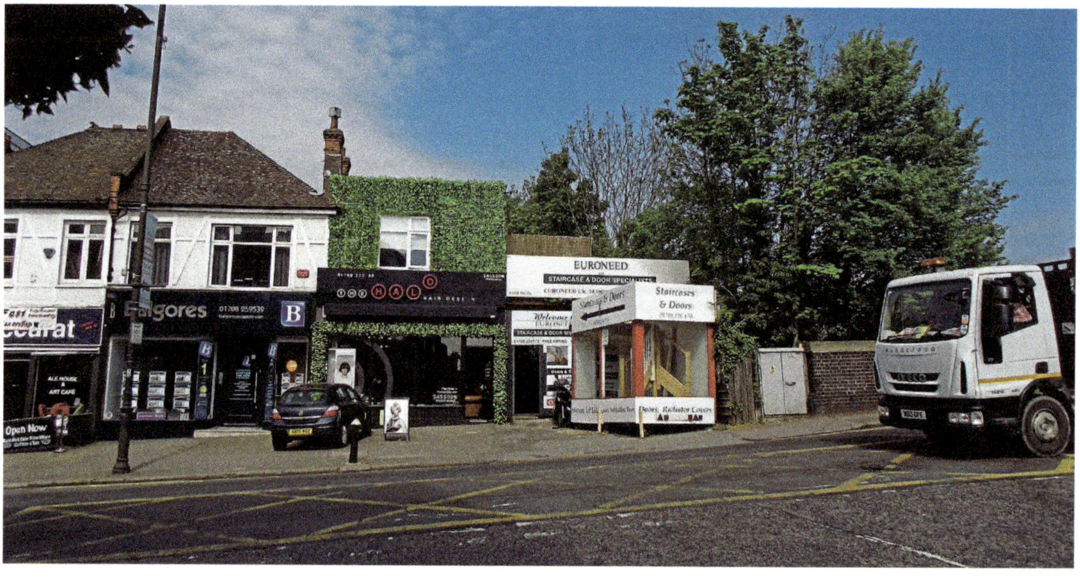

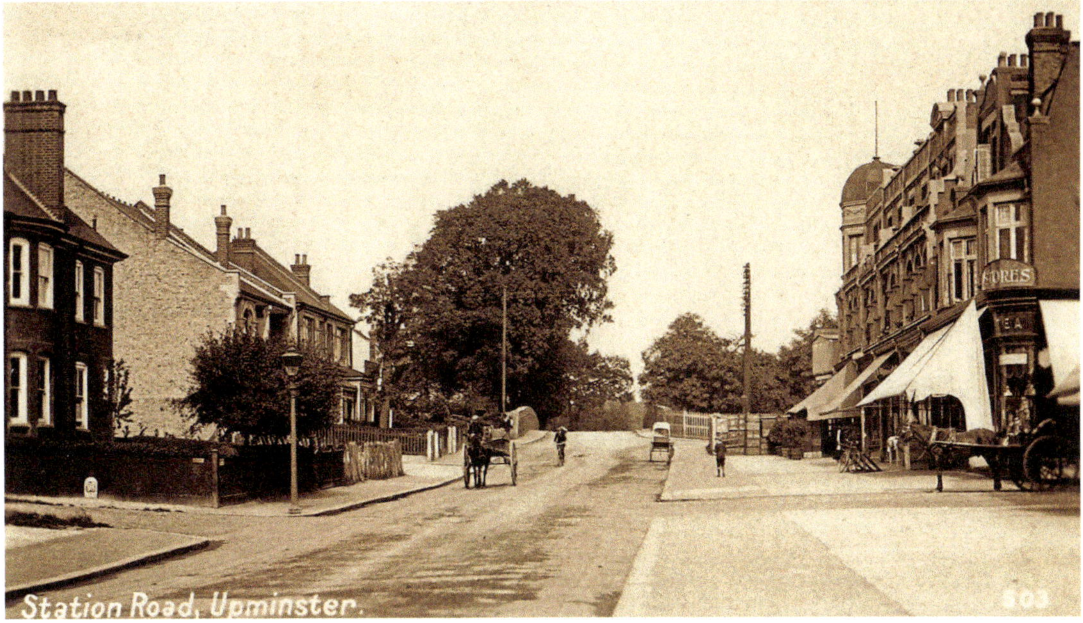

Station Road

The old image is a lovely view of Station Road, showing that the form of transport in this period was mainly one of horsepower. Unlike today, the buildings along the left-hand side of the road, opposite the station, were residential rather than commercial as they are now.

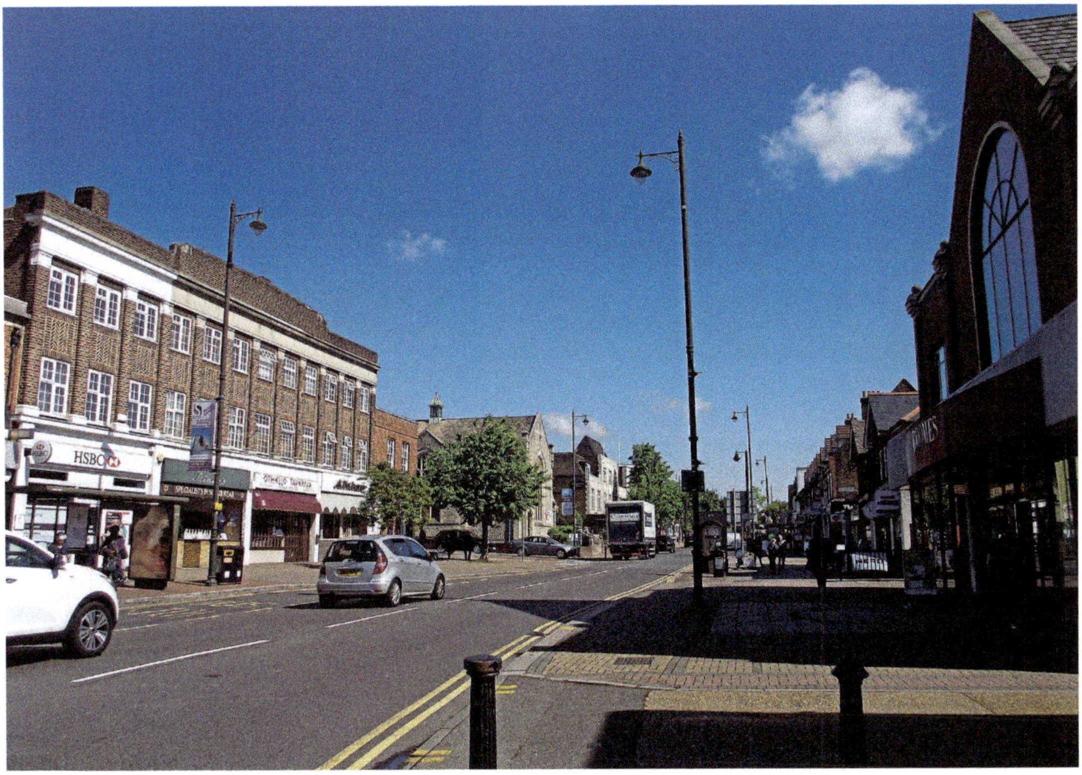

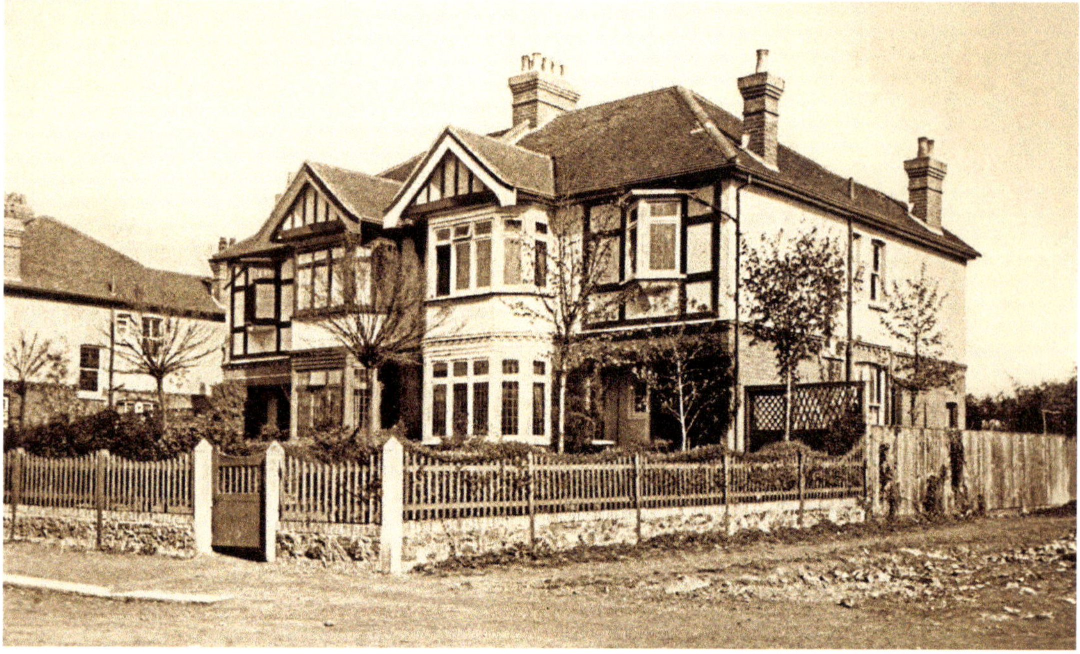

Deyncourt Gardens

Deyncourt Gardens was one of the earlier sites where houses were built in the early twentieth century on the Upminster Hall Estate. It is situated where Station Lane and Hall Lane meet. Houses in the area were built in later years and were even advertised in the *Manchester Guardian* as late as 1931. One of the selling points was listed as only being 7 miles from the Ford Works at Dagenham. Would workers at the plant have been able to afford the price of £595 rising to £2,500? As the modern image shows, there has been an increase in development to the area in recent years.

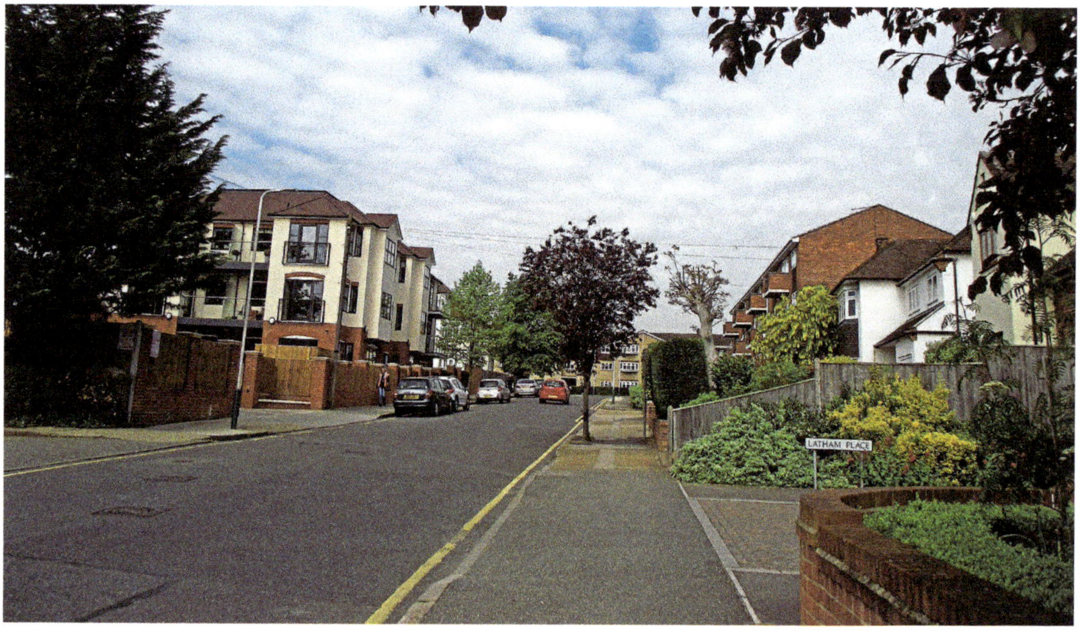

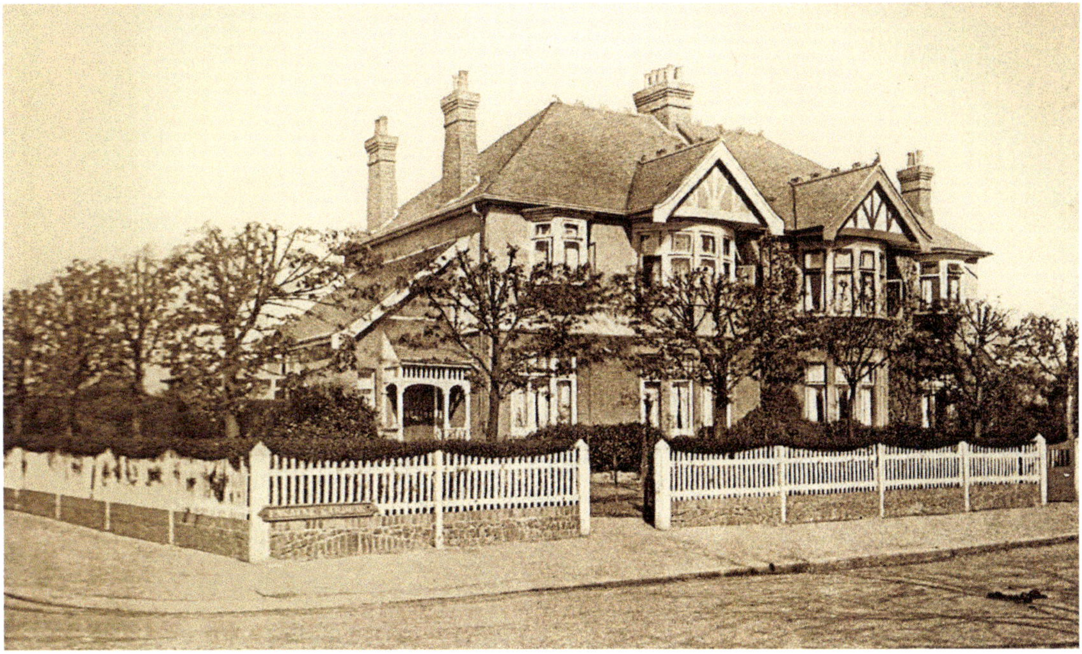

Endgyme Gardens

Endgyme Gardens was another of the earliest sites to be built on. Only part of the Hall Lane Estate had been purchased at this time, while the rest of the land still belonged to the owner of the Hall. The image of the houses show quite a substantial property, with a large garden that was no doubt aimed at the better-off house-hunters. The area has retained much of its earlier character.

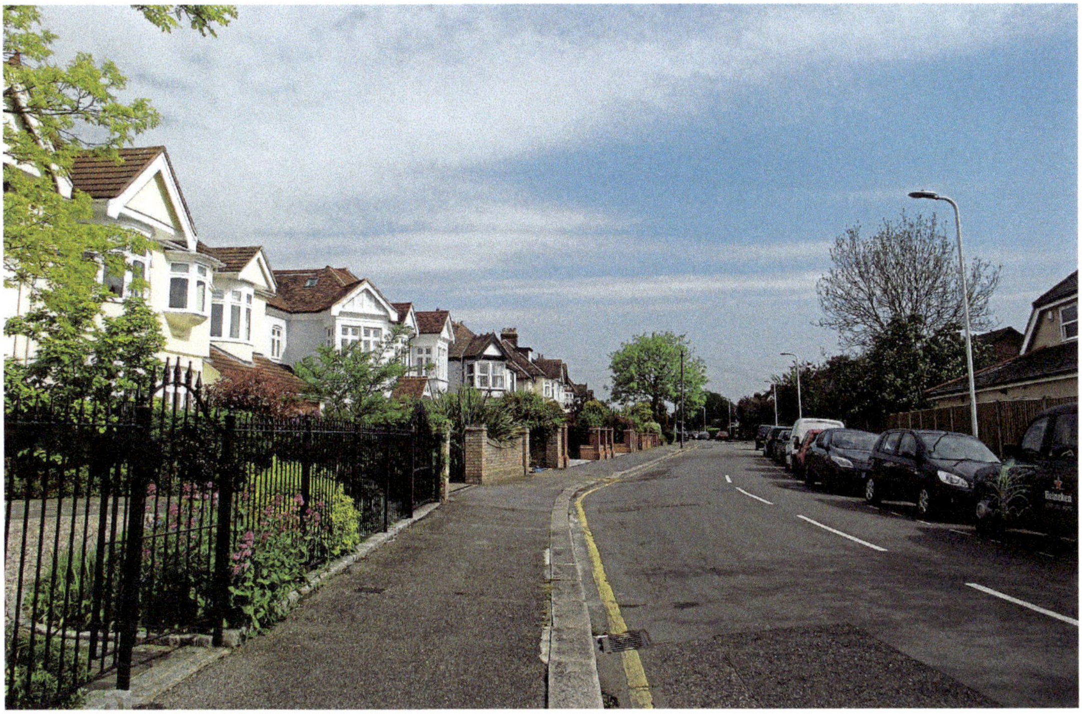

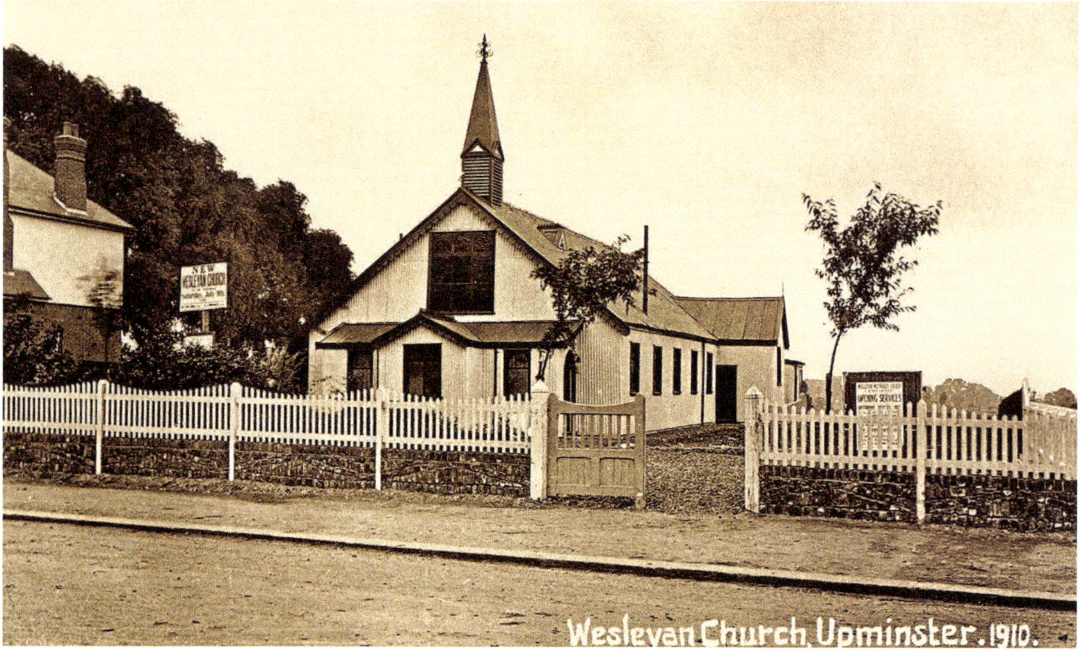

Wesleyan Church

The old image shows what is described by the poster outside as a new Wesleyan Church. This was in 1910. *The Times* reported in 1921 how a new Wesleyan Church was to be built in Upminster. The church would cost £6,600 with a grant of £3,500 but a debt of £1,600 would be left on the building. The church is still standing today, so what was a high price then has proved to have been good value.

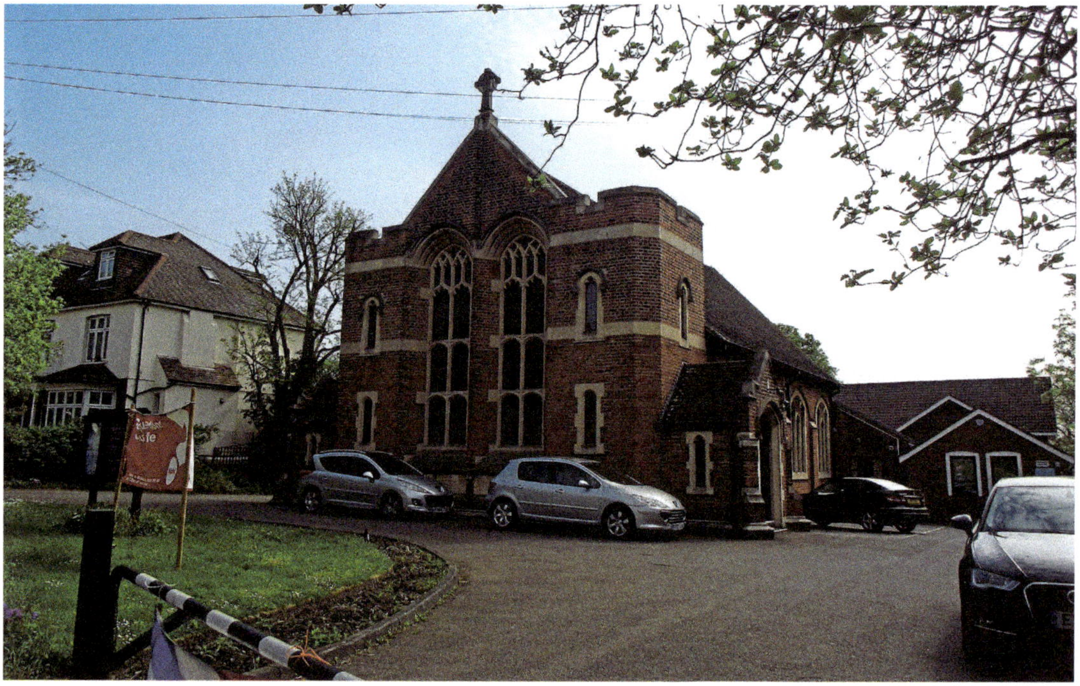

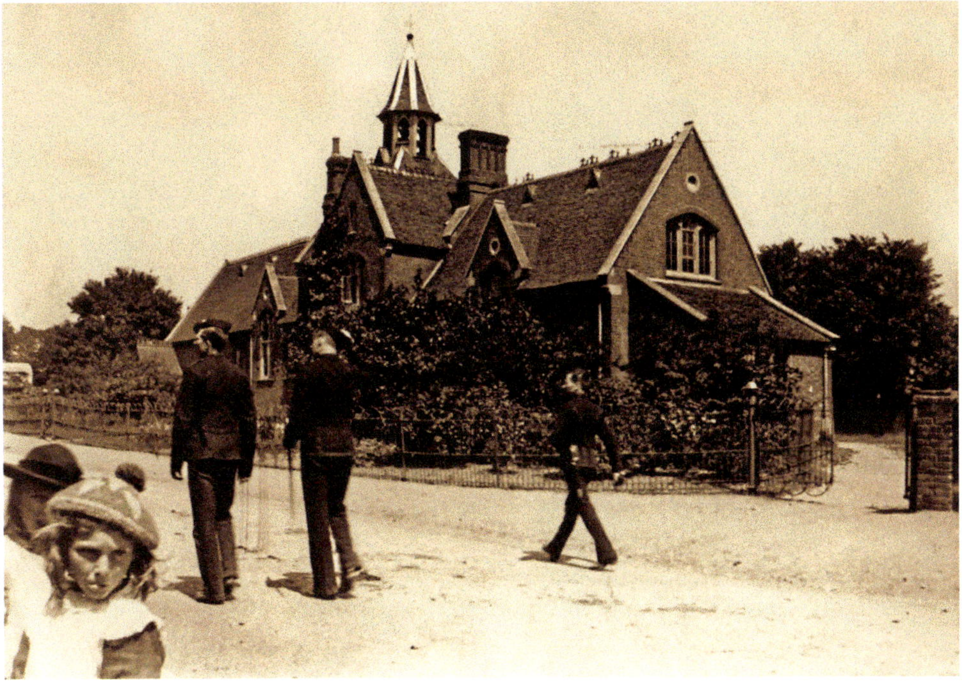

The School

There was originally a national school for boys in Station Road where the National Westminster Bank is now and a girls' school where Barclays Bank now stands. The old image shows the National School during the First World War, hence the presence of the soldiers. The present school in St Mary's Lane was built in the late 1920s and enlarged in the 1930s as the new homes led to an increase in the population. The old national school also reopened for a time to take in the increasing numbers of children. (With thanks to Havering Libraries Local Studies Dept)

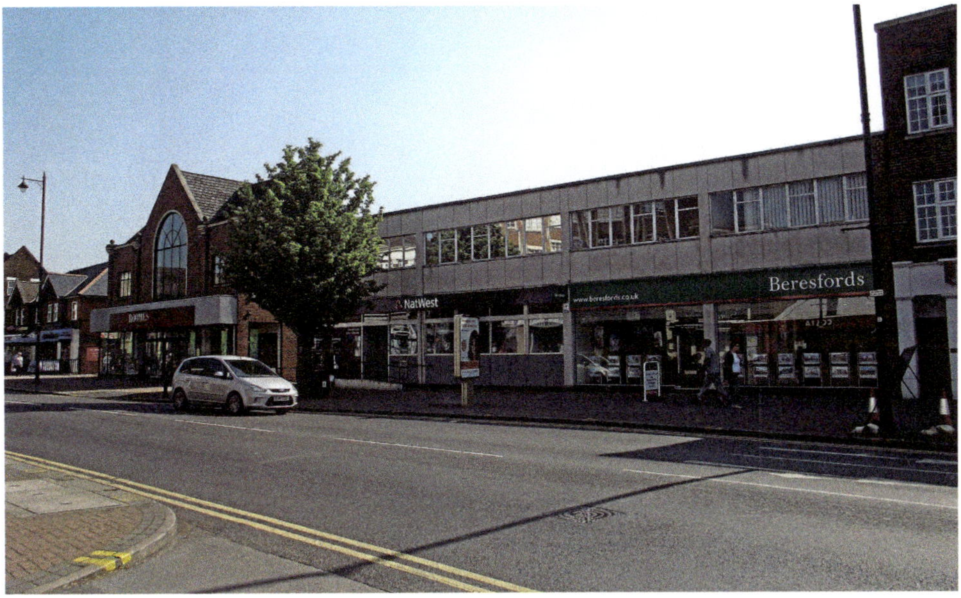

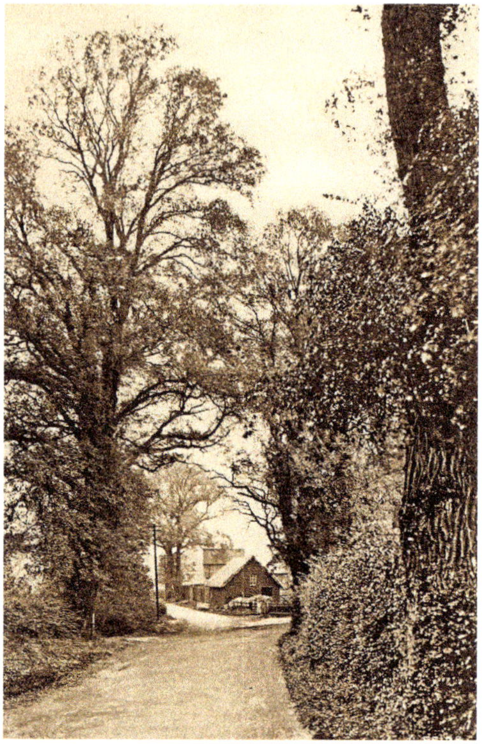

Hall Lane I

Hall Lane used to reach as far as the Broadway (also known, at the time, as Bell Corner) and there were gates into the Hall estate positioned there. When the railway arrived, part of the lane became Station Road from Bell Corner up to just north of the station. In the late nineteenth century, land near Hall Lane was considered as the site of a new cemetery for the town. The old image shows how the lane looked before widespread development took place. Despite the number of houses in the road, it still retains a rural image.

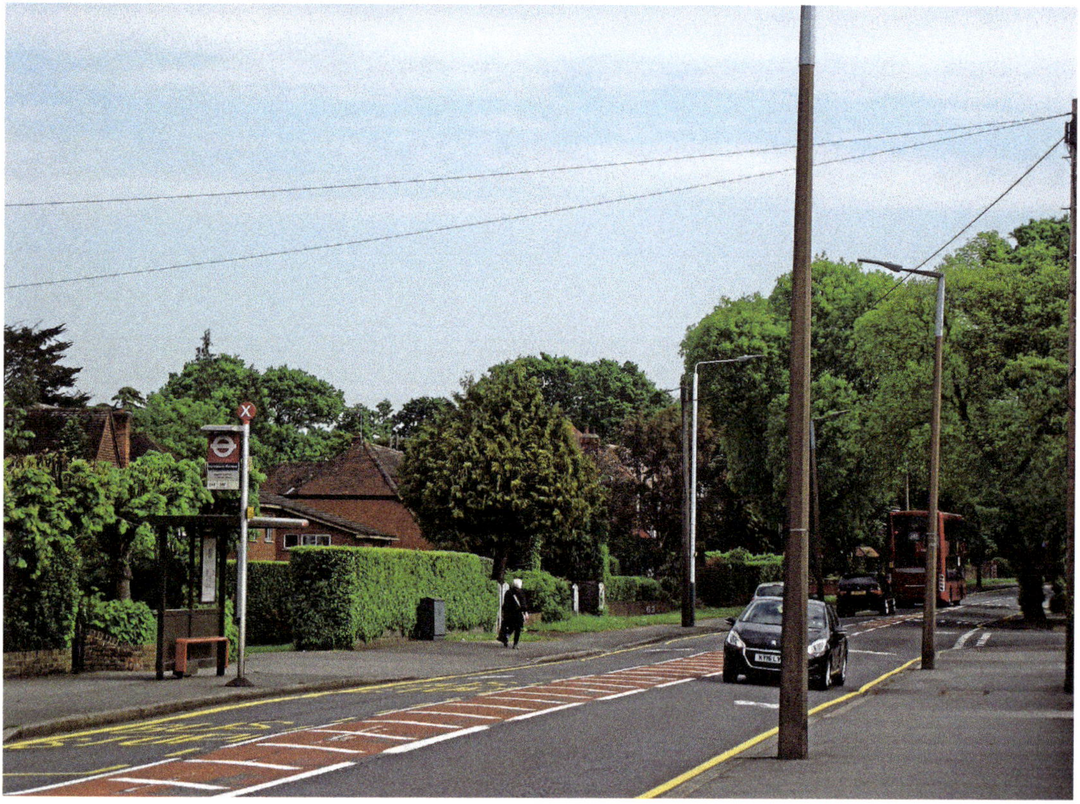

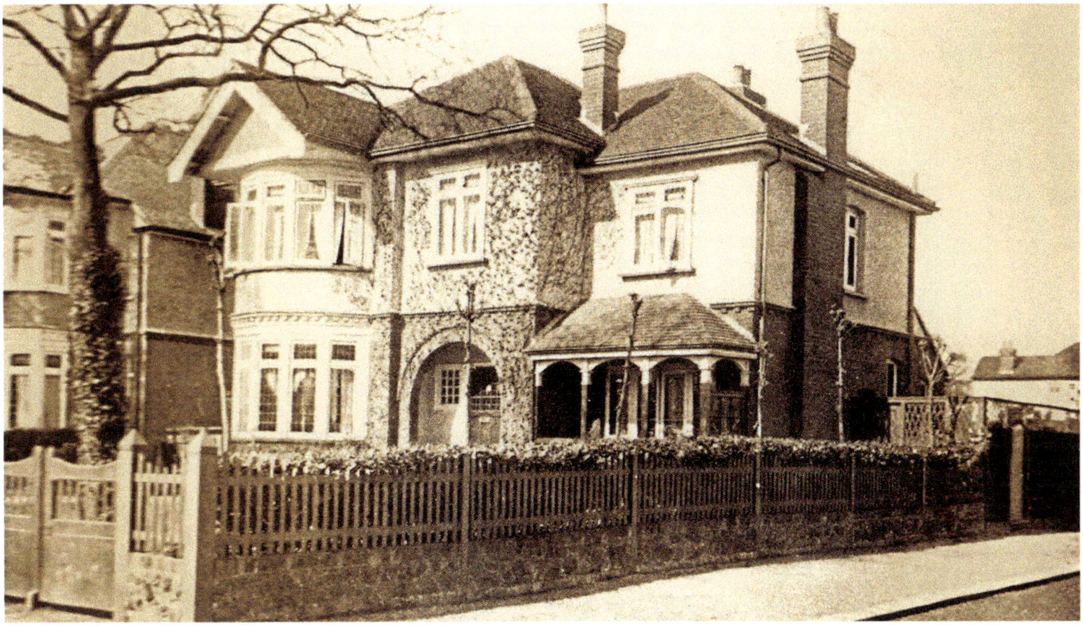

Hall Lane II

The old photograph shows one of the smaller houses built in the area. There was an event nearby that must have aroused local interest in February 1938. During a heavy snowstorm, a light aircraft crashed on the golf course. It hit a tree and turned over. The passenger was thrown clear but the pilot was left hanging upside down in the plane. Neither of the men were seriously hurt. The modern image shows that not all of the homes in Hall Lane date back to the early part of the twentieth century – some are much more recent.

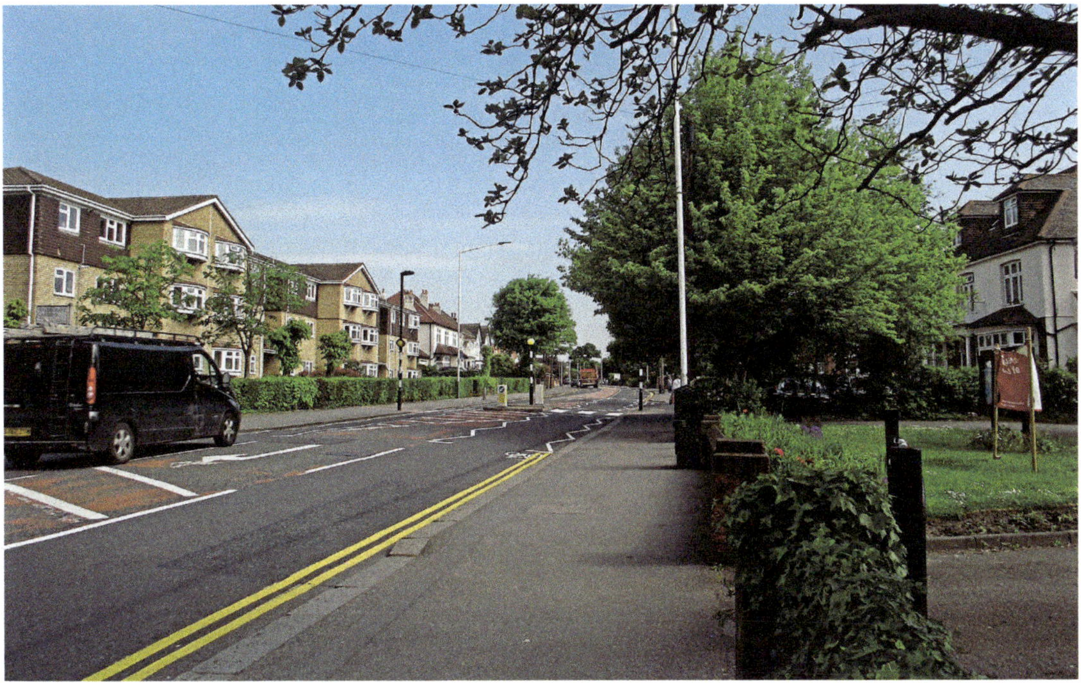

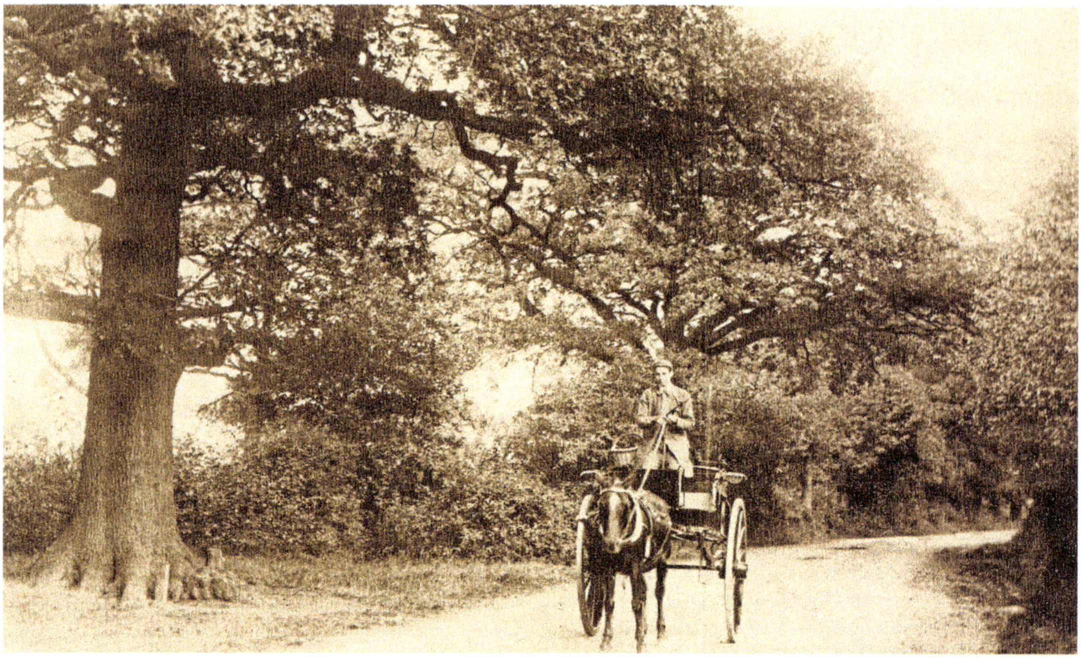

Hall Lane III

Hall Lane was the road towards Warley and was 2 miles long. Although parts of what was the estate have now been built on, the lane still has some wonderful views over open countryside, as well as some of the grandest houses in the area. The old image shows its rural character. It now also passes over the Southend arterial road – the A127. In September 1948, a number of lorries were used to block the road between Upminster and East Horndon so that a pony trap race could take place. The police stated that the lorries had seats so were used like grandstands. There were eight men who were fined a total of £63 despite claiming that they were just caught in traffic. The modern image shows the lesser-developed northern end of Hall Lane.

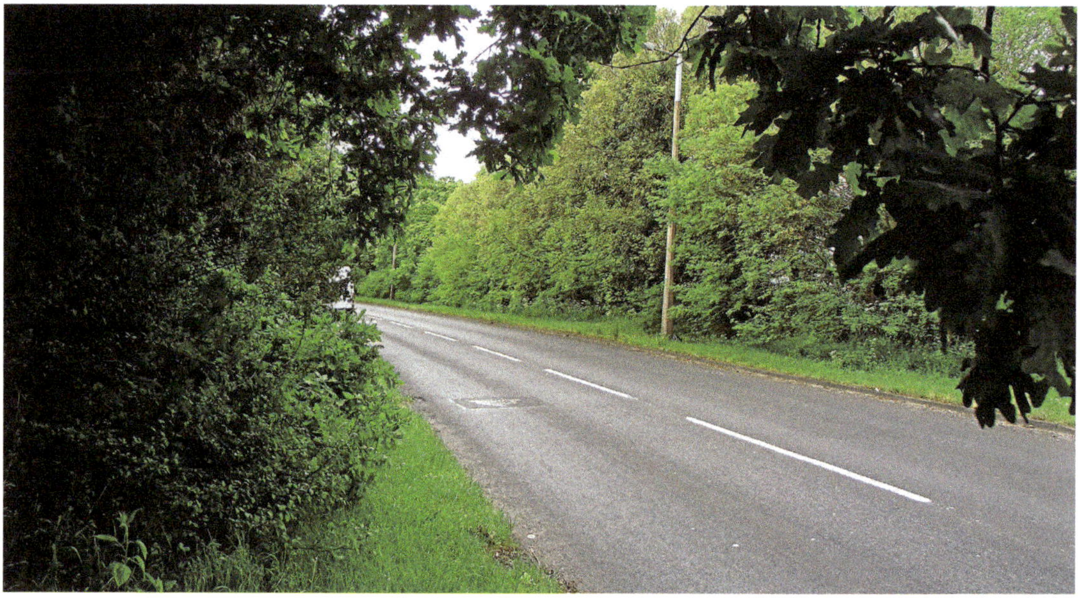

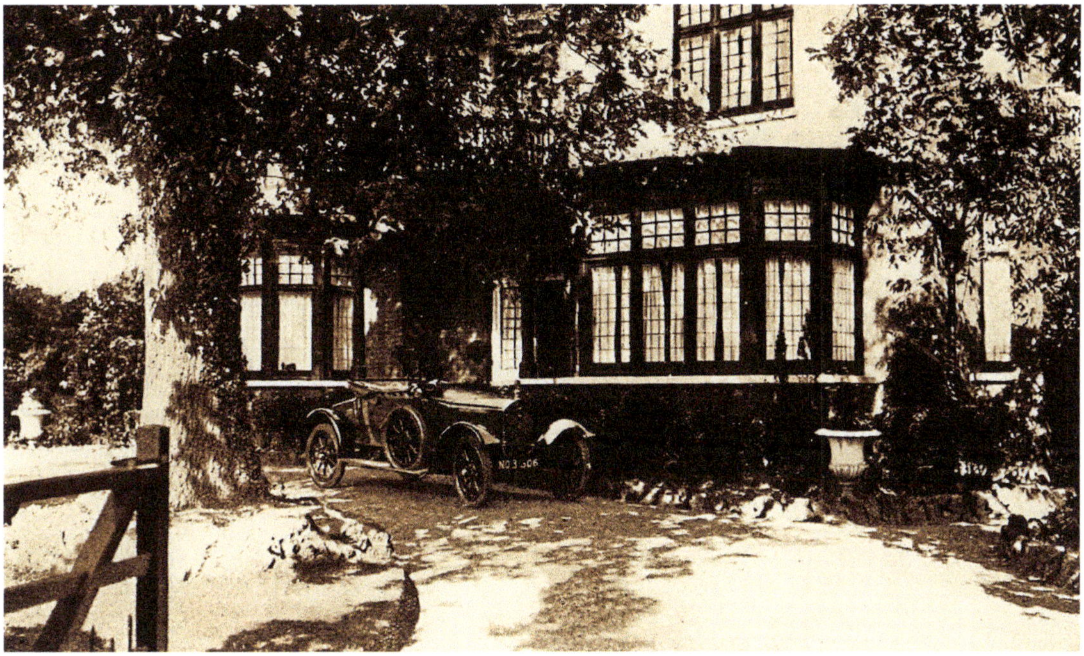

Hall Lane IV

The house shown in the old image is obviously one of the more affluent ones and it looks as though the owner could also afford a car. There was an interesting report in the *Essex Standard* in 1890 concerning a visit by members of the Essex Field Club to Upminster. After meeting at Harold Wood Station, they crossed the Ingrebourne River and went to the northern part of Upminster on the common. From there they could see the spire of the church at Hornchurch and the stone tower of South Weald's church. On a clear day, they claimed to be able to see as far as the hills of Kent and the Crystal Palace. The modern image shows that the road is now a busy thoroughfare.

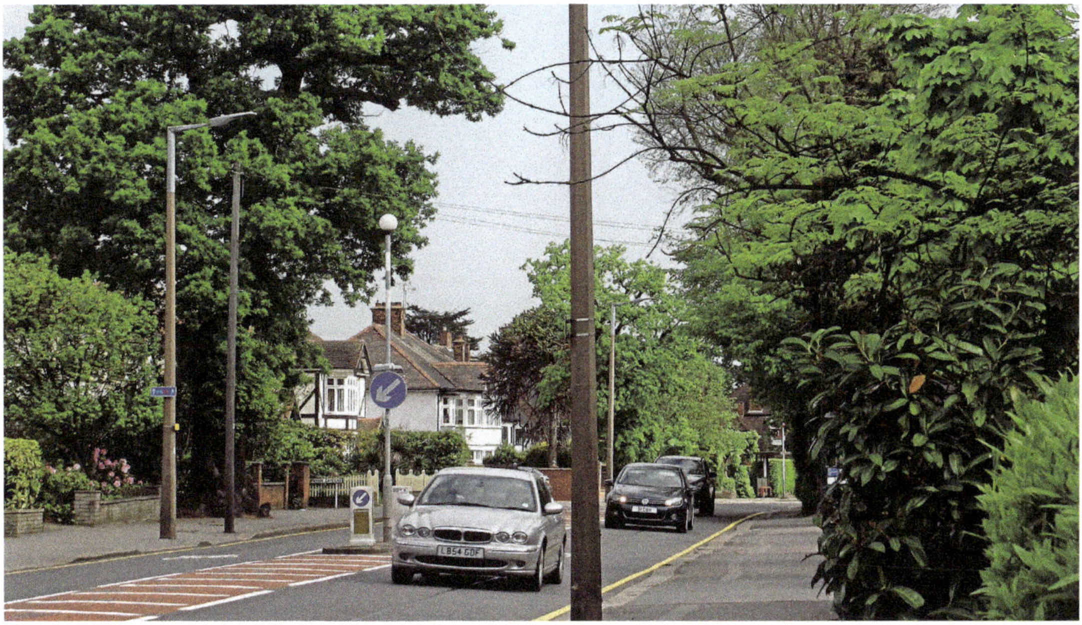

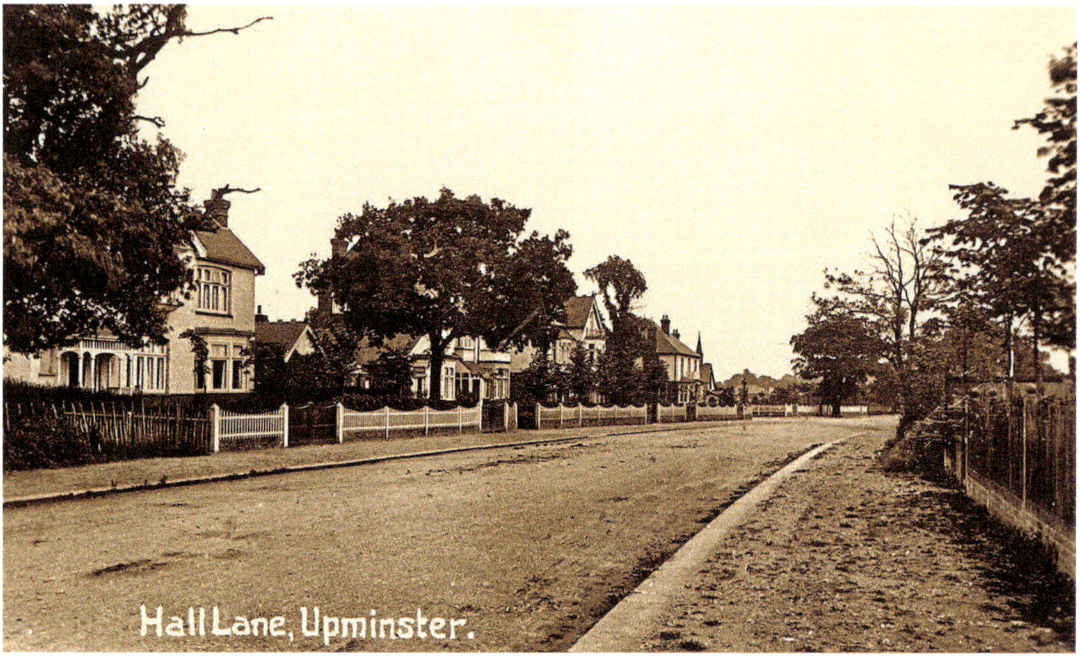

Hall Lane V

One of the oldest buildings in Upminster is situated in Hall Lane in the driveway to Upminster Hall. This is the old tithe barn that dates back to the fourteenth century. It was rethatched in the 1960s and is now a museum, which has been maintained by the Hornchurch and District Historical Society. The majority of the buildings lining the road are much more modern and, as the image below shows, have not changed very much since they were built.

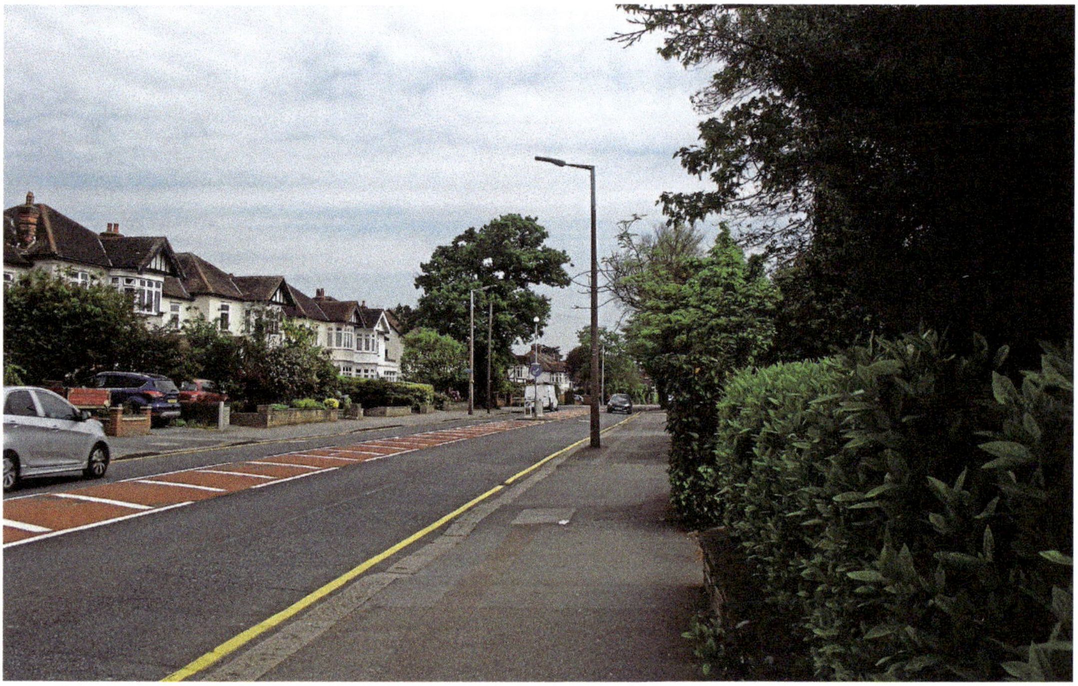

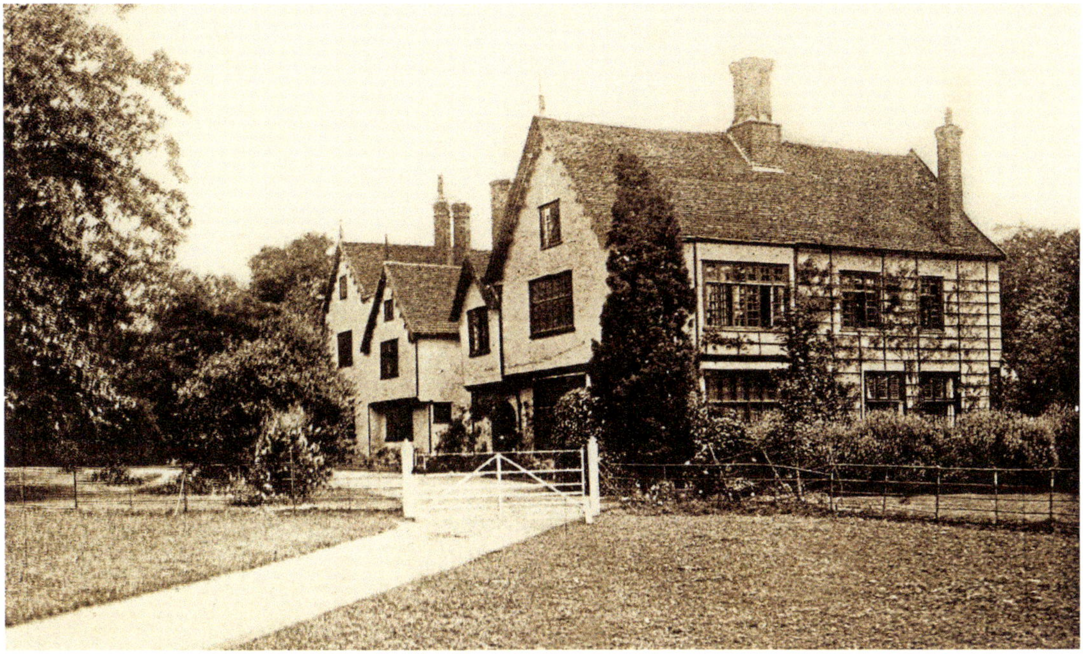

Upminster Hall

There was a good example of the life of a country gentleman who would have lived in the hall in the past. When the Essex Field Club visited the hall in 1890, the owner, Mr G. P. Hope, served them tea on the lawn and showed them his fine collection of fossils, algae and birds. One of the members also displayed a butterfly never previously seen in England. Another member showed a palaeolith (a Stone Age implement) he had found on Tyler Common. In 1921, there was an advertisement for a parlour maid and needlewoman at the hall, which was described as a non-basement building with electric light. The hall has been the home of Upminster Golf Club since 1927.

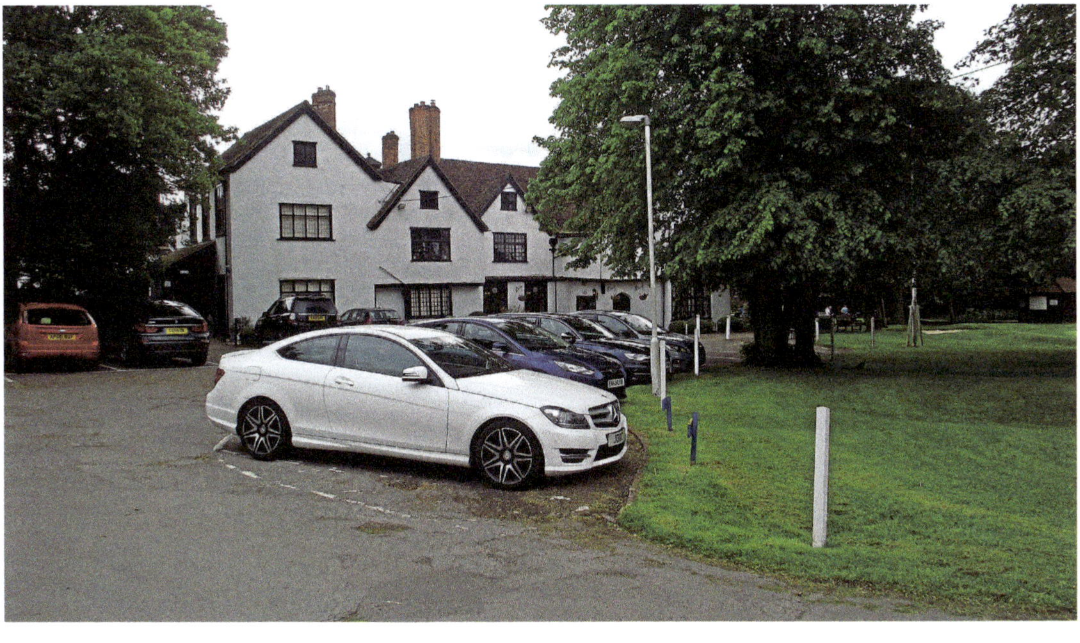

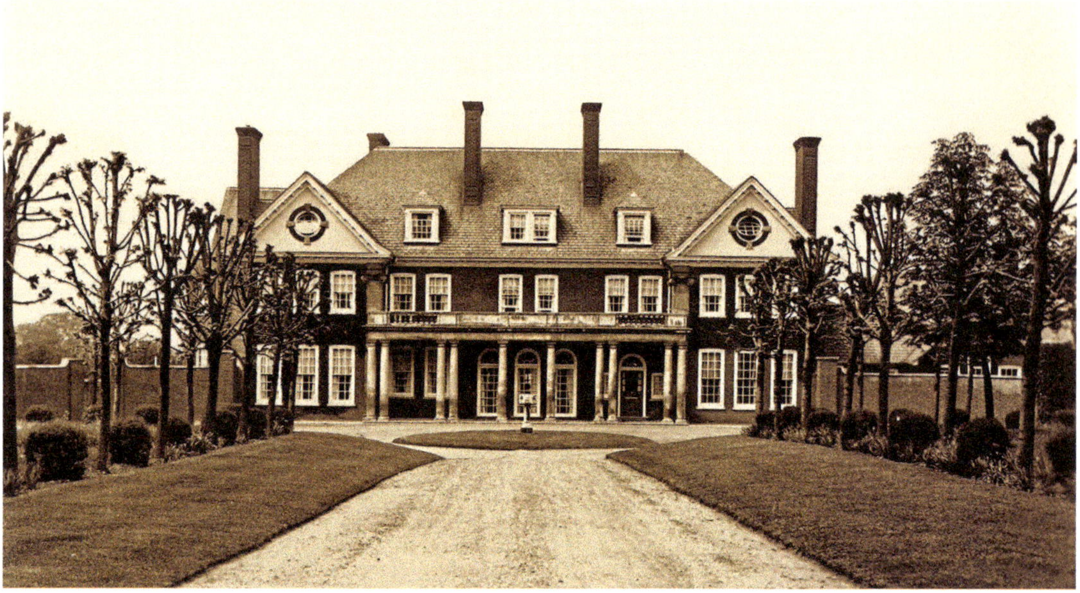

Upminster Court

Unlike many of the other large houses in Upminster, the court was not built until the early twentieth century. It was built for Arthur Williams who was a director of the Samuel Williams Co. at Dagenham Dock. During the Second World War, it was used to house refugees and since then has not been used as a private home. The Essex County Council owned it and used it for education offices. It has also been a retirement home and a college until sold in 2007 to a private company for use as offices once more.

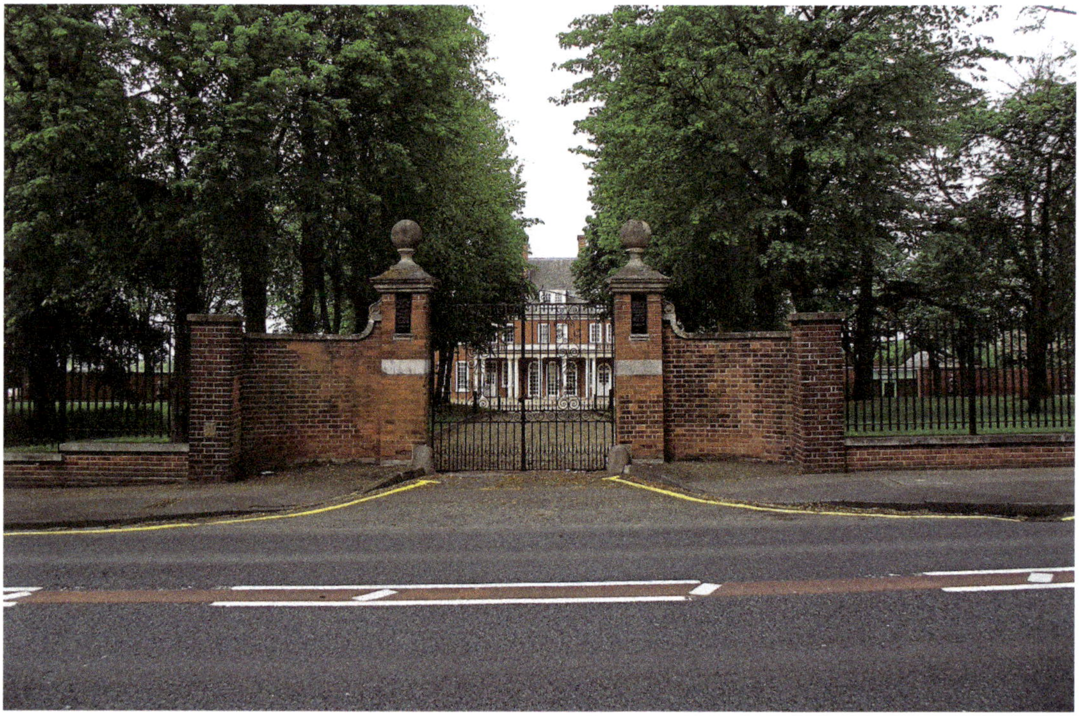

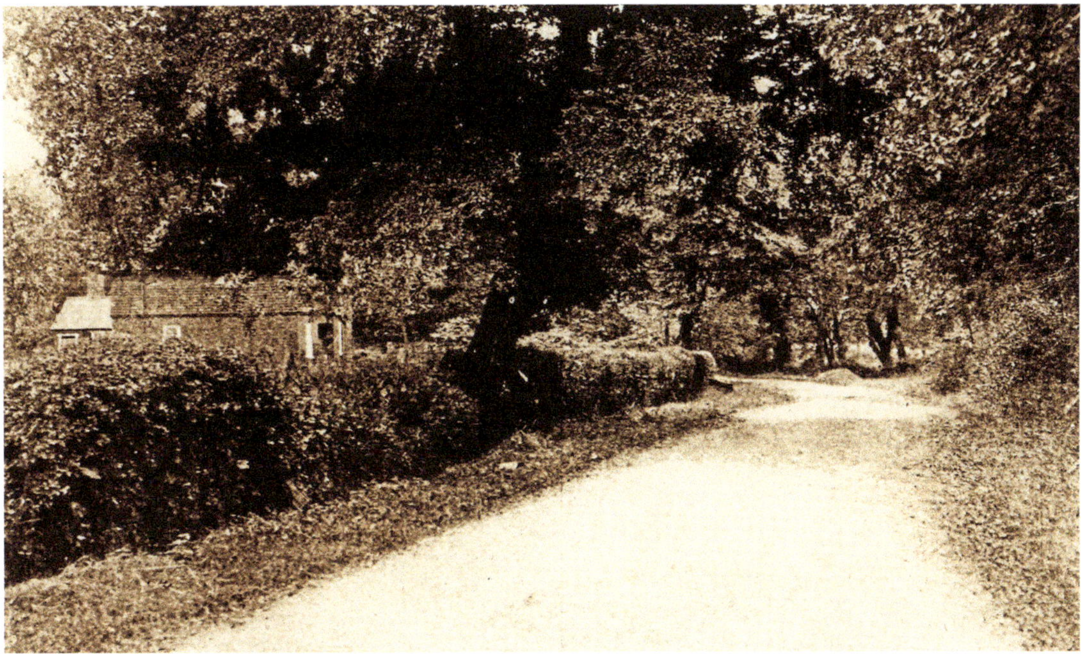

Centre of Garden Suburb

The Garden Suburb was an idea that evolved from the Garden City movement of Sir Ebenezer Howard in the late nineteenth century. The idea was to combine town and countryside as an alternative to crowded cities. The idea proved to be too expensive and was diluted to Garden Suburbs examples, which were built in Romford and in Ilford. One of those involved in the Ilford Garden Suburb was Peter Griggs, who also did much of the early building in Upminster. The old image was used in the Upminster Estates booklet to promote the area. The modern image shows that there are still rural homes in the town; this one is situated in the Chase, leading to Cranham Church.

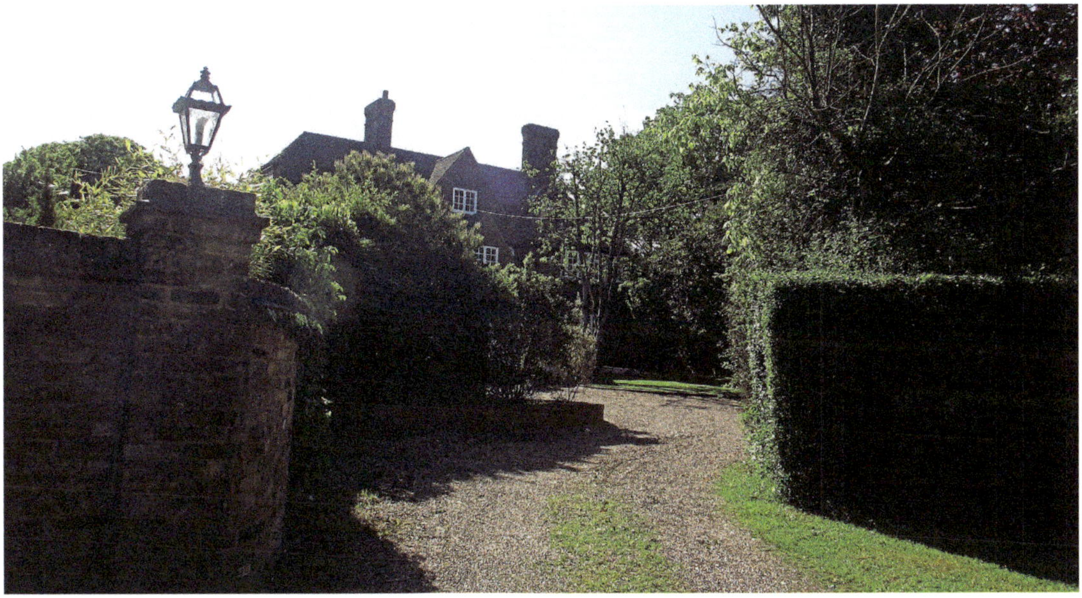

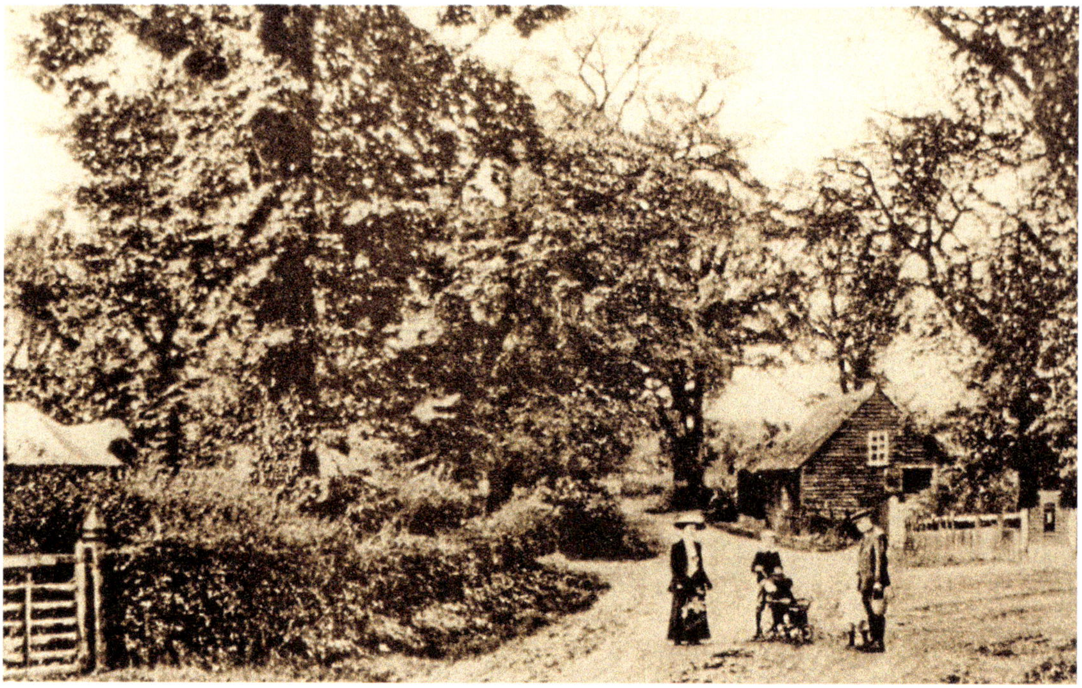

Bird Lane I

Bird Lane has retained much of its rural image. In the past, it was once the centre of brickmaking in Upminster and employed up to twenty men. The trade seems to have been widely pursued in Essex and, in nearby Ilford, brick-making led to the discovery of well-known fossils, but I haven't heard of any being discovered in Upminster. Farming survived the brick-making trade; the farm shown in the modern photograph is situated at the junction of Bird Lane with Hall Lane. (With thanks to Swan Books)

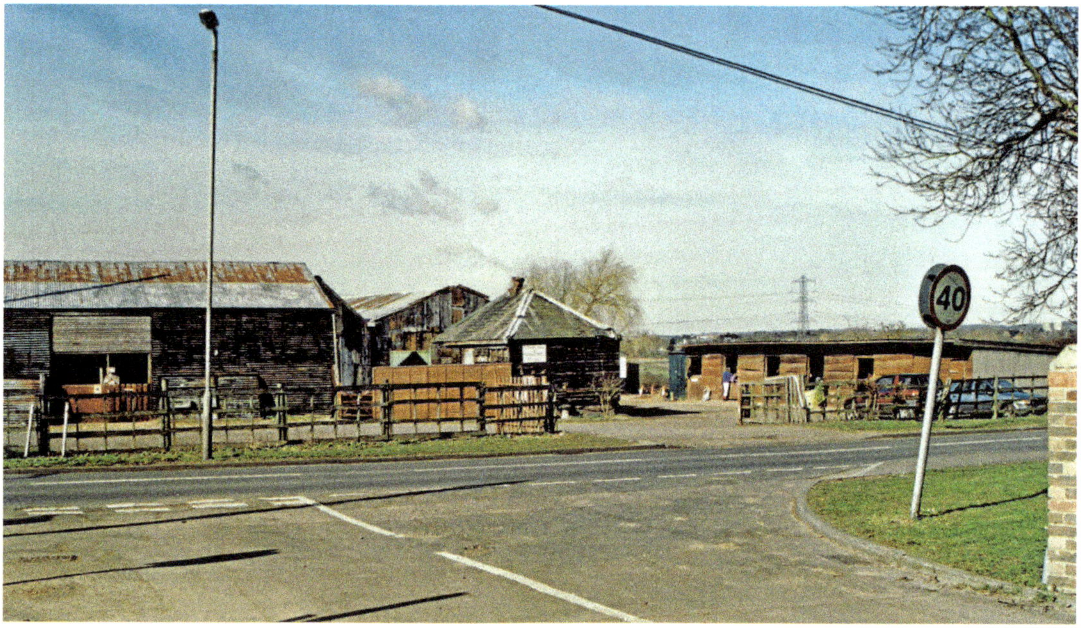

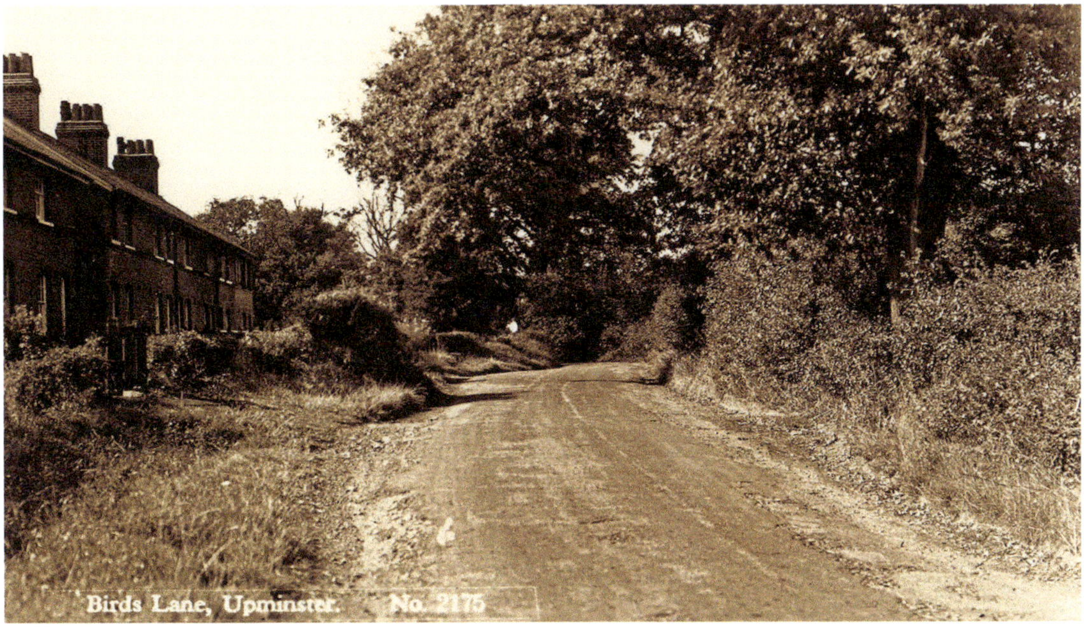

Bird Lane II

The lane is the site of the Pantile Cottages, which were built for workers of the brick-making industry in the late nineteenth century. The area is still mainly farmland and the lane itself leads into Tomkyns Lane and then into Warley Road. There has been very little development in the area, as the modern image shows.

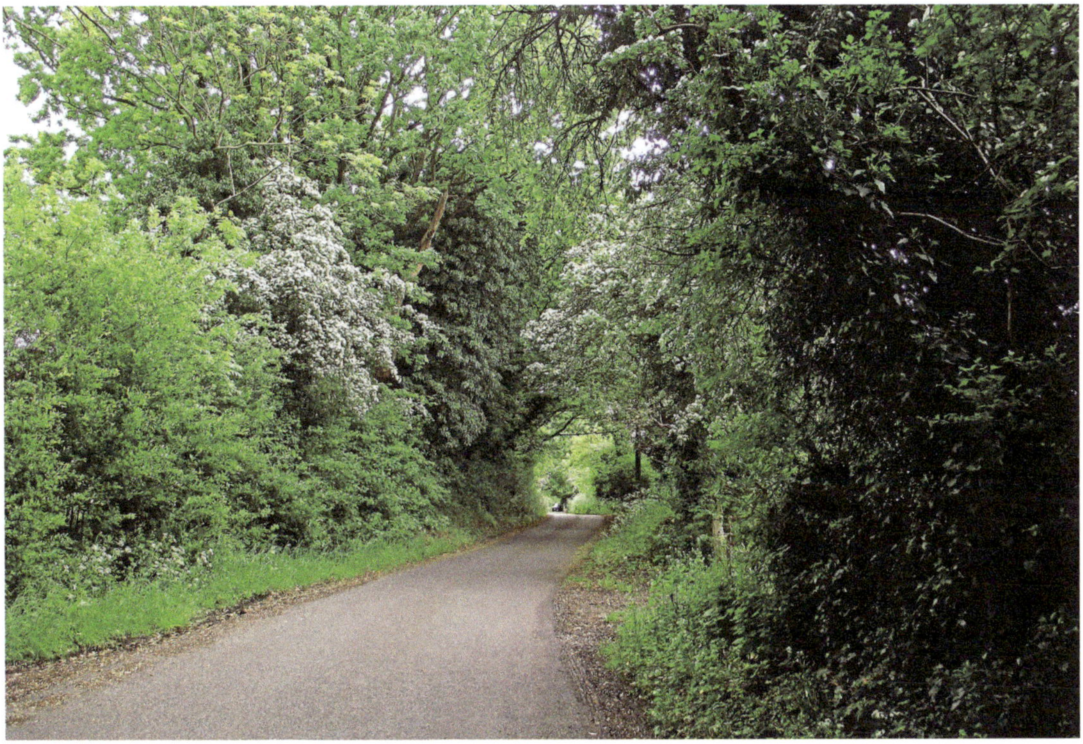

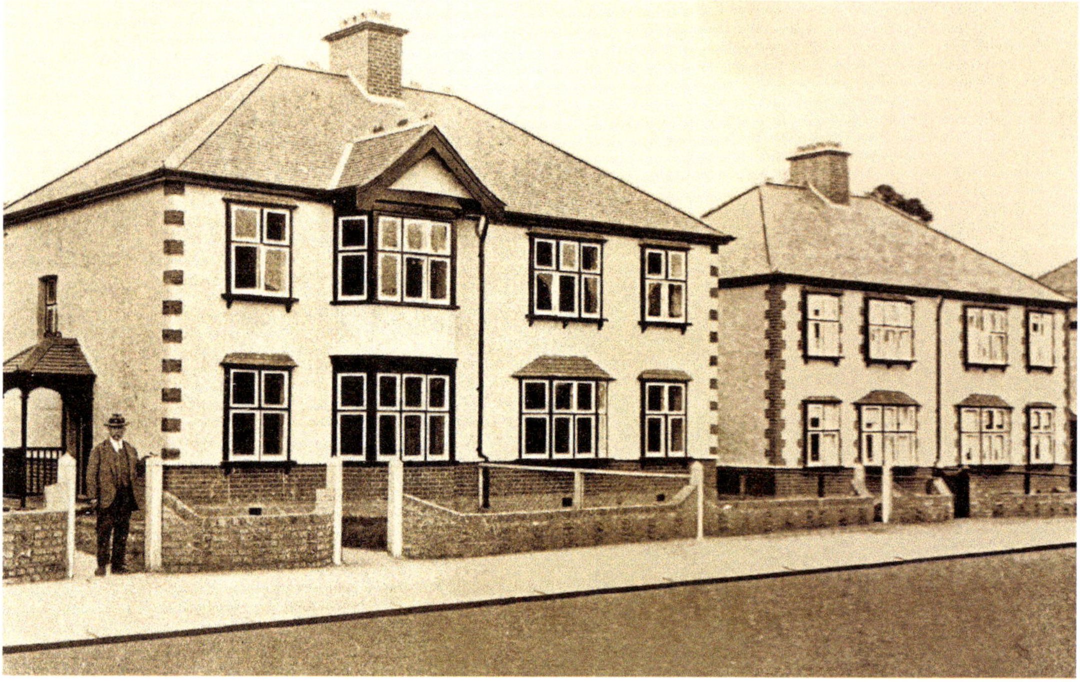

Sunnyside Gardens

Sunnyside Gardens is situated on what was the limit of the estate known as New Place. The house on New Place estate was demolished in 1924, allowing development to take place, although the stable block known as the Clockhouse was saved by the council. The gardens have changed since the houses were built, with a number of bungalows now in evidence.

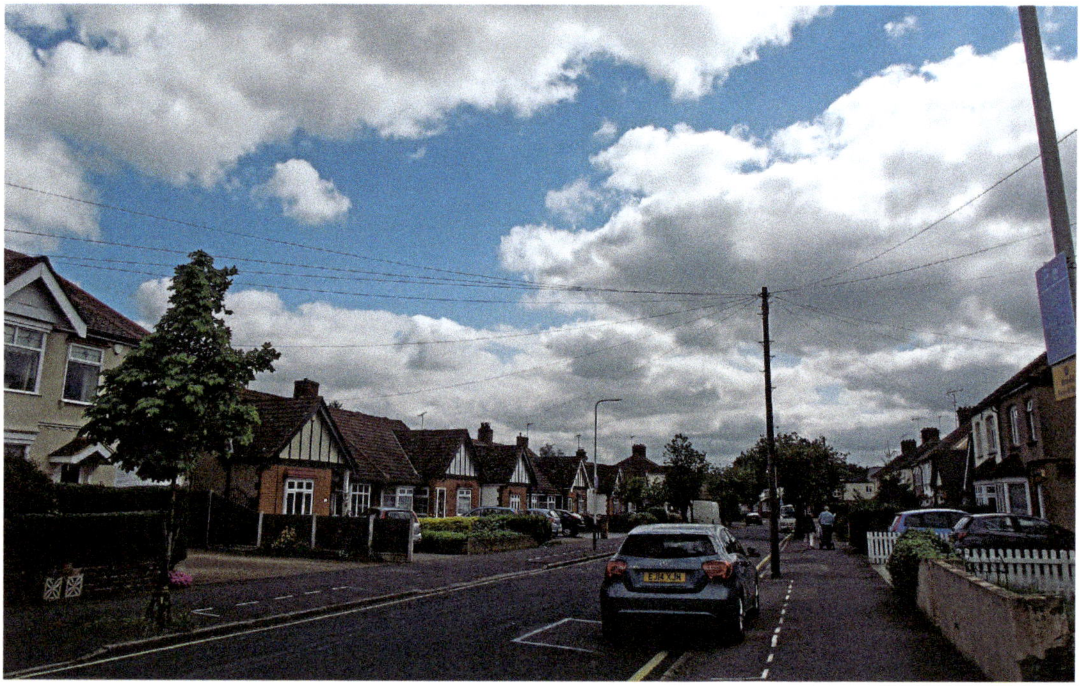

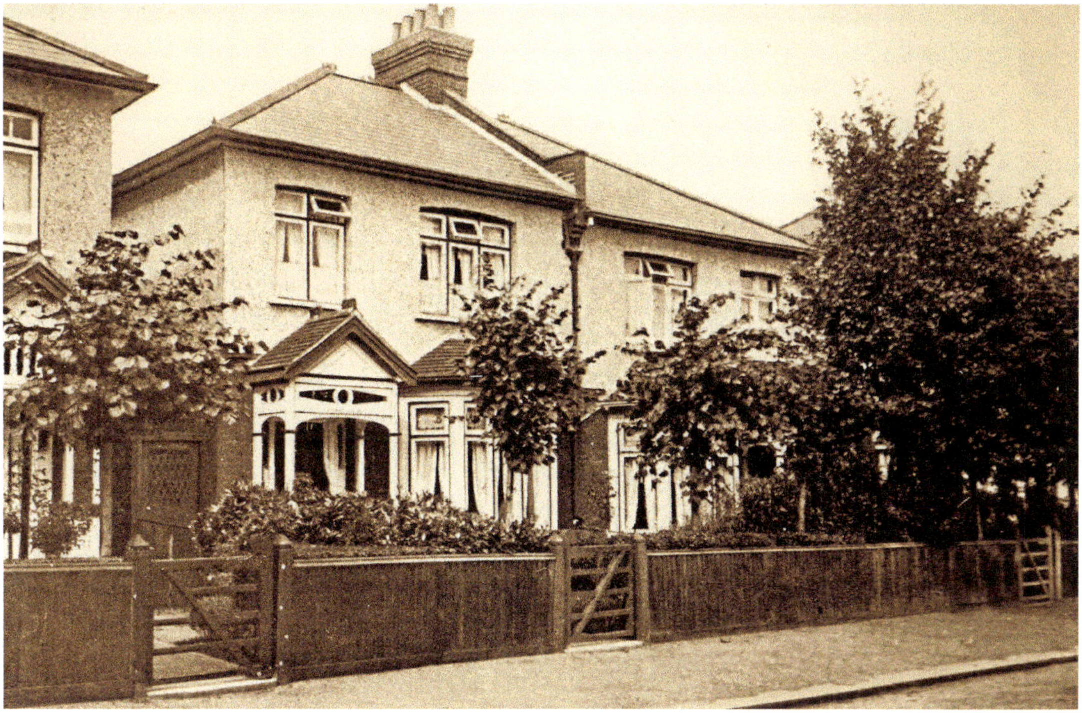

Argyle Gardens I

The point where Argyle Gardens meets St Mary's Lane was once the boundary between the parishes of Upminster and Cranham. It was also the site of a manor house called New Place. This went through a number of redevelopments and the final house built and lived in by Sir John Esdaile was demolished in the 1920s. The houses were built soon after and their original designs are still evident today.

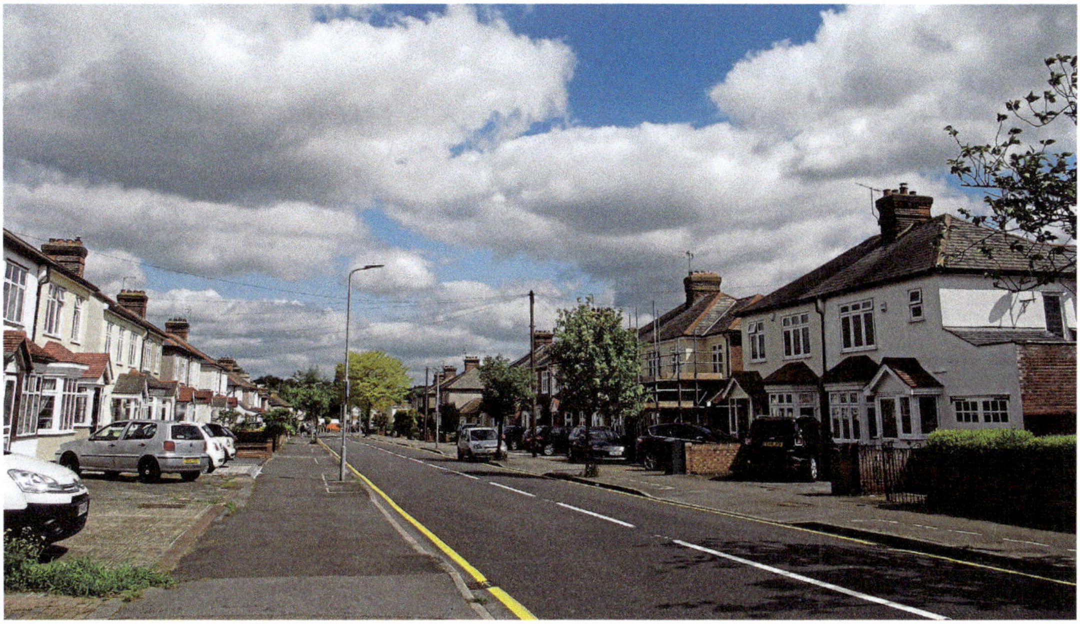

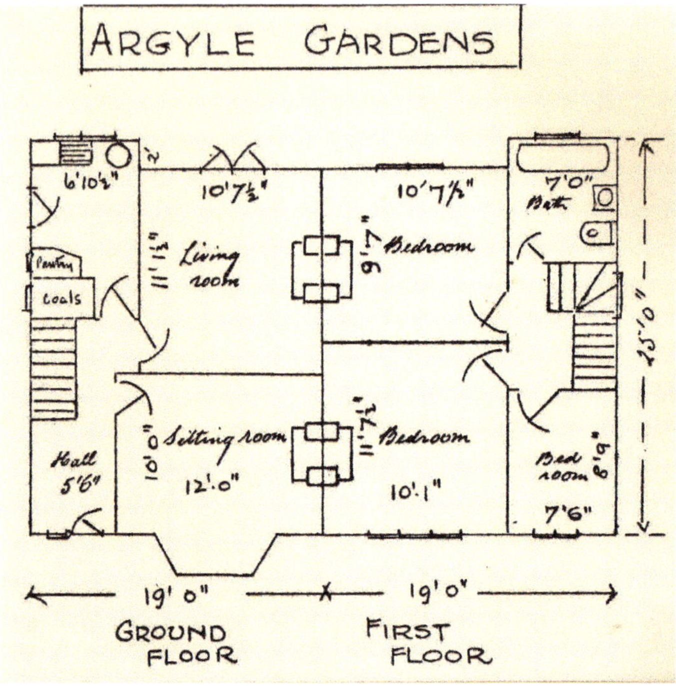

Argyle Gardens II

The booklet issued by the Upminster Estates contained a plan of the interior of one of the houses in Argyle Gardens. Although many of the houses in Upminster being built at the time were rather grand, such as those in Hall Lane, the size of the rooms in the plan show that this was not the case in all of the new homes. Argyle Gardens was the site of some of the less expensive homes.

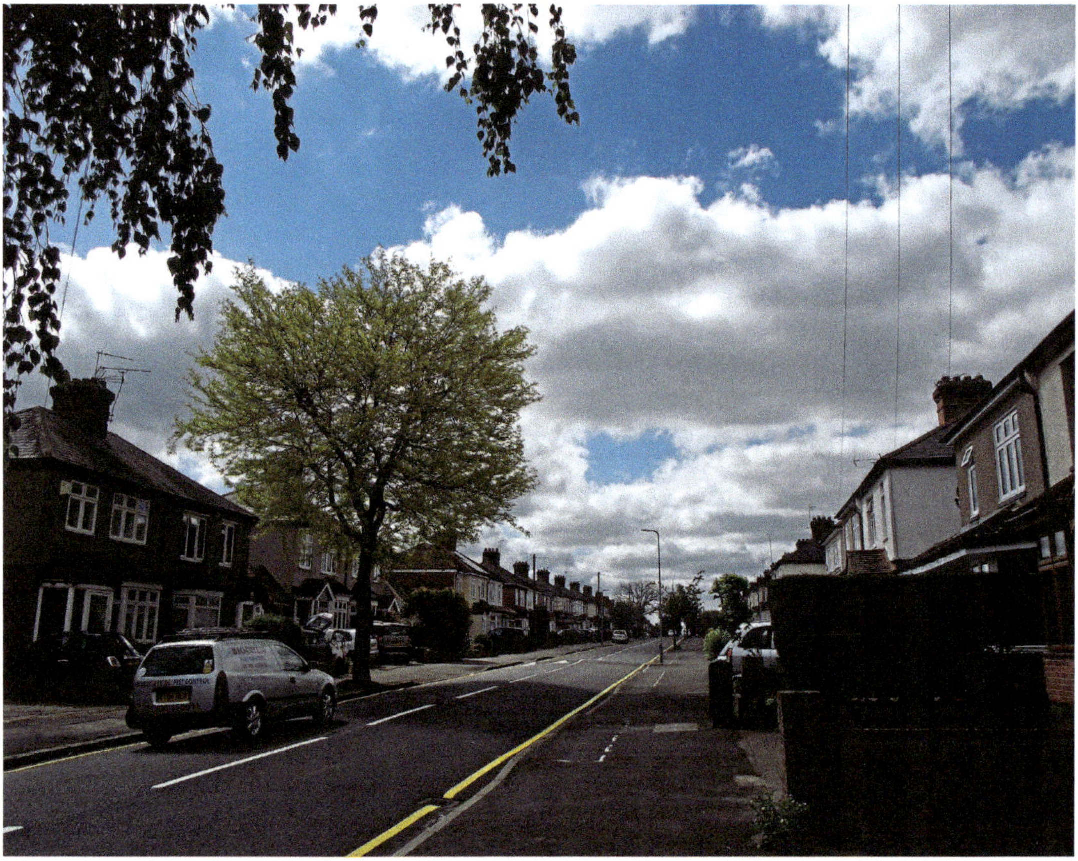

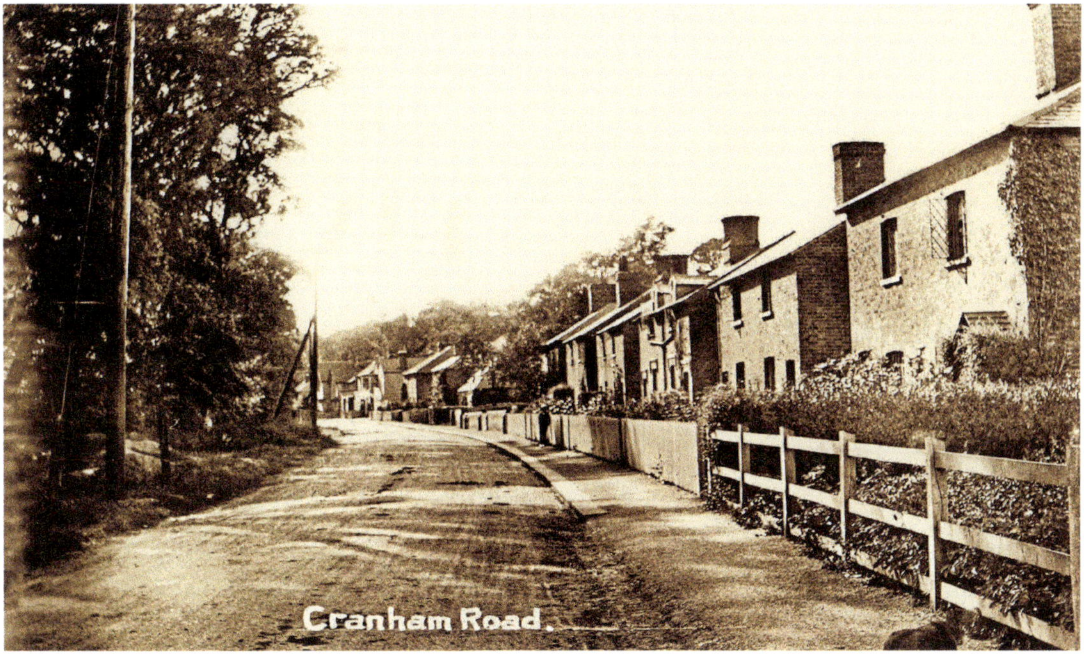

Cranham Road

The old image shows what was once known as Cranham Road but is now St Mary's Lane. Although there is a way into the main part of Cranham from St Mary's Lane, this is under a low railway bridge; double-decker buses to Cranham are therefore forced to take the longer route to the estate along Hall Lane. The modern image shows some of the older buildings in what was Cranham Road and the shops at the junction with Station Road.

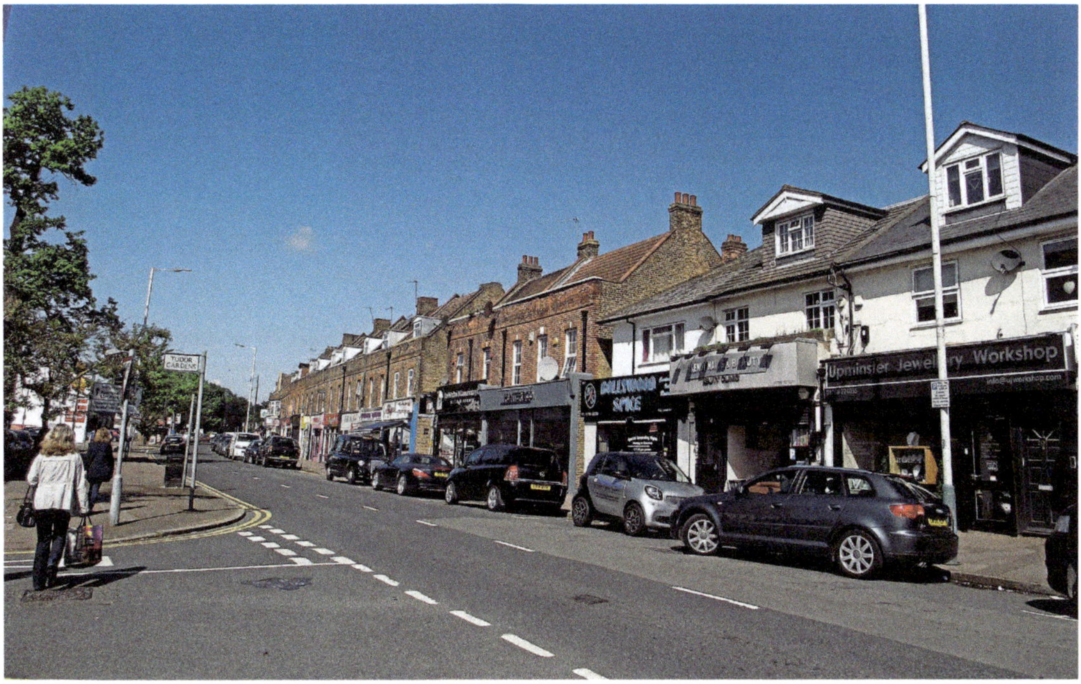

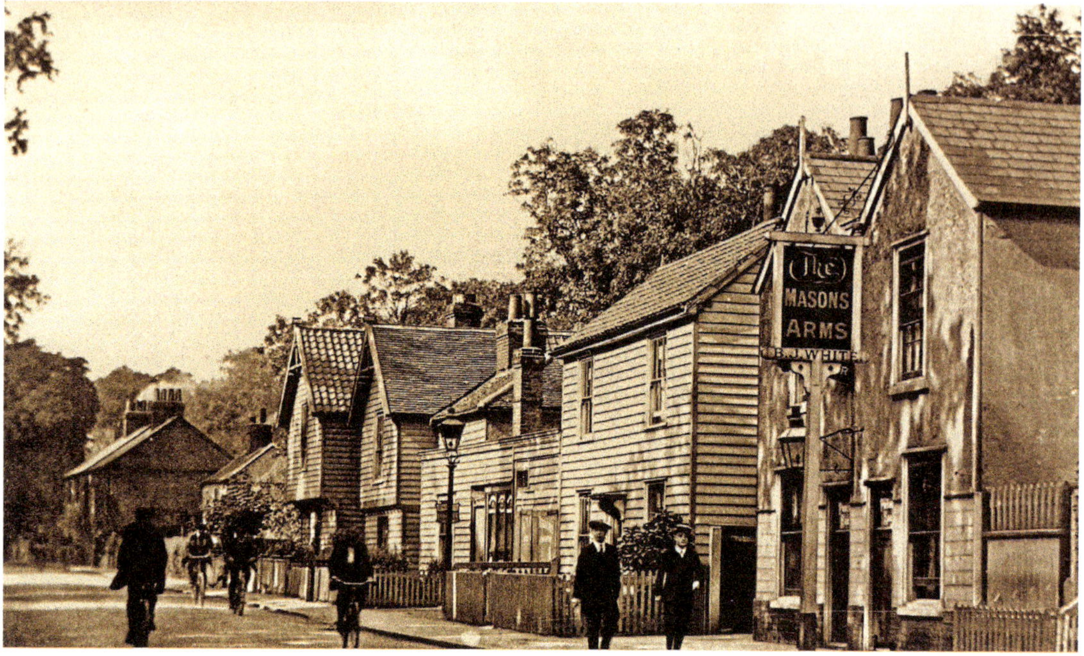

Mason's Arms

The Mason's Arms once stood on the boundary between the parishes of Upminster and Cranham. There was a row of very old cottages alongside the inn. The Mason's Arms was rebuilt in the late 1920s on the site of a previous inn. The buildings along this part of the road were once part of the old Upminster Hall Estate. As the modern image shows, the Mason's Arms has gone the way of numerous other public houses, having recently been closed and demolished. The site was still empty at the time this photograph was taken.

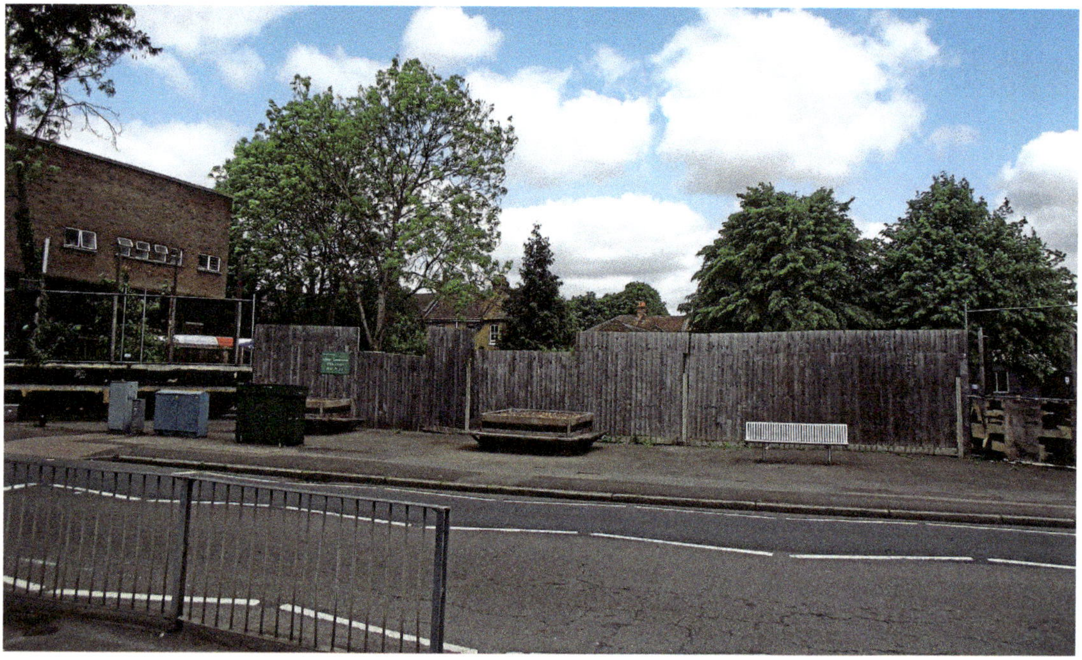

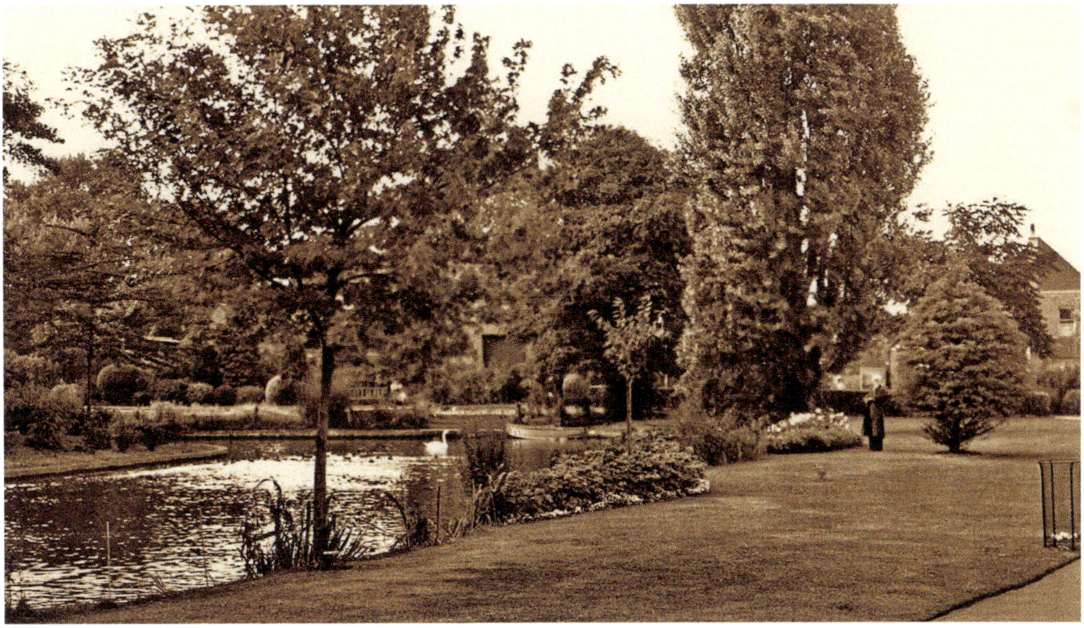

Clockhouse Gardens

The gardens were once part of New Place estate and the water feature in the gardens was once part of the moat of the old house. The gardens, along with the Clockhouse, were saved from development when they were bought by the council. The Clockhouse was once the stable block of New Place, which had a clock set in a turret. It was known as the village clock in the nineteenth century.

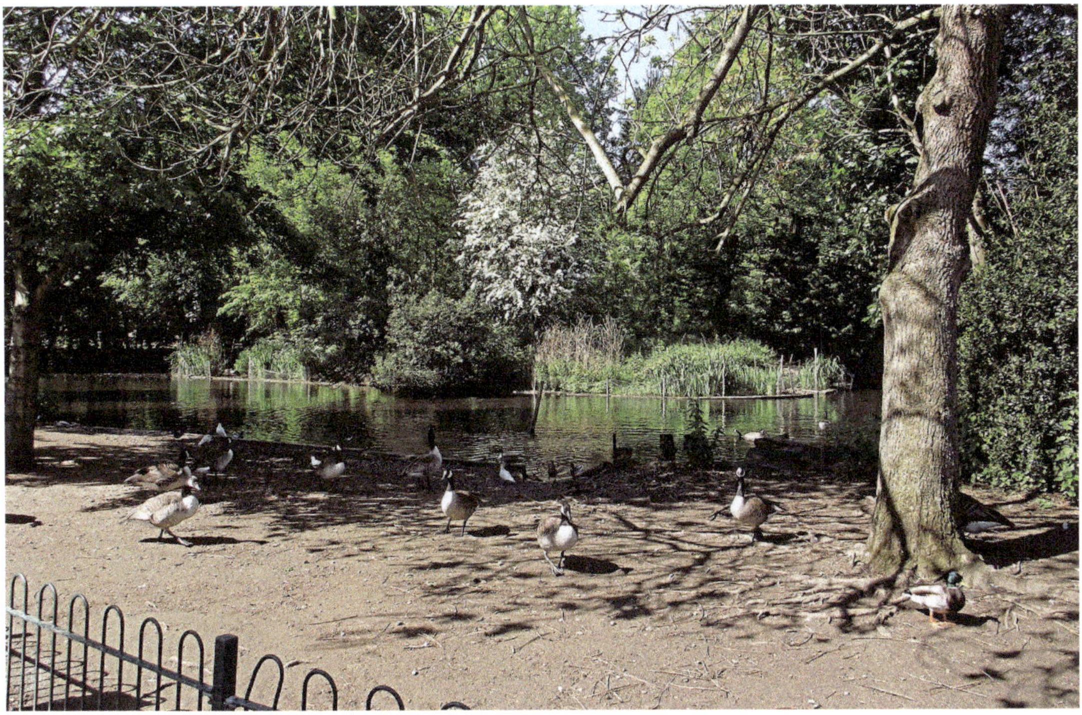

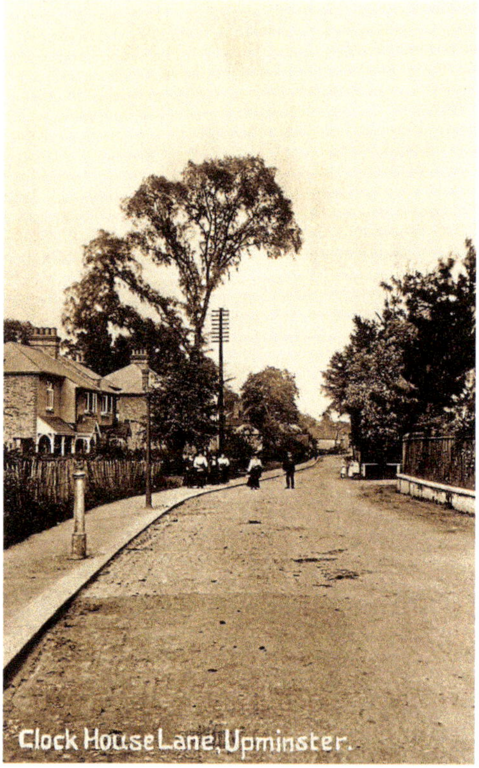

Clockhouse Lane

There were plans to demolish the Clockhouse in the 1920s when housing was planned in the area, but the council bought it for offices, which saved it from demolition. It was also where the Upminster Fire Brigade was based and was later used as a library. Although there is no Clockhouse Lane there now, part of what is now St Mary's Lane was once known by this name when it was Cranham Road.

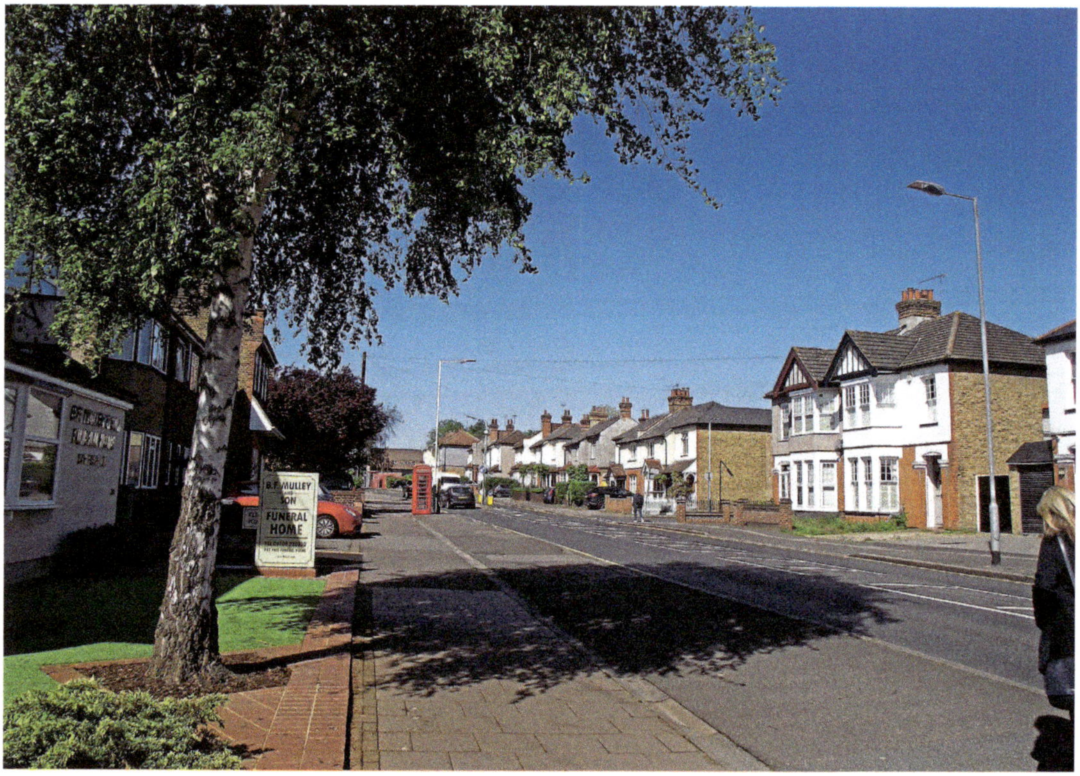

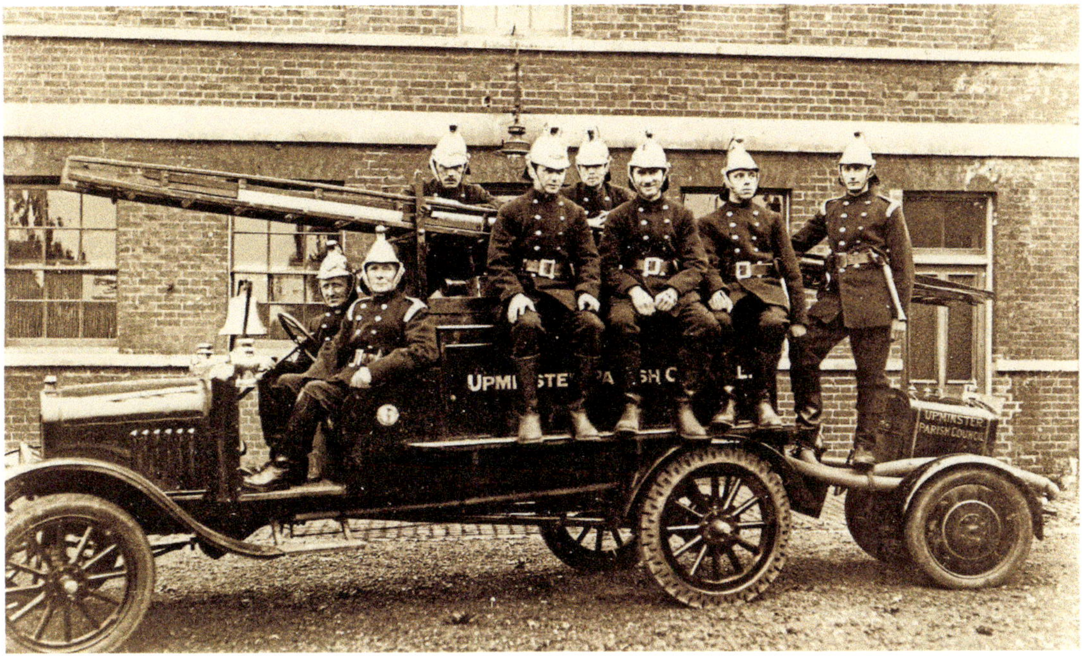

Fire Brigade I

In the early days of the twentieth century, Upminster did not have its own fire brigade – the nearest was at Billet Lane in Hornchurch. When the thatched roof at West Gate Lodge caught fire in 1908, it took the firemen so long to get there that much of the building was lost. Fire hydrants were not built in Upminster until 1908 and a handcart fire engine was bought. Hornchurch Fire Brigade, however, still did much of the work in Upminster but there were often disputes over payment and whether the Hornchurch brigade should have attended fires in Upminster. The modern image shows the front view of the Clockhouse, where the Upminster brigade was based.

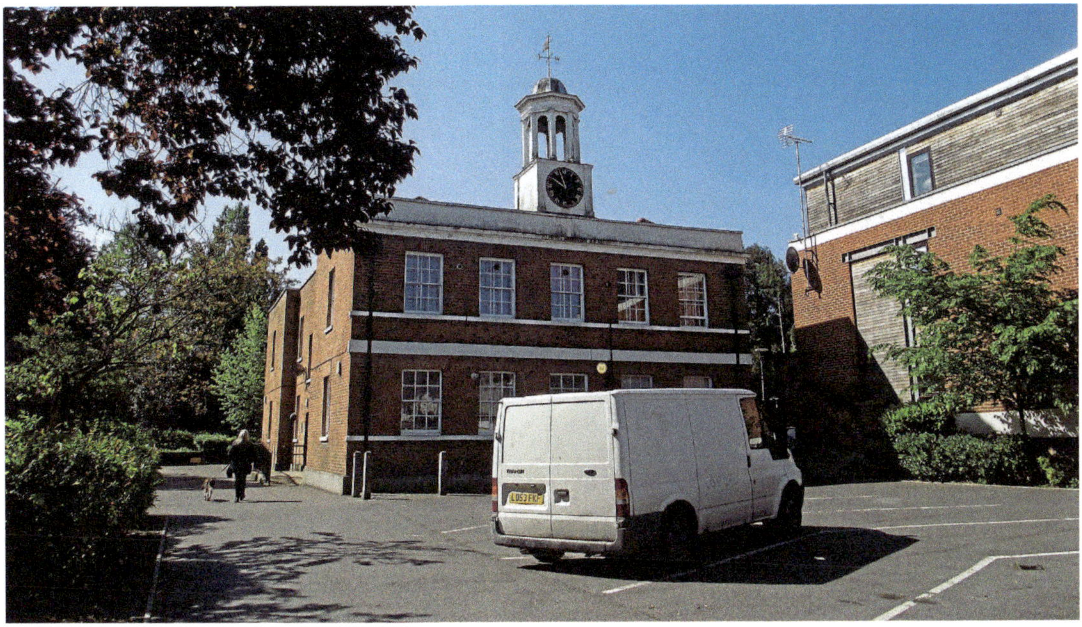

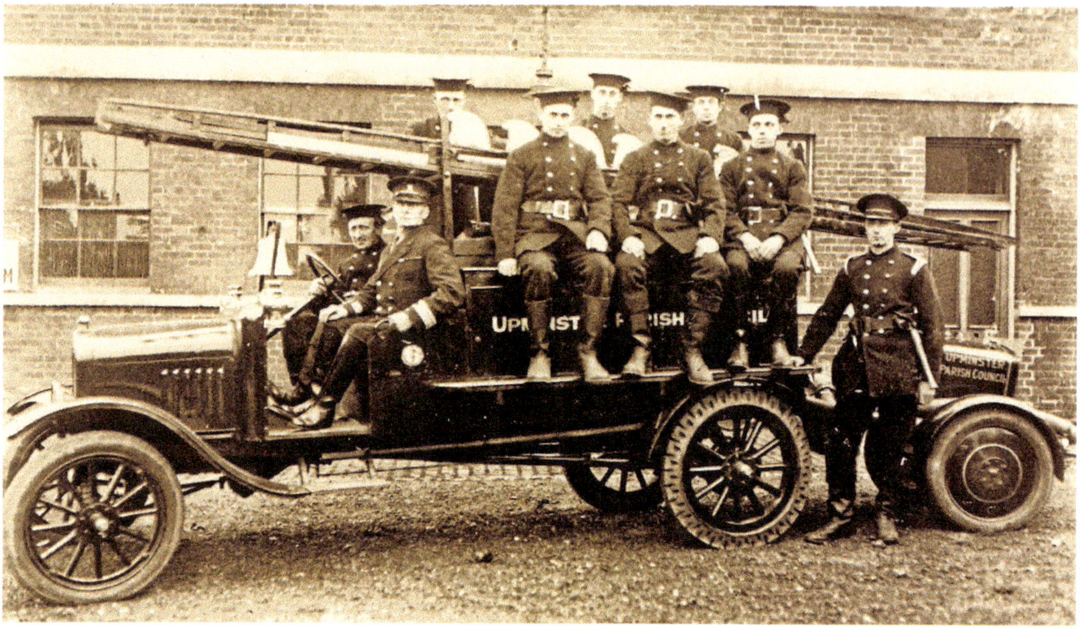

Fire Brigade II

There were obviously some important people in the past who played a large part in the life of the village. In 1904, Hyla Henry Holden became rector of the church. As well as this, he was a parish councillor and a captain of the Upminster Fire Brigade. The brigade had an unusual task in January 1912 when, according to *The Times*, a resident in Waldergrave Gardens went mad and set fire to his house. He kicked a policeman down the stairs and had to be subdued by the firemen turning their hoses on him. It wasn't until 1927 that Upminster had its first motor fire engine. The volunteer brigade was based at the Clockhouse and the modern image shows the rear view of the building.

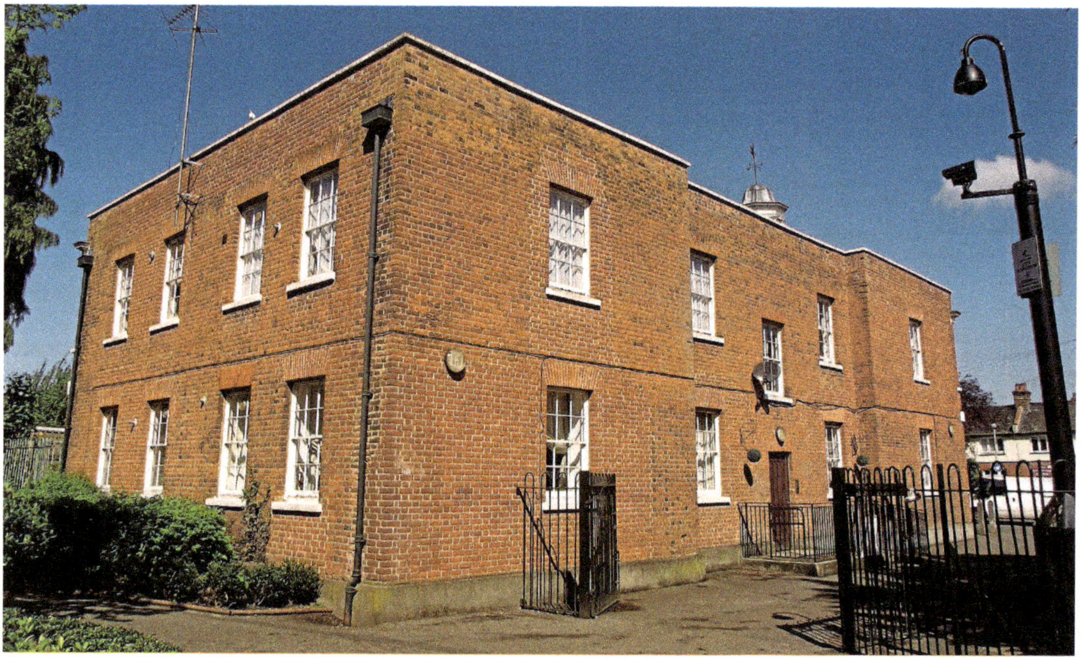

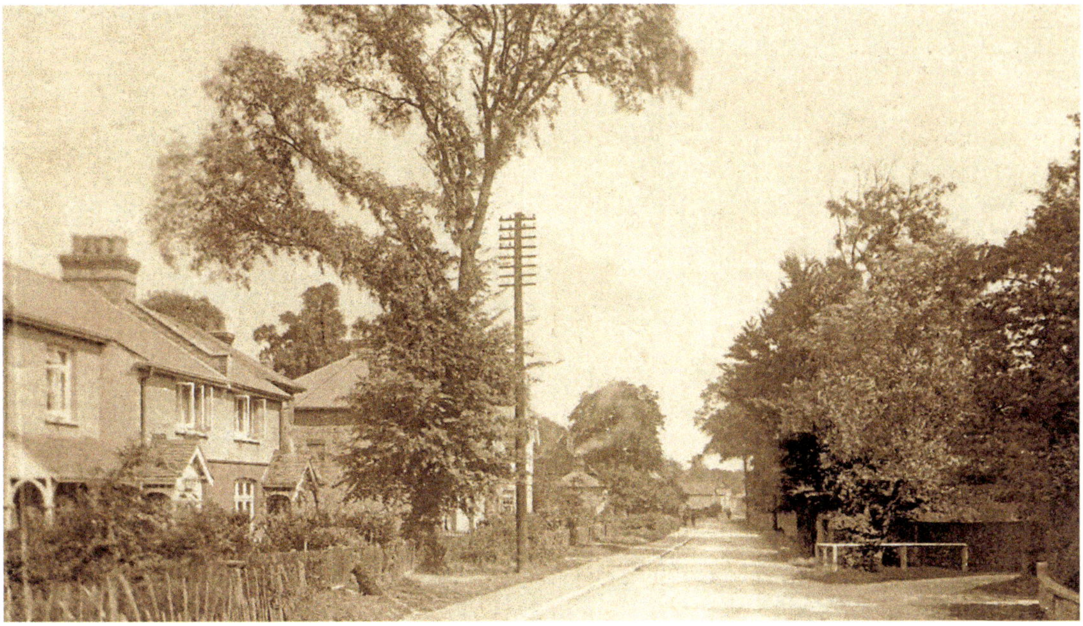

Cranham Road I

Cranham Road was renamed St Mary's Lane in 1922, supposedly after the Lady Chapel in the Church of St Laurence. I had thought that perhaps it had something to do with the fact that it led in a general direction towards North Ockendon, which has a St Mary's Church. Cranham has manged to keep its own identity as it began as a separate village to Upminster. There is little sign now of what was described by Ballard as 'a quaint little village with bridges over the roadside ditches'.

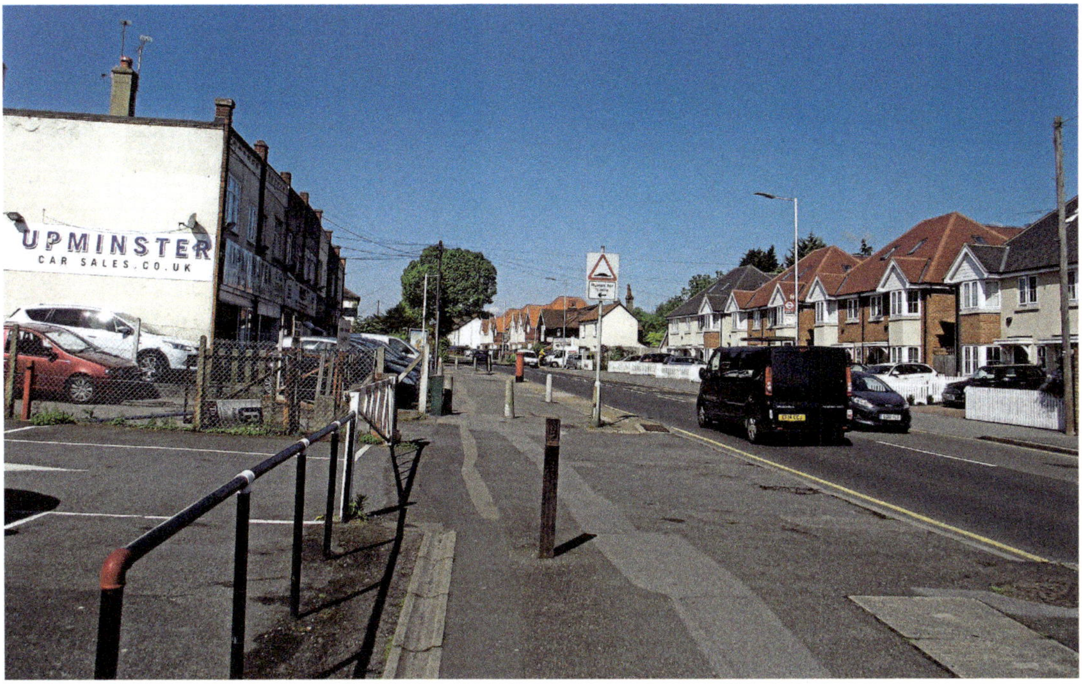

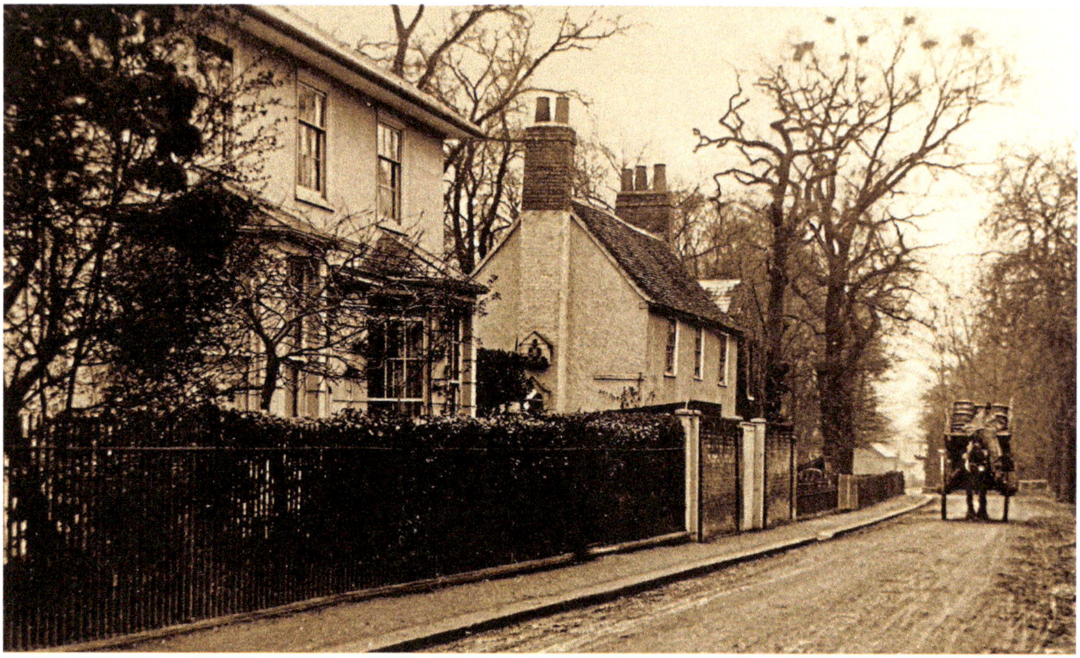

Cranham Road II

The village of Cranham may not have been well known but one of its previous residents at Cranham Hall was. Gen Oglethorpe was the founder of the colony of Georgia in America. Another well-remembered resident was Robert Middlemas who lived at Cranham Court. He had a fleet of double-decker buses that he used to give poor children from London's East End trips to Cranham from the mid-1930s until the outbreak of the Second World War.

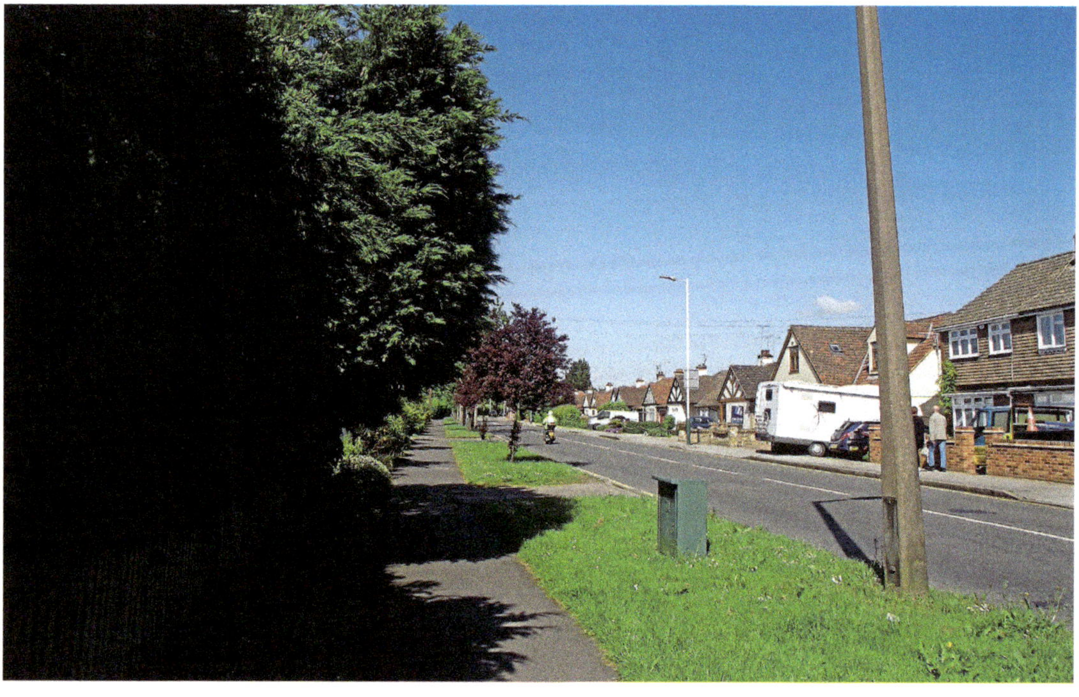

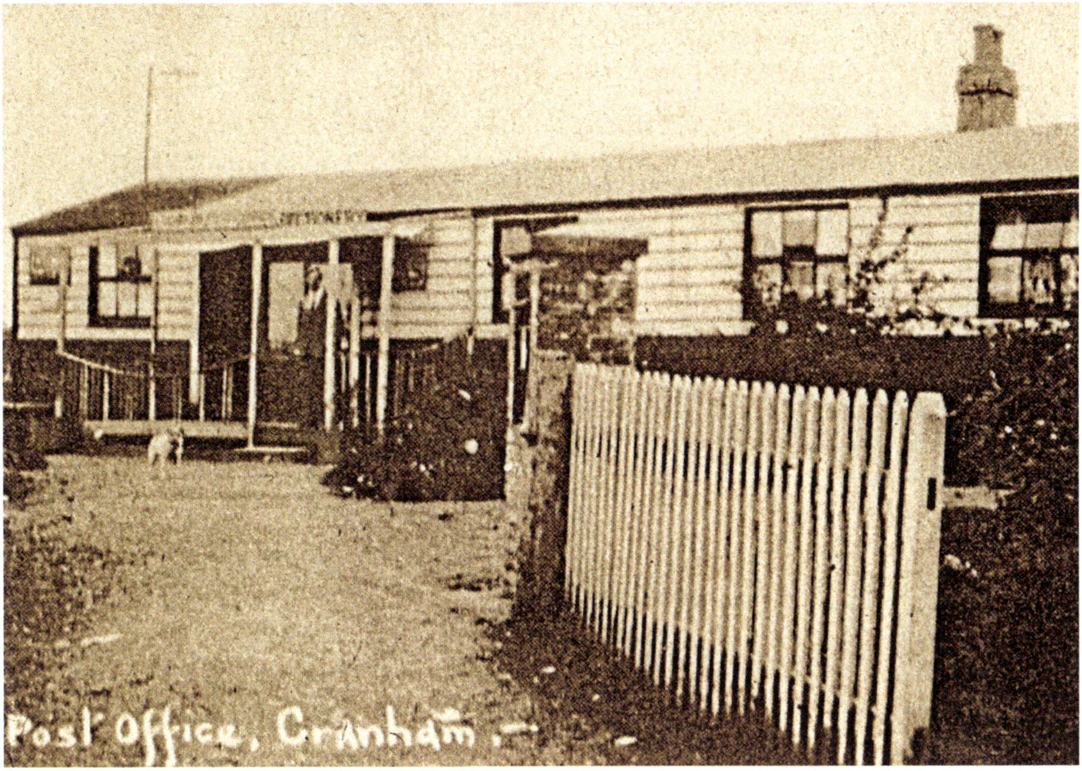

Post Office

The old post office was originally situated in what had been an old army hut that stood where Willow Parade now stands at the junction of Moor Lane and Front Lane. The hut was later a residence until the late 1950s when the present shops were built on the site. Willow Parade is the block of shops to the right of the modern image. (With thanks to Havering Libraries Local Studies Dept)

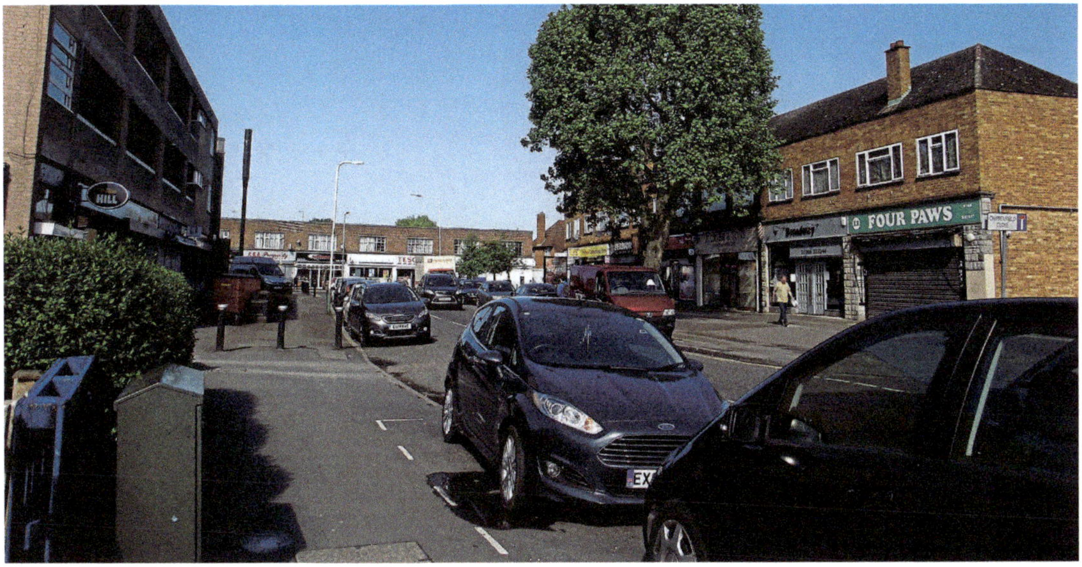

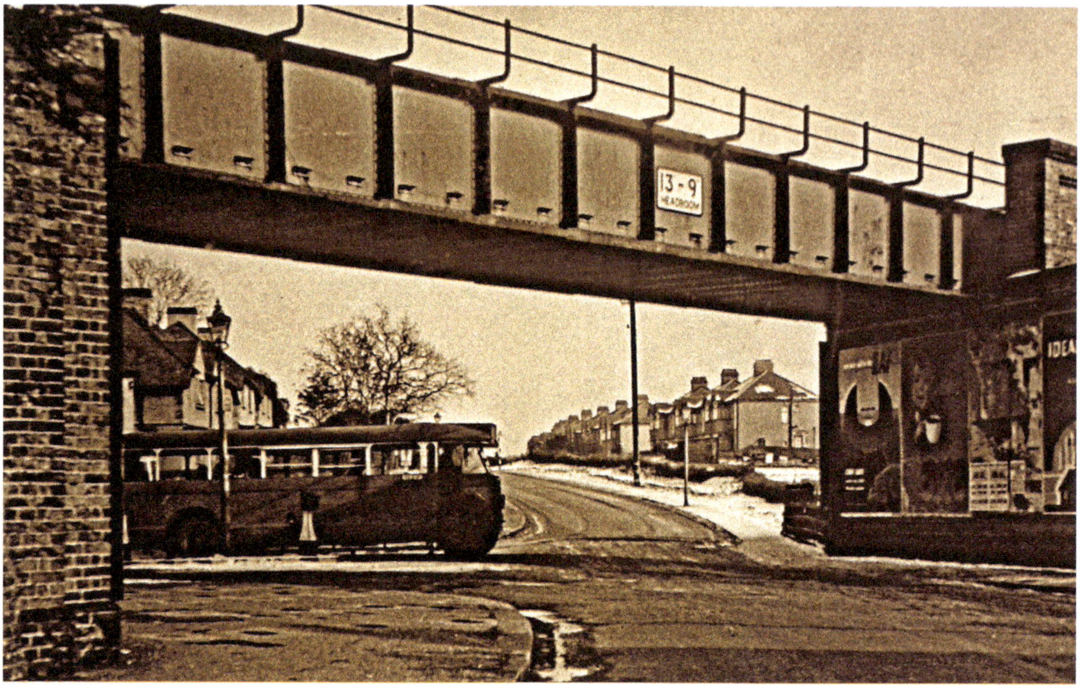

Railway Bridge

The bridge allows access to Cranham from St Mary's Lane. Much of Cranham has been separated from Upminster by the railway lines. The bridge is quite narrow in the old image and also quite low, which explains why the single-decker bus is able to pass under it. Double-decker buses today take the longer route from Upminster to Cranham along Hall Lane, but there is still a single-decker route between Cranham and Upminster that passes under the bridge. (With thanks to Havering Libraries Local Studies Dept)

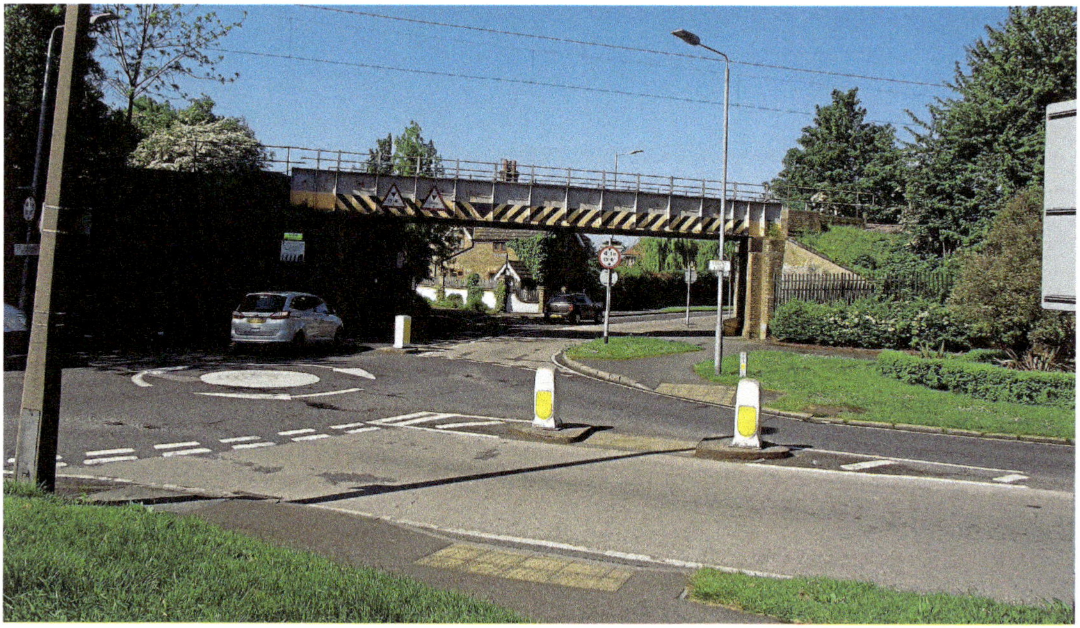

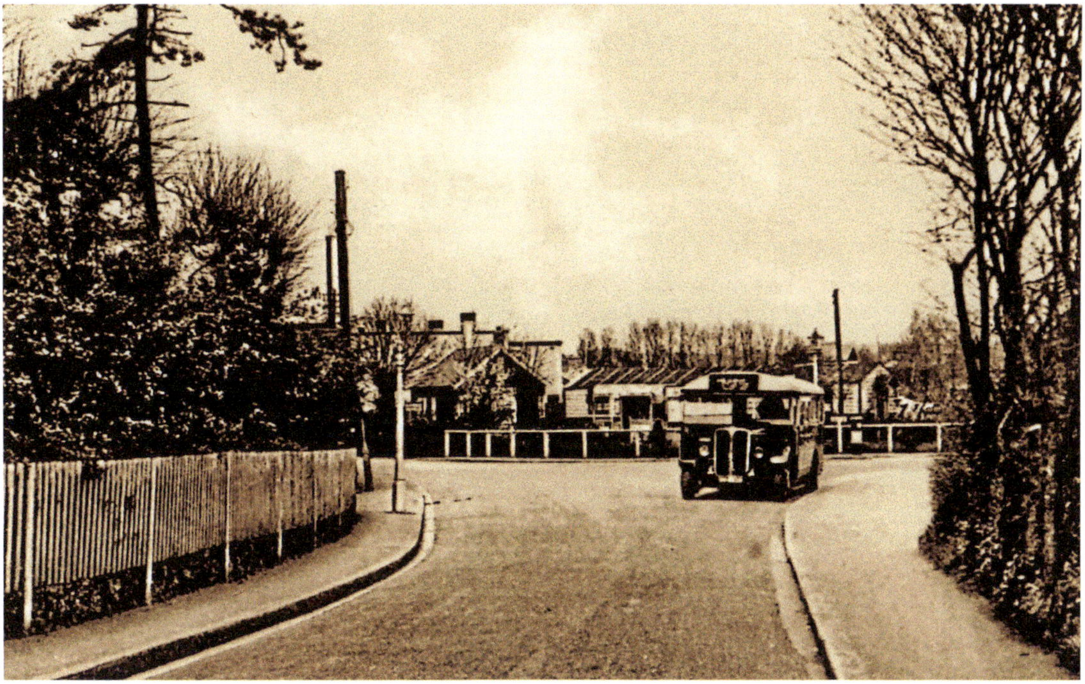

View From the Bridge

The old view of Cranham beneath the bridge shows many of the older buildings that stood in the area before it was widely developed in the 1950s. Very few of the older buildings survived the development of the post-war period. Little has changed however on the southern side of the bridge where the Chase leads to the church. (With thanks to Havering Libraries Local Studies Dept)

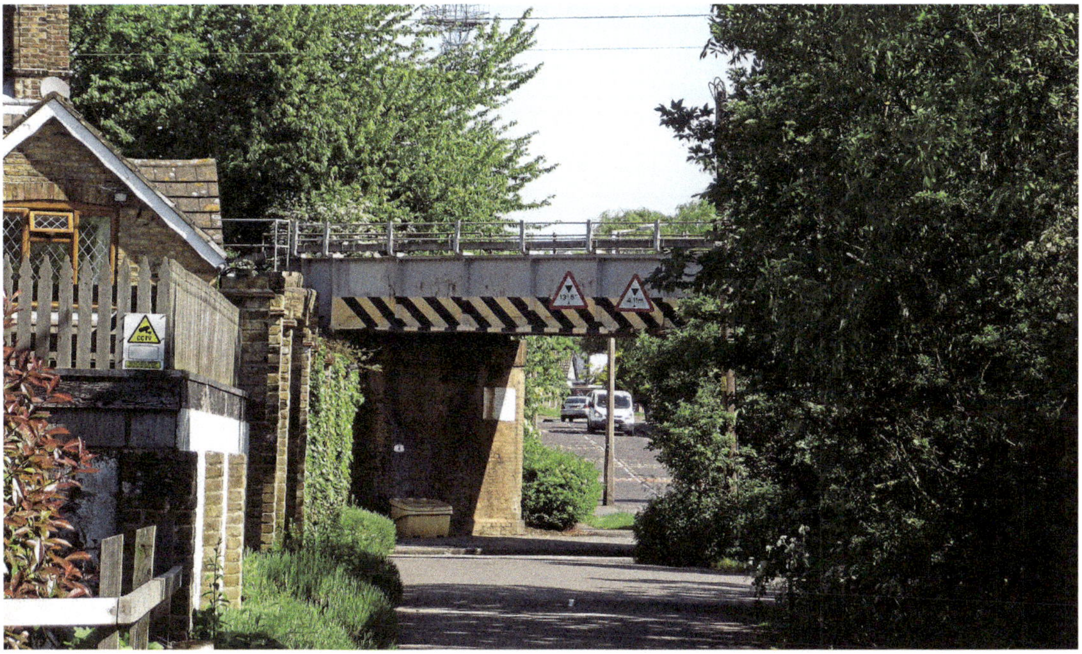

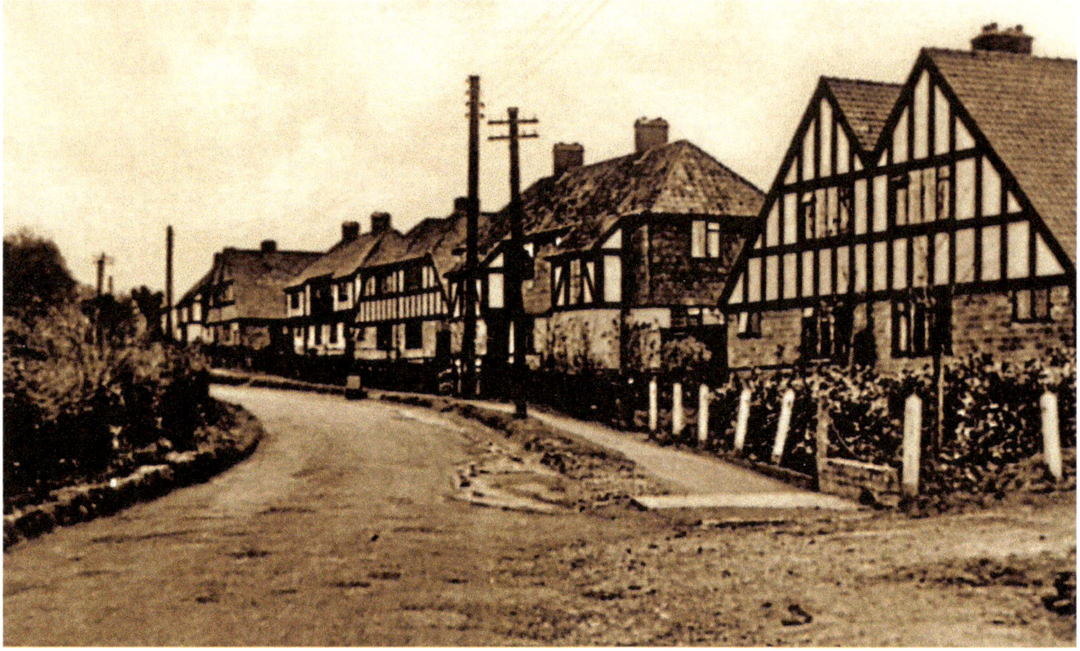

Front Lane I

Front Lane was, in the past, known as Cranham Lane. Where it meets the A127, part of what was once Front Lane is now Folkes Lane. The A127 was built in 1925. Front Lane was one of the first areas in Cranham to be built in the early nineteenth century on what had previously been farmland. A problem with water supply then held up further development. Much of the present housing was built after the Second World War. The modern image shows the same houses that are in the old photograph.

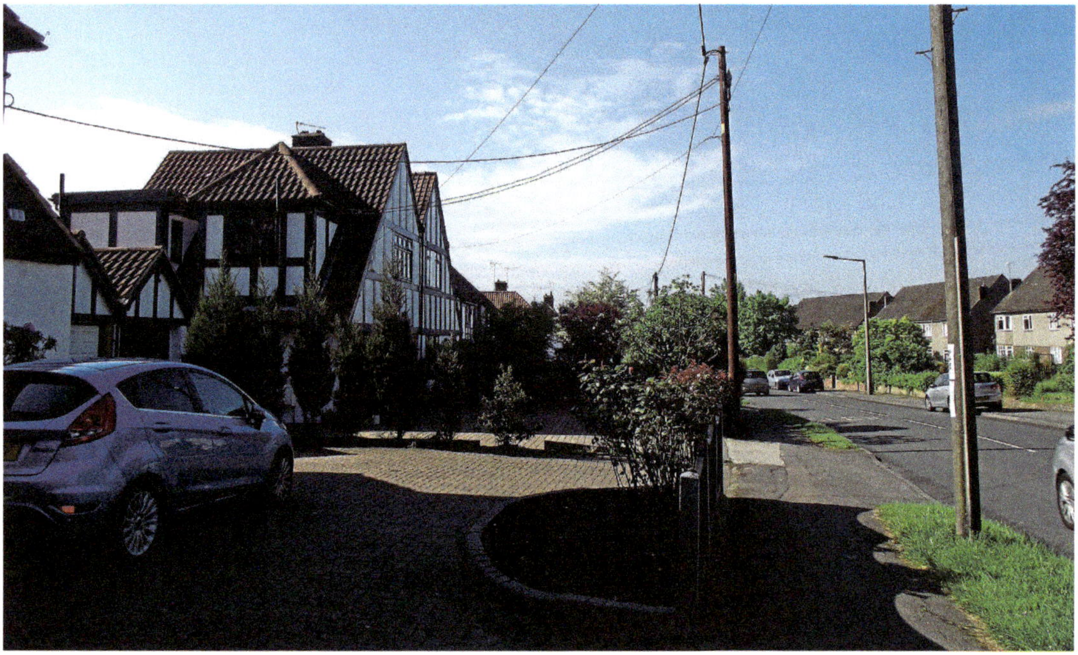

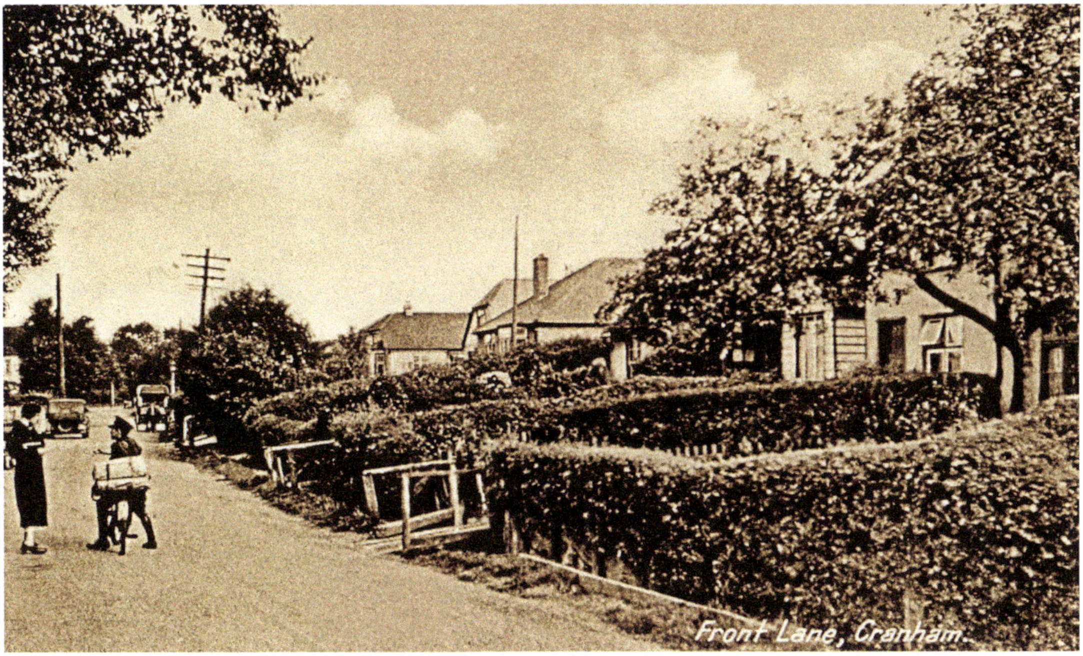

Front Lane II

Before the war, much of Cranham was still rural and a report in *The Times* in January 1943 told how land girls had reclaimed 1,200 acres of ground in Essex. The report said that London was now eating bread from wheat grown on what had, for forty years, been derelict bushland. The reclaimed land was described as stretching from Corringham to Cranham. The old image depicts the area with bridges across the ditches as previously mentioned. The modern photograph shows that there are still some open spaces. (With thanks to Havering Libraries Local Studies Dept)

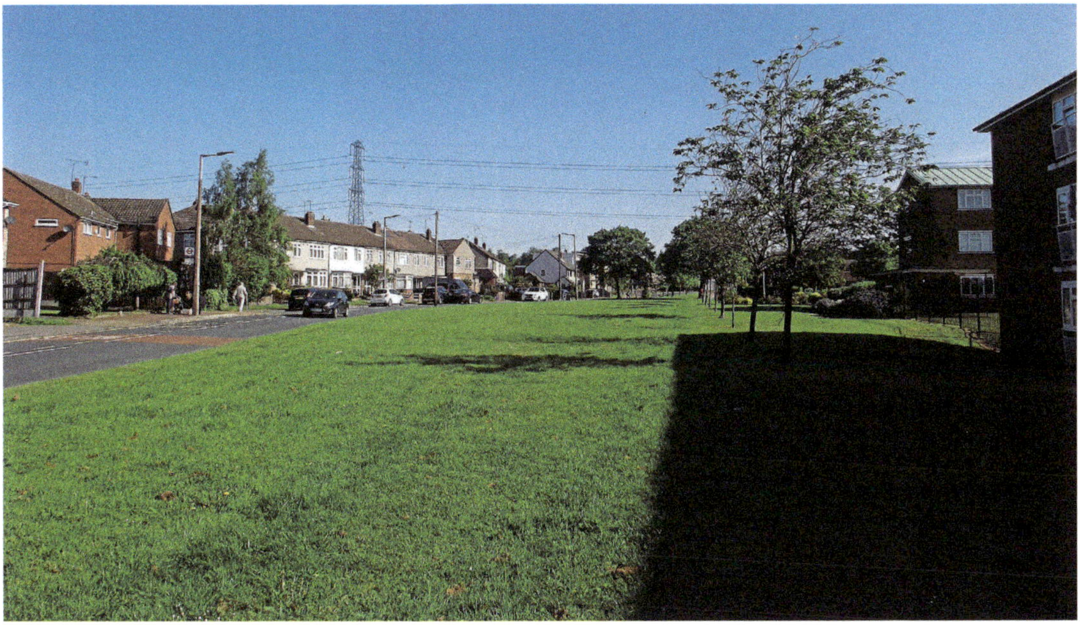

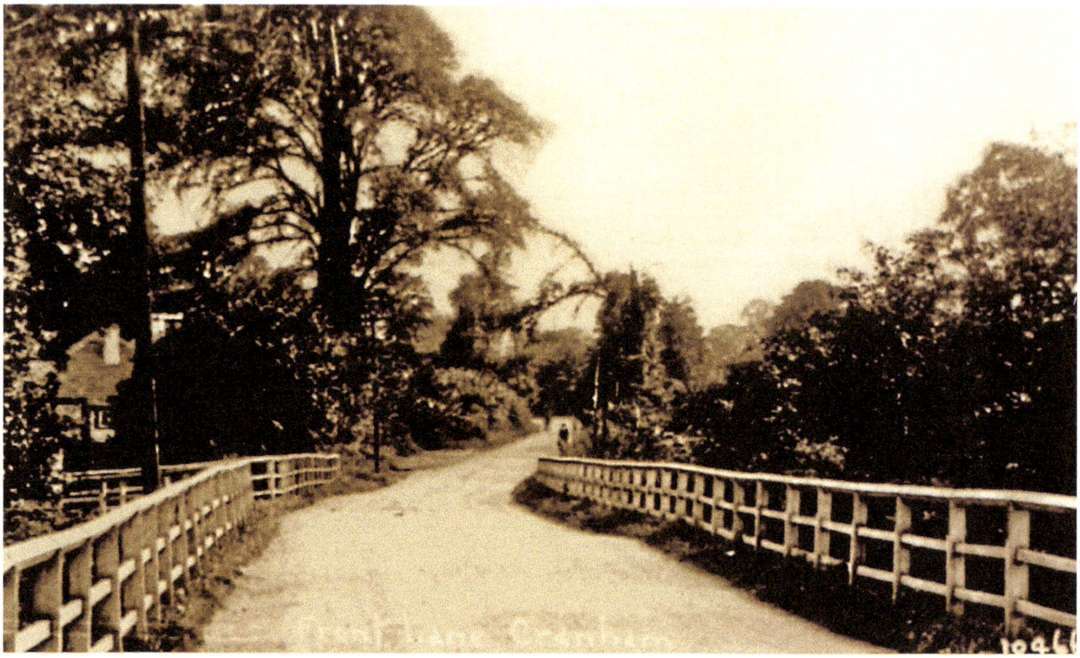

Front Lane III

When Front Lane was known as Cranham Lane it was the main route to the church and Cranham Hall. There is now another church that stands in Front Lane, which is much nearer for local residents as the old church by the hall is quite a distance away. St Luke's Church was built in the mid-1950s and is shown in the modern image.

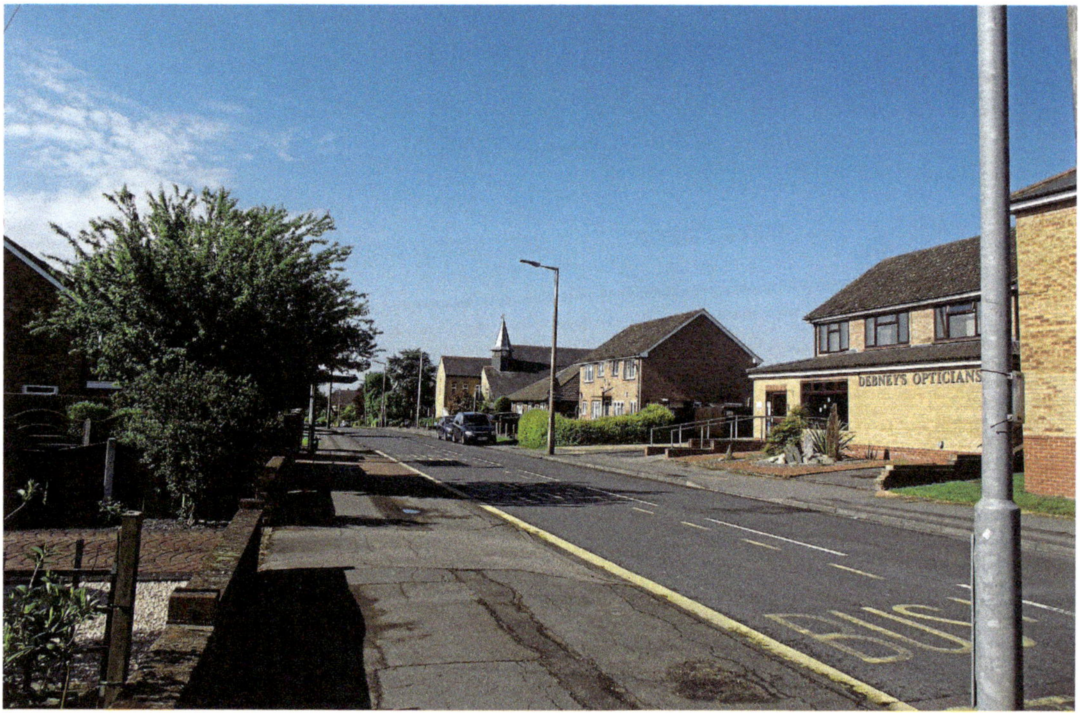

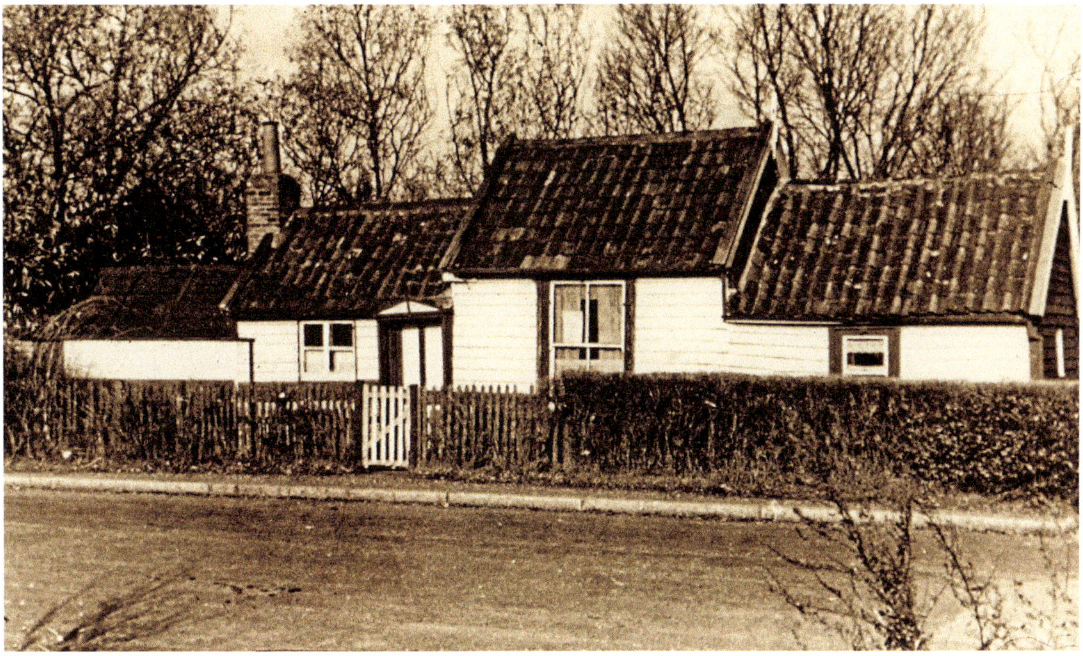

Moor Lane I

Moor Lane was known once as Cranham Back Lane. Where the A127 now dissects the lane it has changed its name to Folkes Lane. Moor Lane was, along with Front Lane, one of the first areas in Cranham to be built upon in the early twentieth century. In 1931, twelve council houses were built in Moor Lane called Oglethorpe Cottages. Much of the present housing in the area, however, was built after the Second World War. Both images show that bungalows were, and still are, popular.

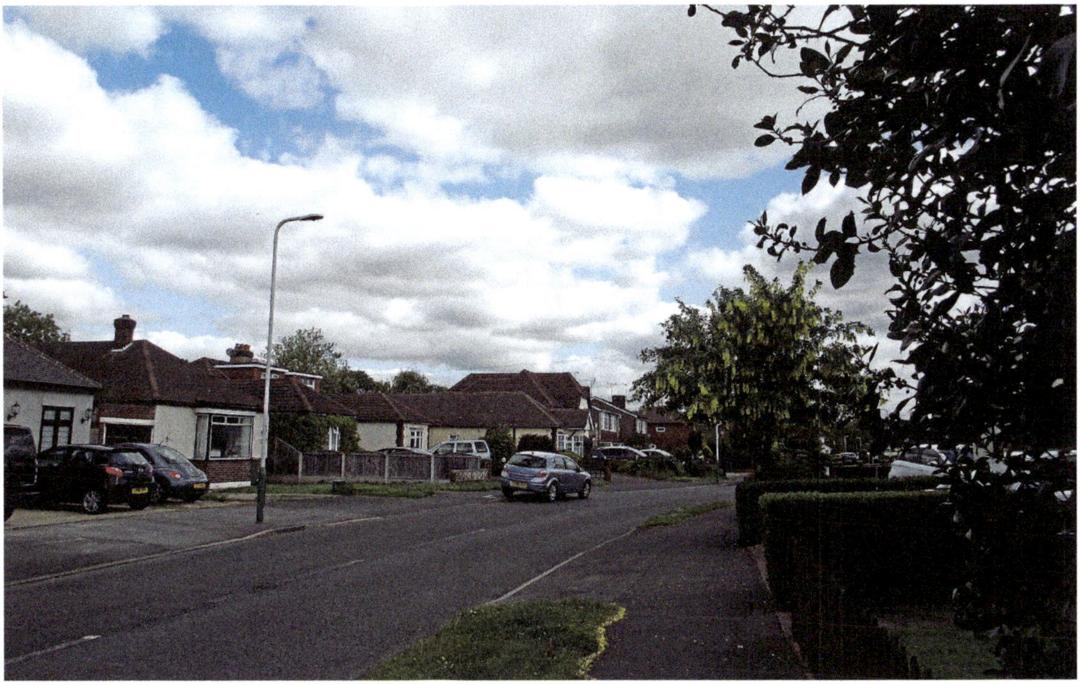

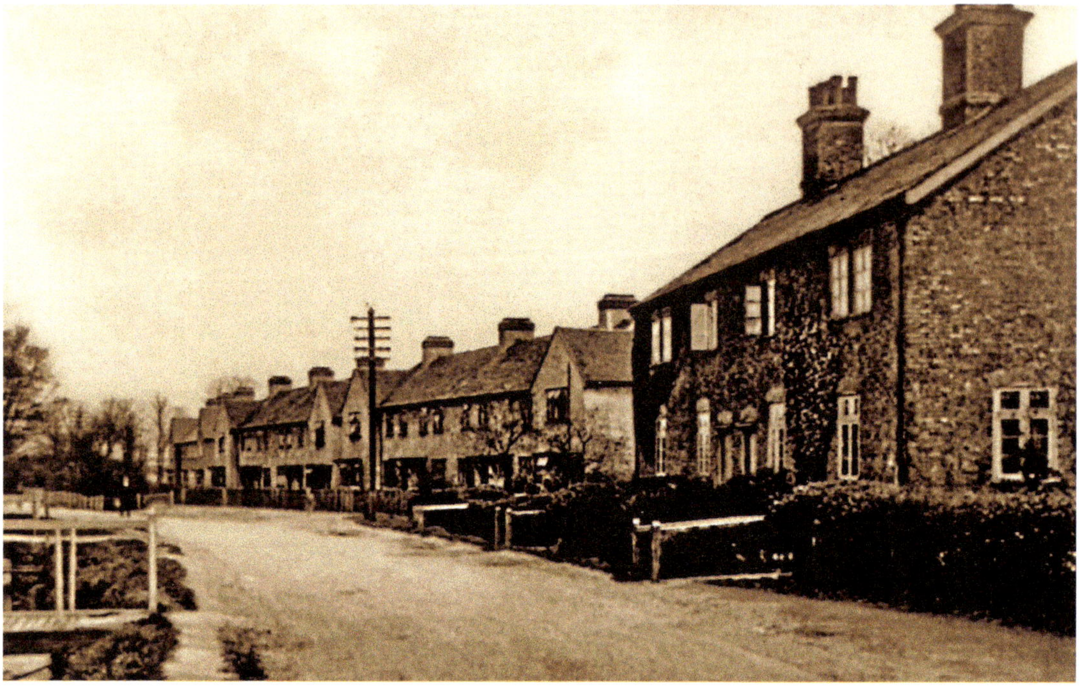

Moor Lane II

Moor Lane runs close to where Cranham Brick Works were situated during the First World War. They had their own railway siding and a road that led into Moor Lane. Before the area was built up in the 1950s, it led to Brickfield Woods. When *The Times* reported on the construction of the Victoria and Albert Museum in 1909, they said that the building was lined with Cranham Bricks. The large holes caused by the workings survived up until the Second World War.

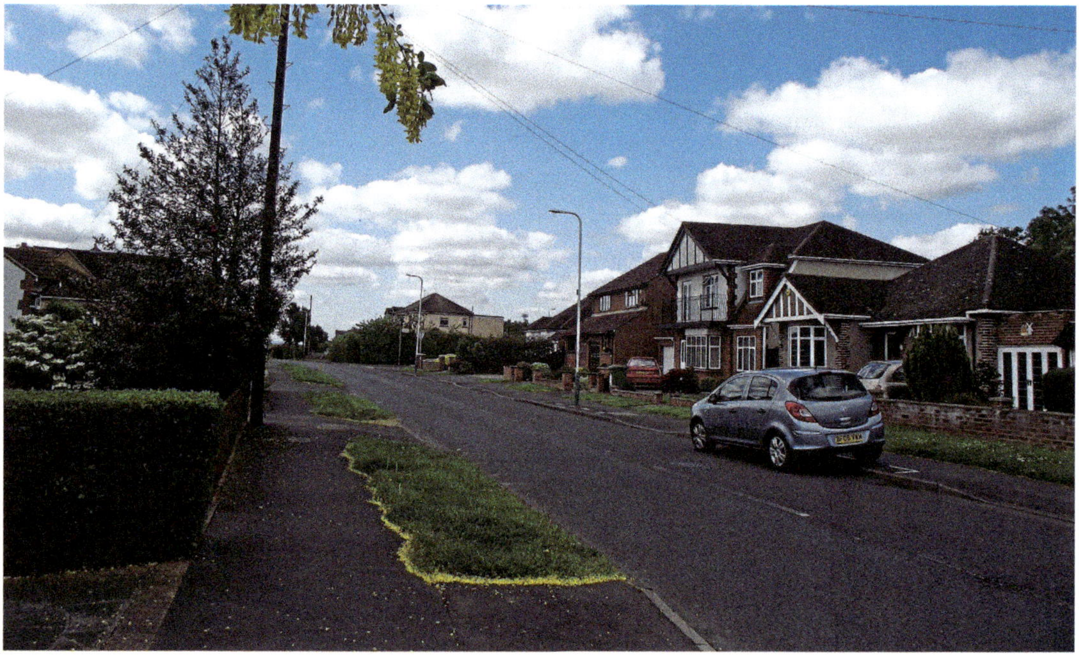

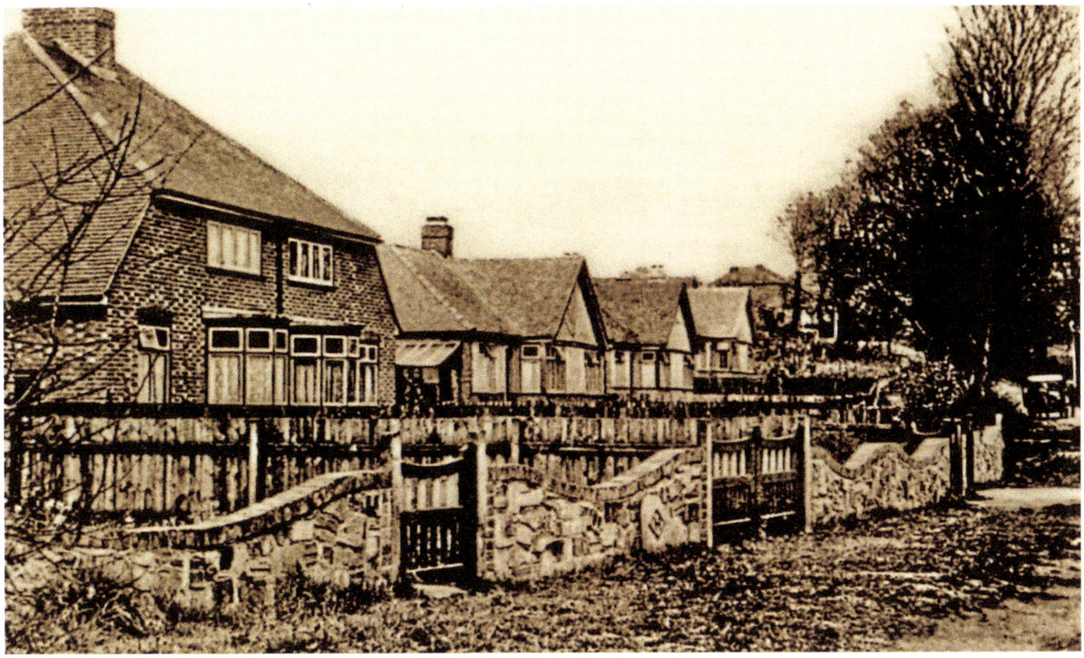

Moor Lane III

A development that had an effect on Cranham was the construction of the M25 nearby. Not everyone in the area agreed and one local resident of Cranham held up the construction for some time in 1980. The lady tried to overturn compulsory purchase orders on land needed for the motorway, which ended up in a High Court hearing. Of course, the road was eventually built. The modern image shows another development that affected the area. The tower is situated in the railway sidings.

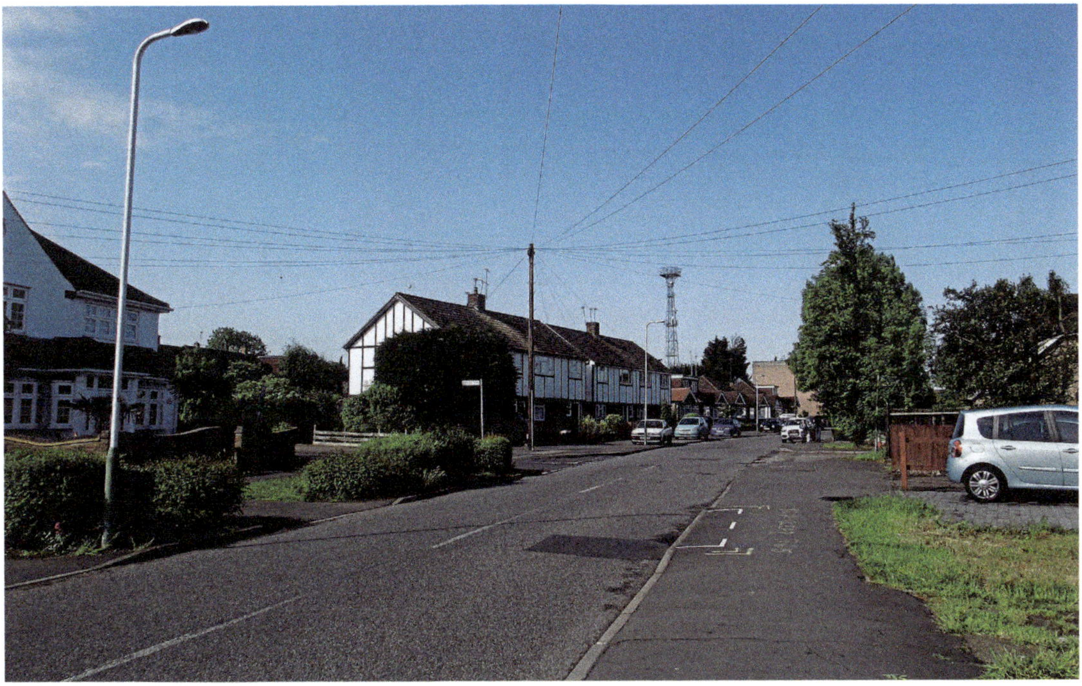

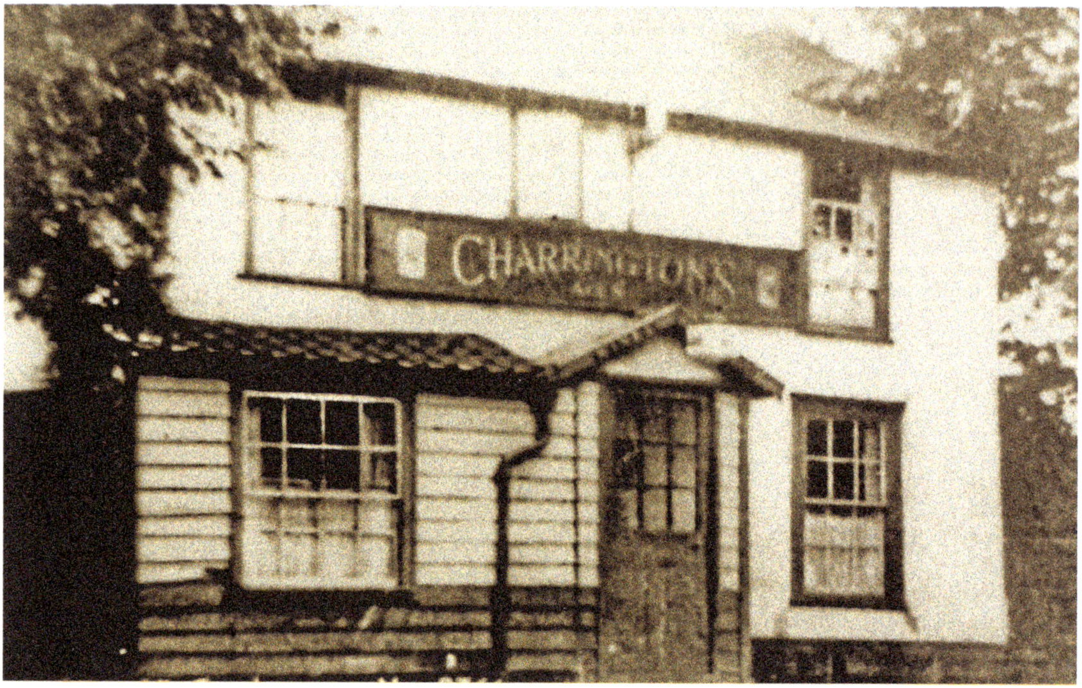

The Plough

Dating back to the mid-nineteenth century, the Plough has a long history. It did not stand on the present site shown in the modern image but was closer to Plough Rise further back along Front Lane. The present building was built in the mid-1950s when much of the housing development in the area took place.

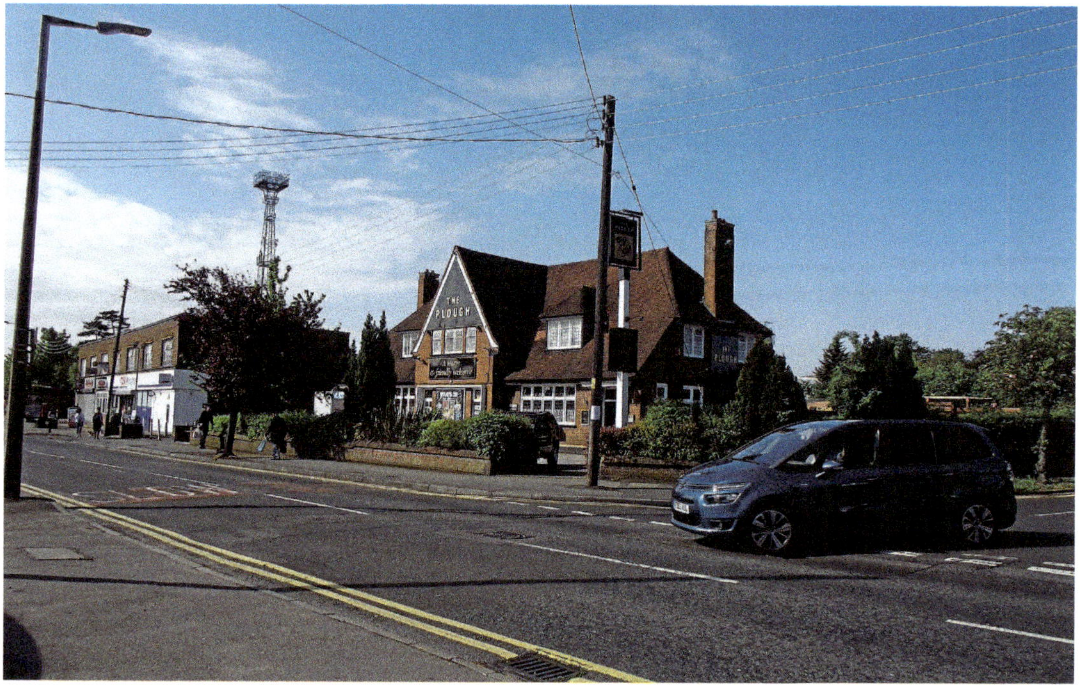

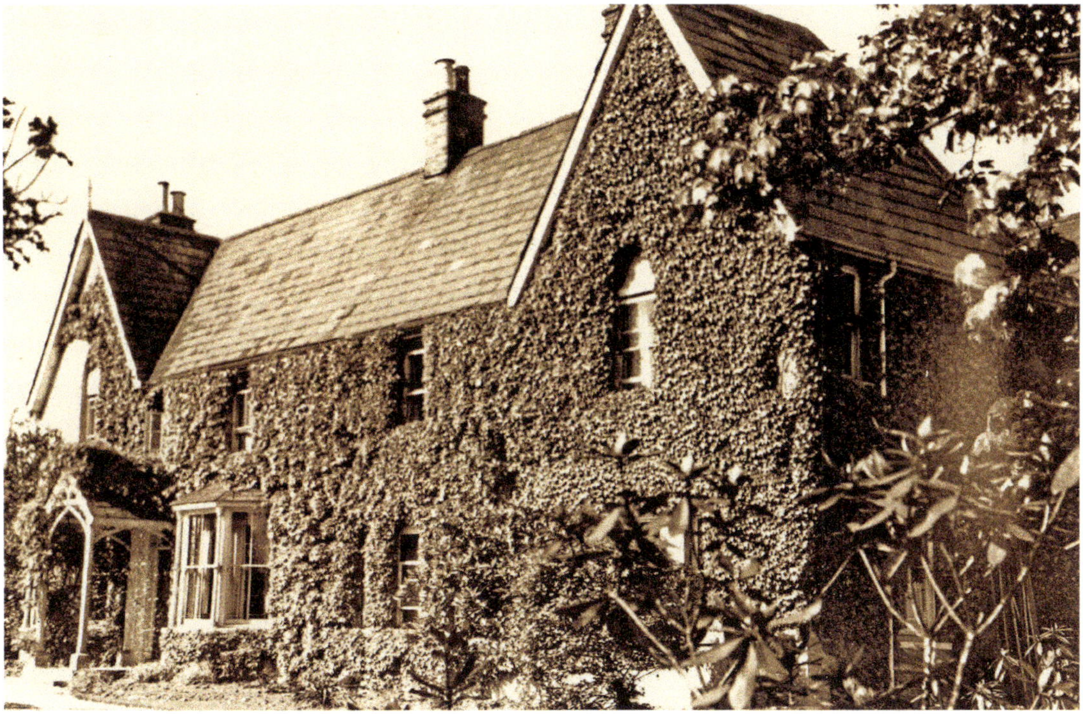

Crouches

Crouches stood where Front Lane and Moor Lane meet. Although it survived the widespread development of the area in the 1950s, it was then demolished when the London Transport Depot by the station was extended in the 1960s. The entrance to the depot is shown in Front Lane. (With thanks to John Drury)

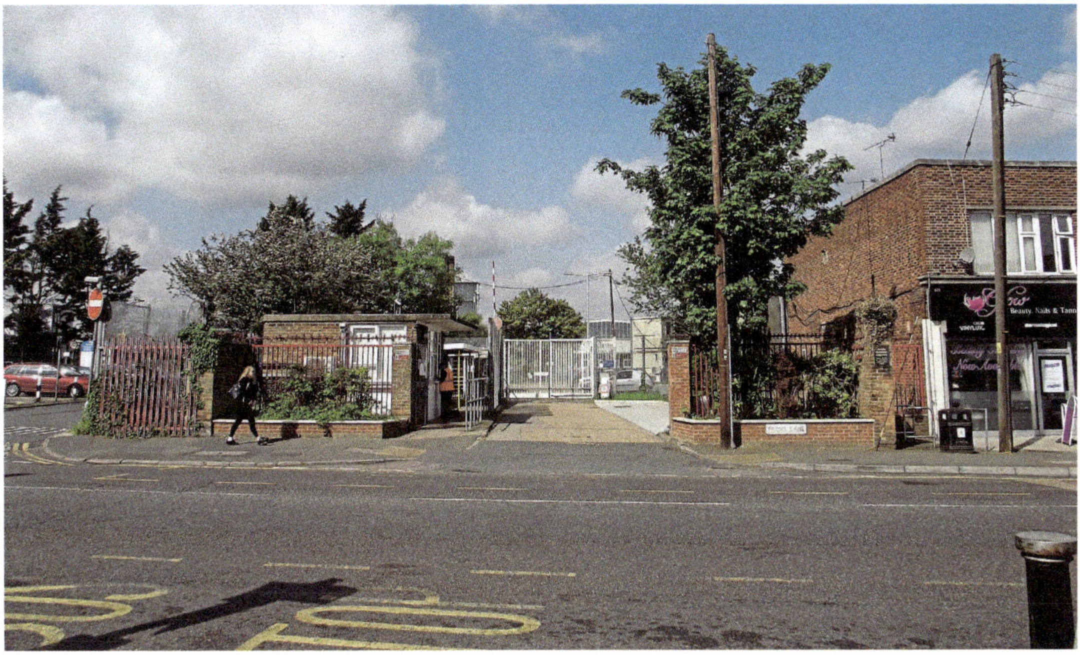

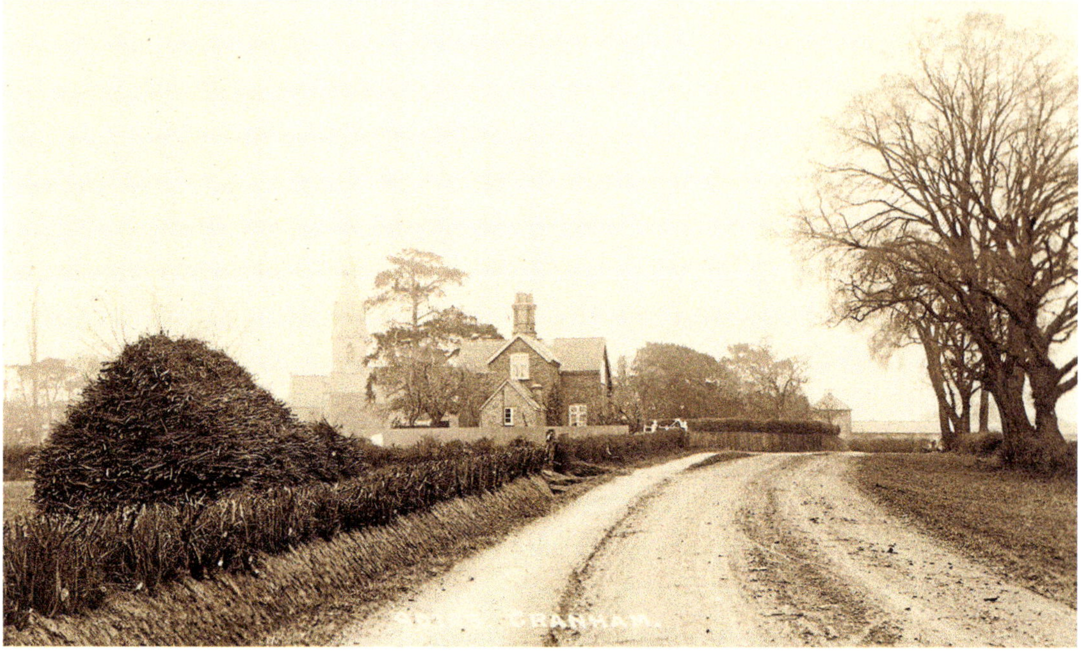

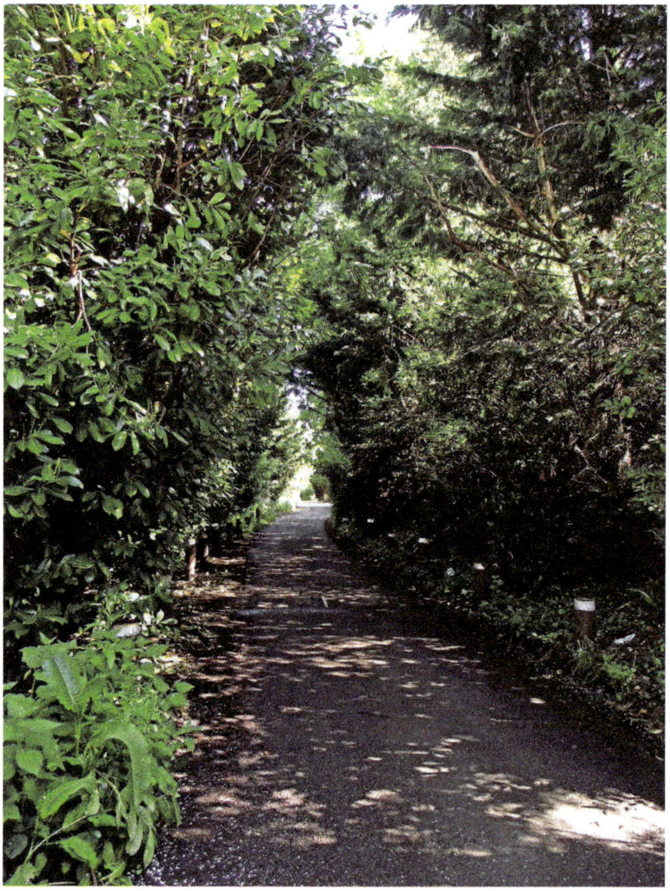

Cranham Church I

The route to Cranham Church is along the Chase and, as the old image shows, it was much less overgrown than it is today. It is now impossible to see the church until you are very close to it, due to the growth of the trees on both sides of the Chase.

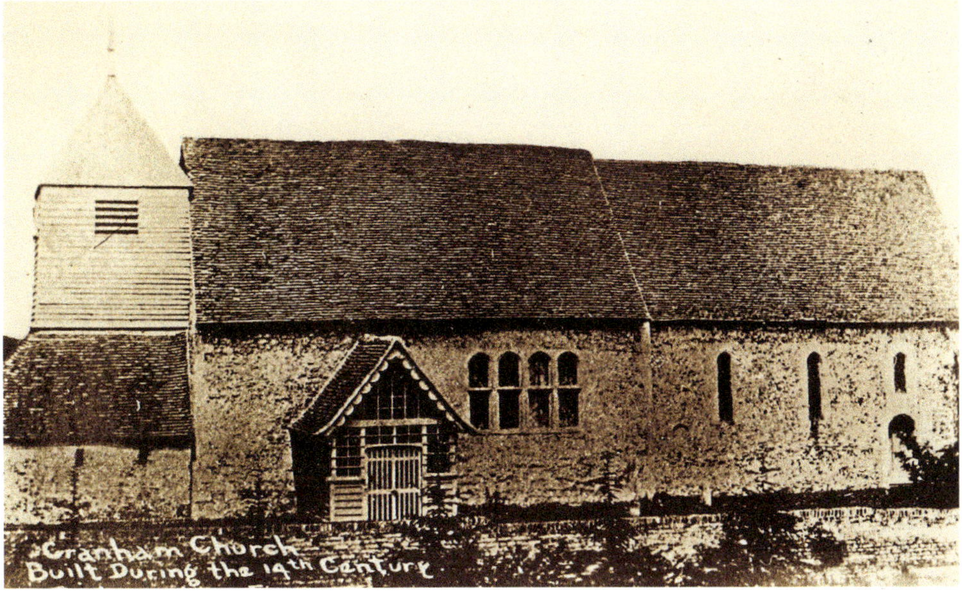

Cranham Church II

The building in the old image above is the old church that stood until the mid-nineteenth century when it was replaced by the present church. Cranham Church was to become the centre of attention in 1923 when there was a proposal to have the remains of Gen Oglethorpe removed from his resting place in Cranham Church and taken to Georgia in America, which he founded. The request arose after the coffin of the general was found after excavations in the church. The debate raged in the national press over whether this should be allowed. The general of course stayed where he was but wreaths often turned up from the University of Georgia. In 1933, the rector refused to allow one wreath into the church as it was so large that it blocked the chancel. (With thanks to John Drury)

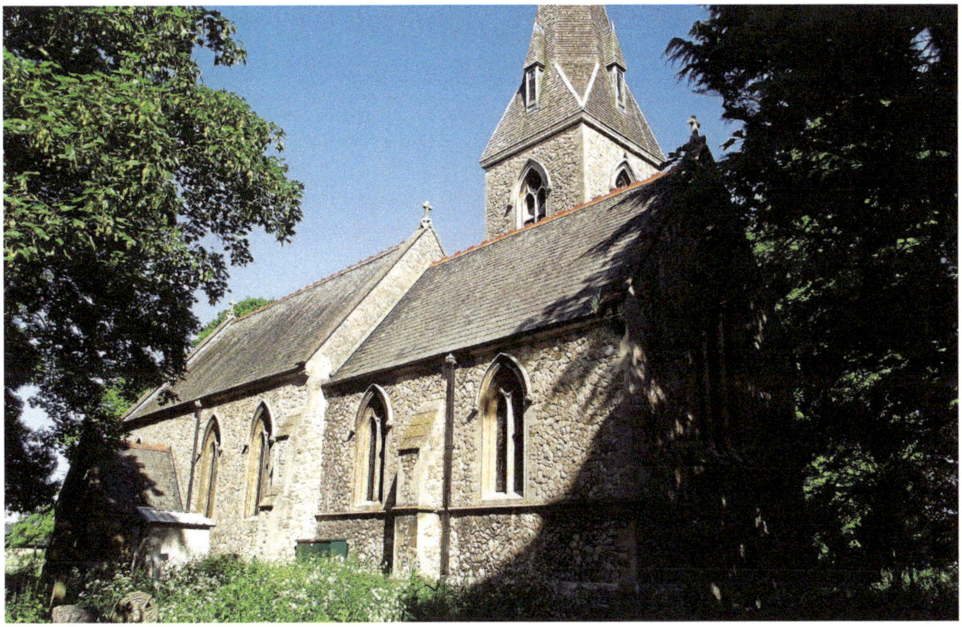

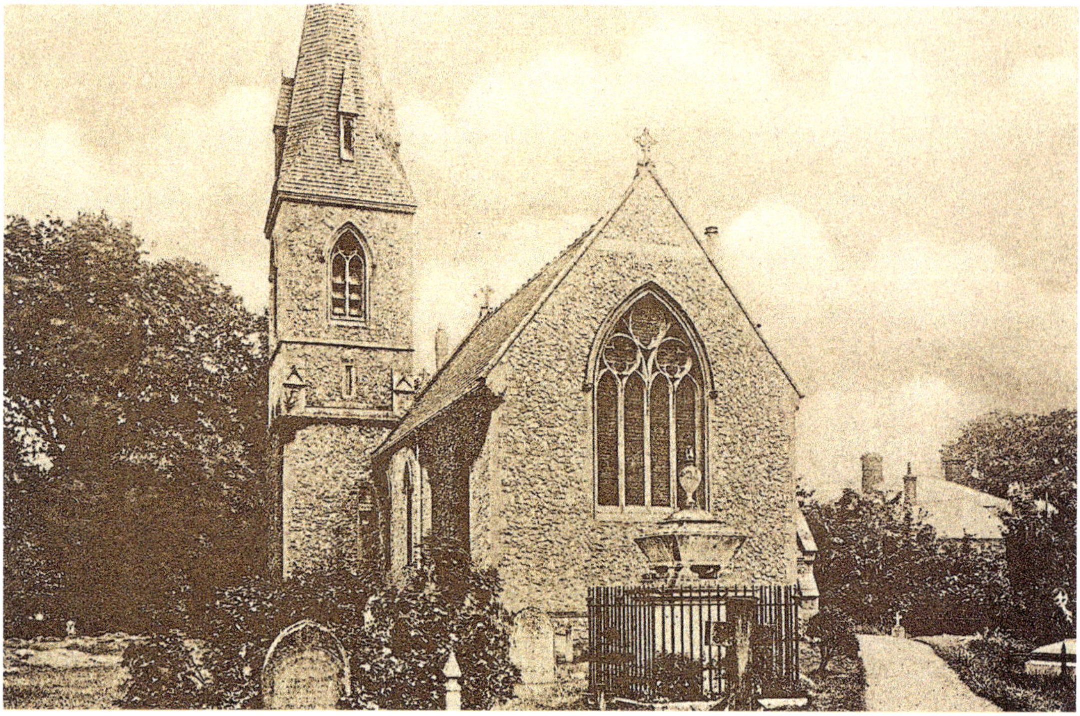

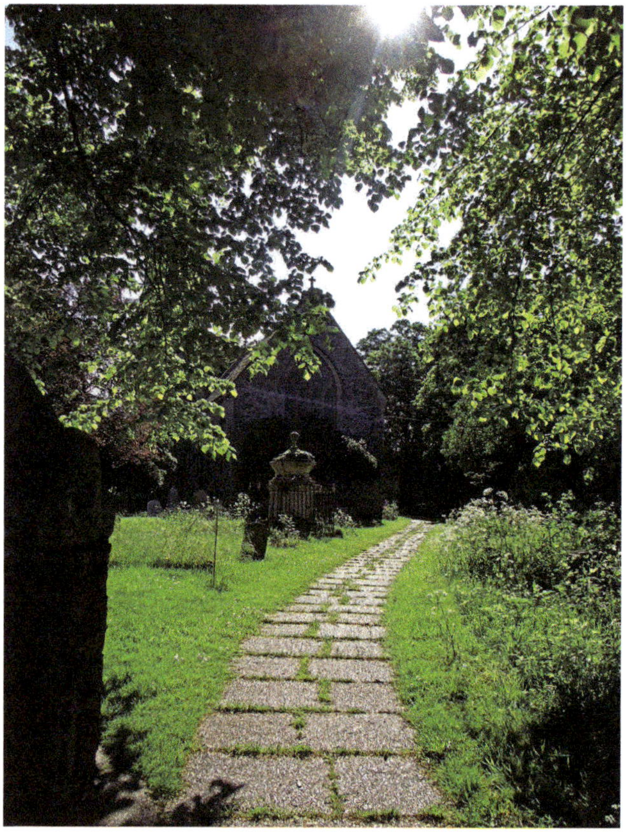

Cranham Church III

The church in the photo was built in the late nineteenth century after the one that previously stood on the site was demolished in 1873. There has been a church on the site since the thirteenth century, although there have been a number of new buildings over this time. The church is next to Cranham Hall, once the home of General Oglethorpe who is still buried in the family vault in the church. The site of the church is quite remote at the end of a long overgrown lane and the churchyard itself is also in a similar state.

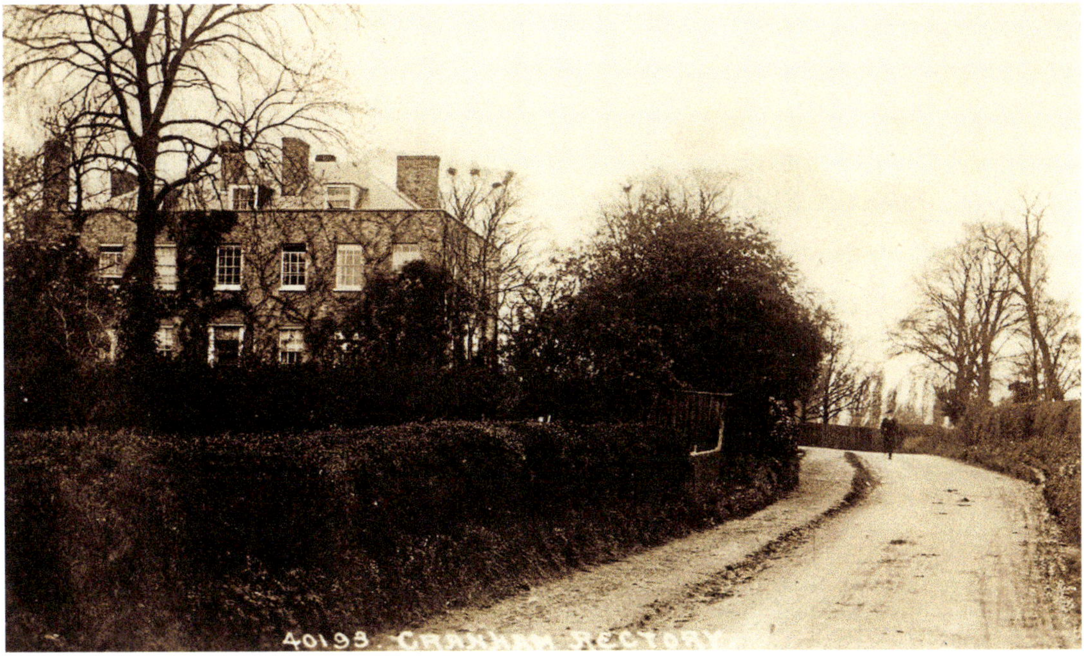

Cranham Rectory

The rectory was situated in what is now Rectory Gardens and was the home of the Rector of Cranham. The building dates back hundreds of years and it is thought that the most recent rectory building was built in 1790. The surroundings included stables and other farm buildings. The rectory was sold to a private owner some years ago and a new housing estate, Rectory Gardens, now stands on the site. (With thanks to John Drury)

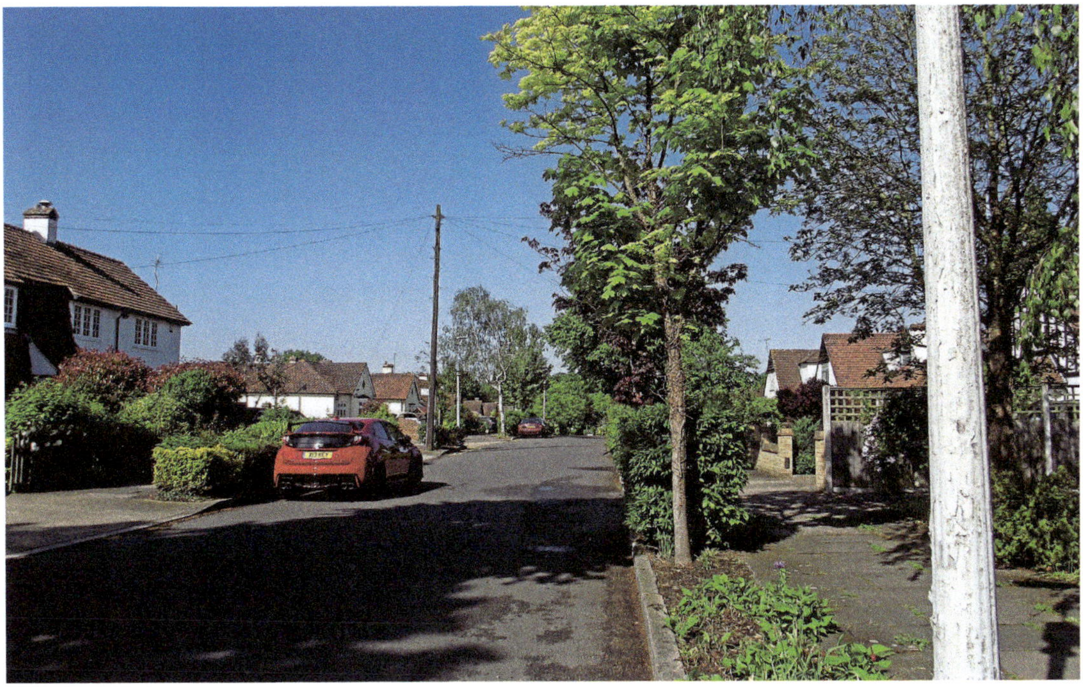

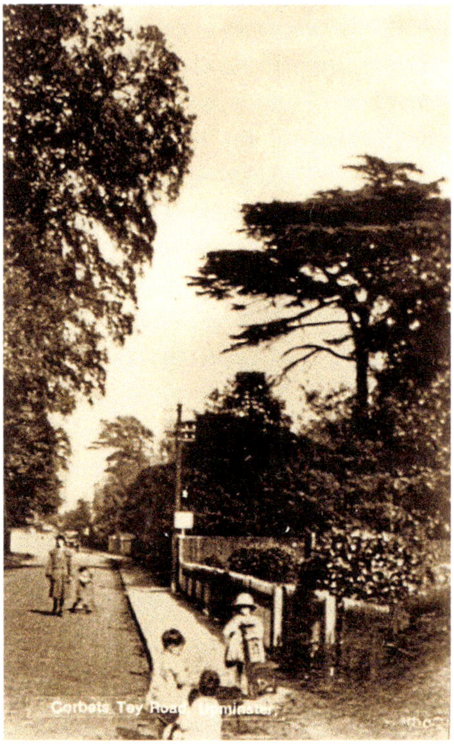

Corbets Tey Road I

Corbets Tey was another nearby village that has become part of Upminster with which it has always had close connections. The village once had four inns. The village was very rural and it wasn't until 1924 that the first bus ran through it. There were also a number of large houses, such as London's and Fox Hall, which have now gone. Most of the road is now lined with houses dating from the mid-war period and, of course, shops.

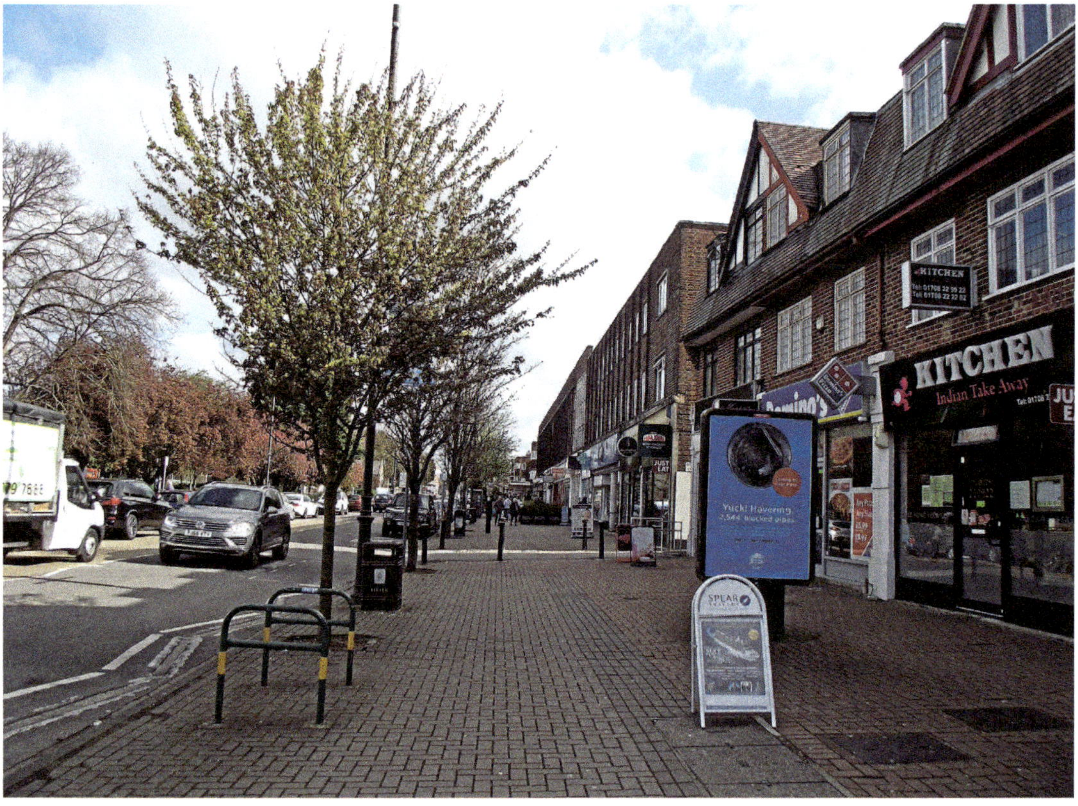

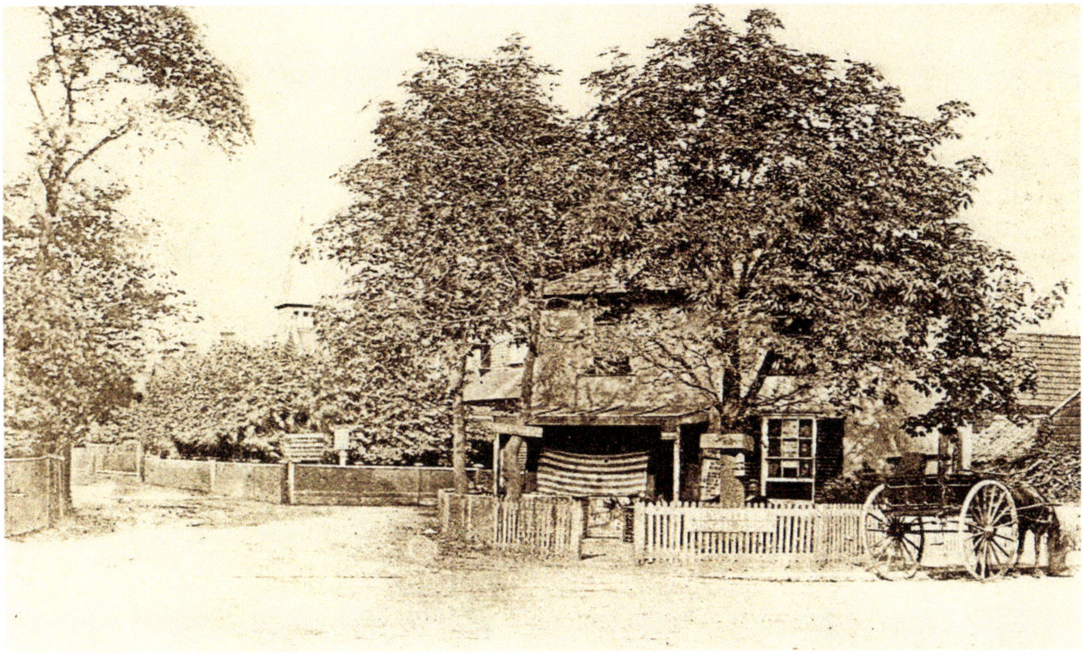

A Quaint Broadway

The old image was published in the booklet produced by Upminster Estates, one of the companys building houses in the area, to show how the area was still surrounded by open countryside. Much of the land was being built on and it was only council action that preserved some open land in the centre of the town when they paid £7,000 for the land to be turned into a park in 1929. The modern image is of a house in the Chase that is still in a semi-rural position.

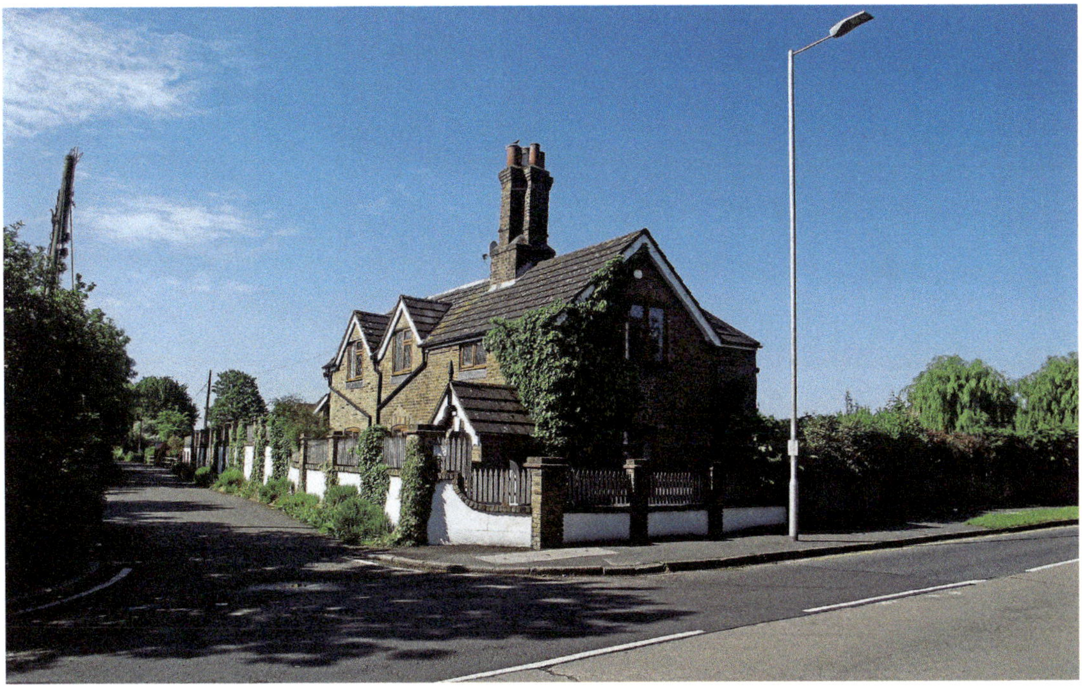

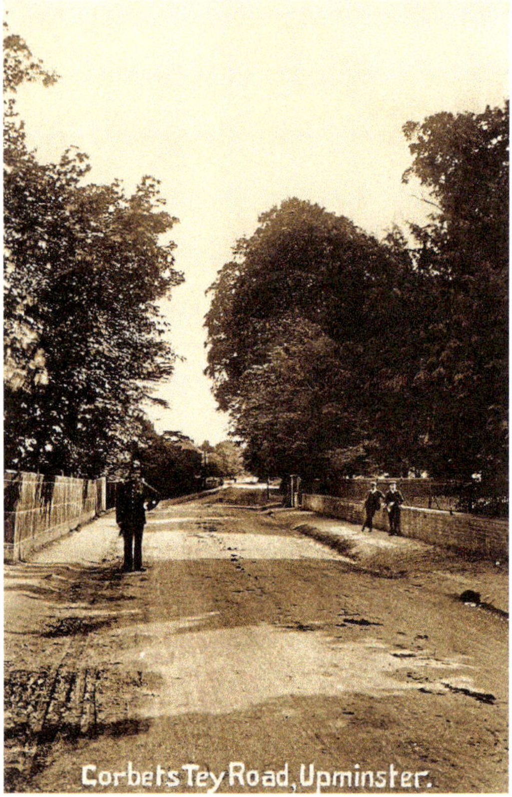

Corbets Tey Road II

There is some dispute as to how Corbets Tey got its name. One view is that it was once owned by a man named Corbet, and *tey* is a Saxon word meaning 'enclosure', hence 'Corbets enclosure'. A more exciting explanation is that when Elizabeth I was on her way to review the troops at Tilbury waiting to face the Armada, she said to a man named Corbet who was with her, 'Corbet stay.' The modern image shows some of the houses in the road.

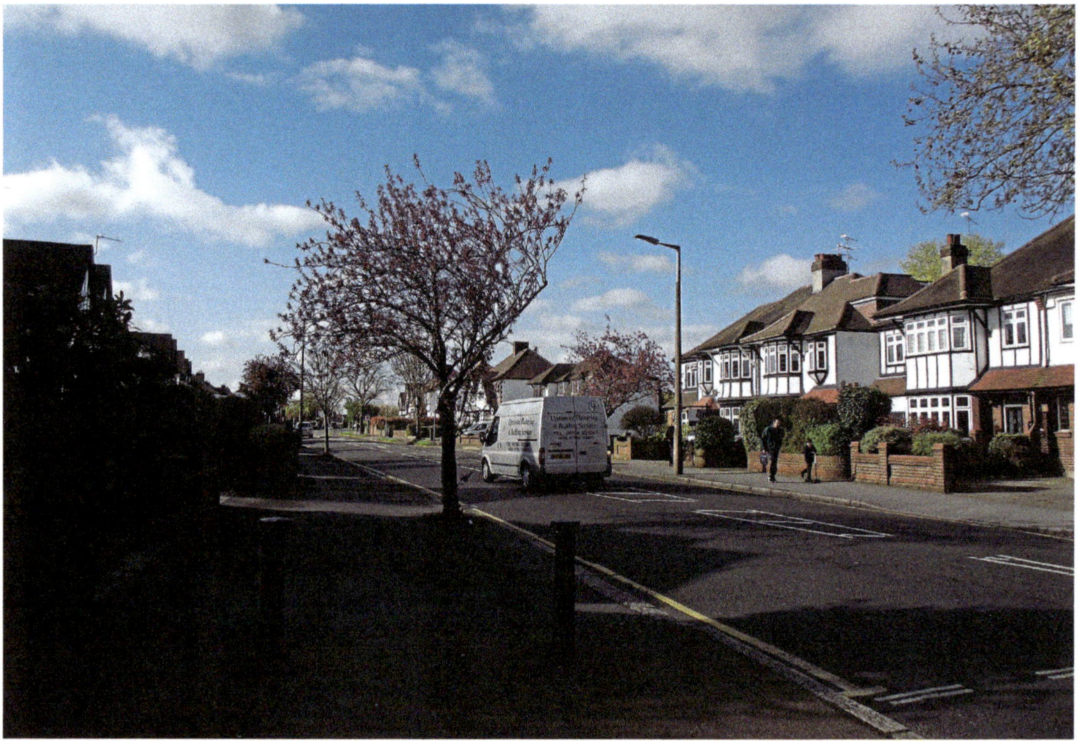

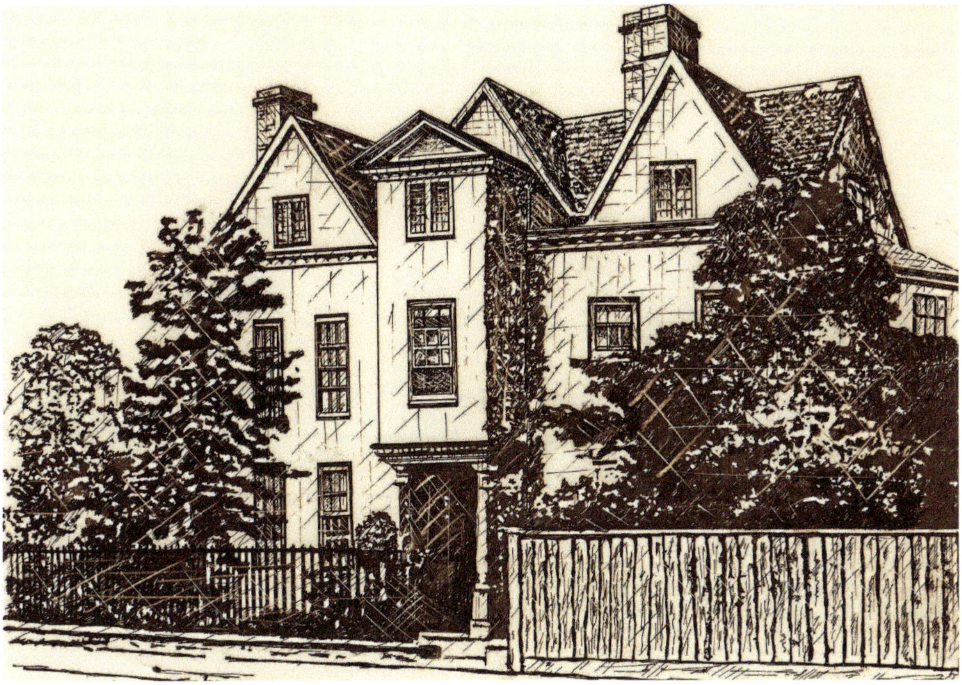

High House

High House stood opposite the church in Corbets Tey Road. It dated from the sixteenth century and was demolished in 1935 having been replaced with shops and flats. The shops are called Byron Parade as Lord Byron was supposed to have stayed in the house when it was occupied by Maj. Howard in the early nineteenth century. The residences above the shops are known as Byron Mansions. Maj. Howard died at the Battle of Waterloo. The house was also the home of Dr Derham when he was rector of the Church of St Laurence. (With thanks to John Drury)

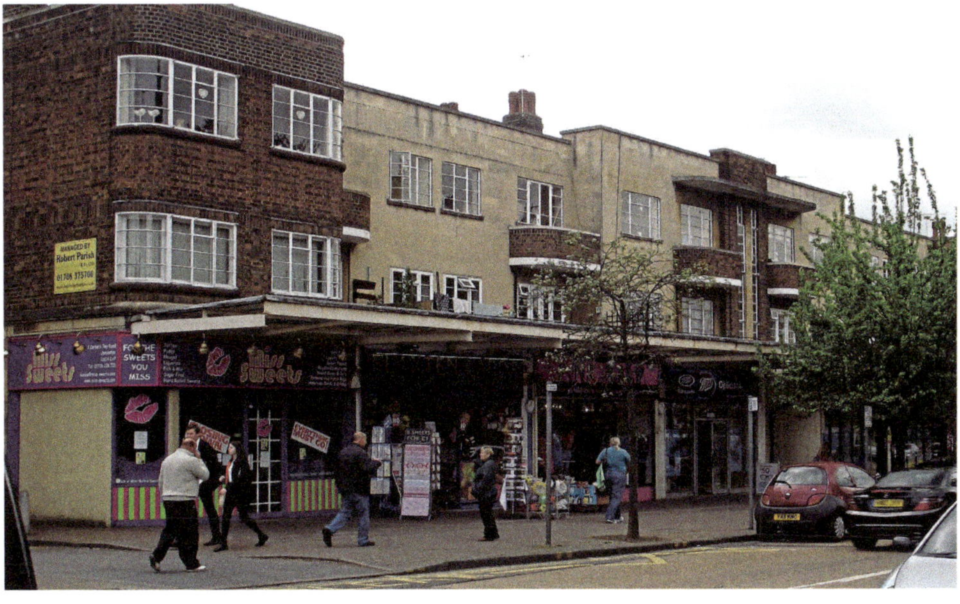

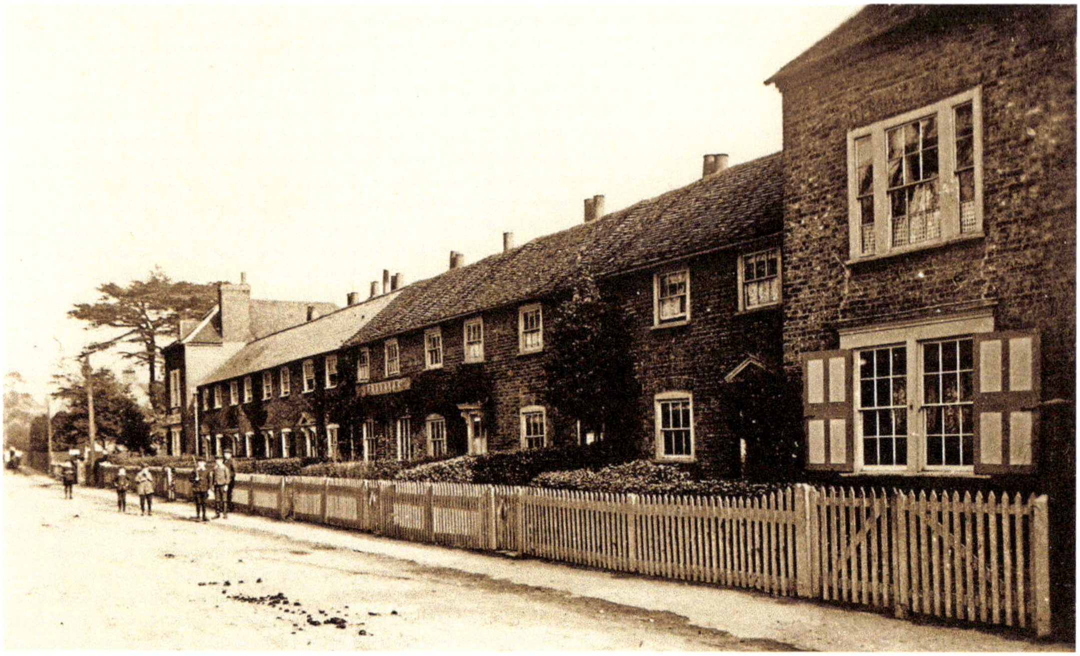

Post Office Cottages

The Post Office Cottages stood in Corbets Tey Road and the post office was in one of a row of cottages. The actual post office was at the end by the Bell Inn, and was one of the first shops in Corbets Tey Road. More shops were built in the 1930s when housing was built on the Springfield estate in the 1930s and others after the war. (With thanks to John Drury)

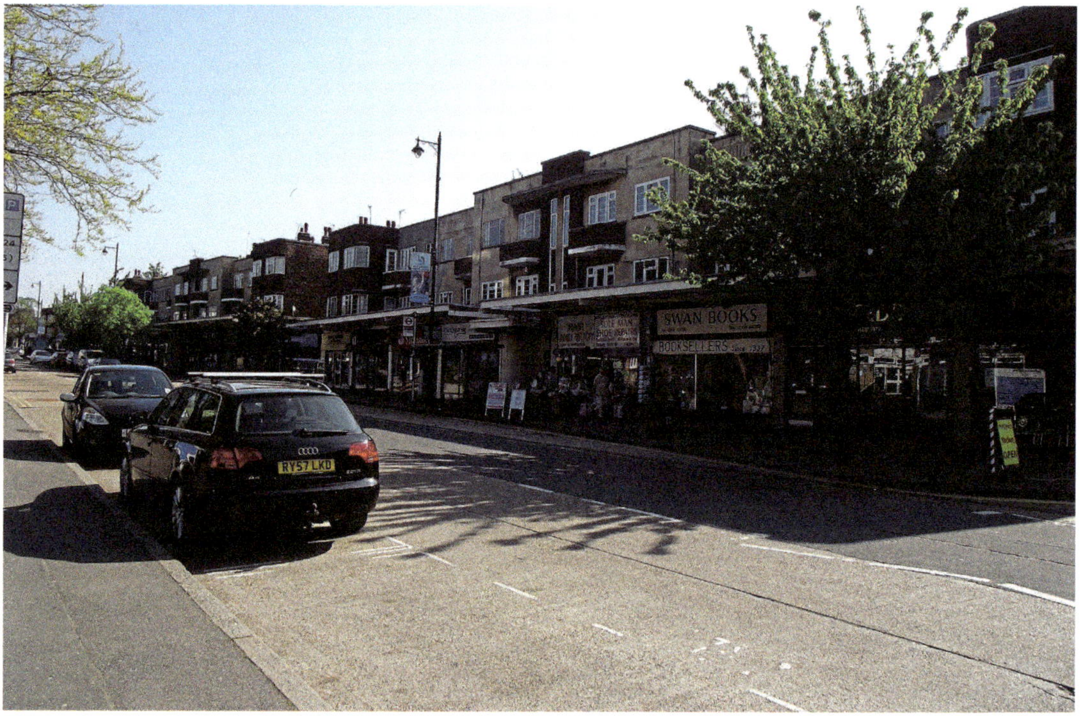

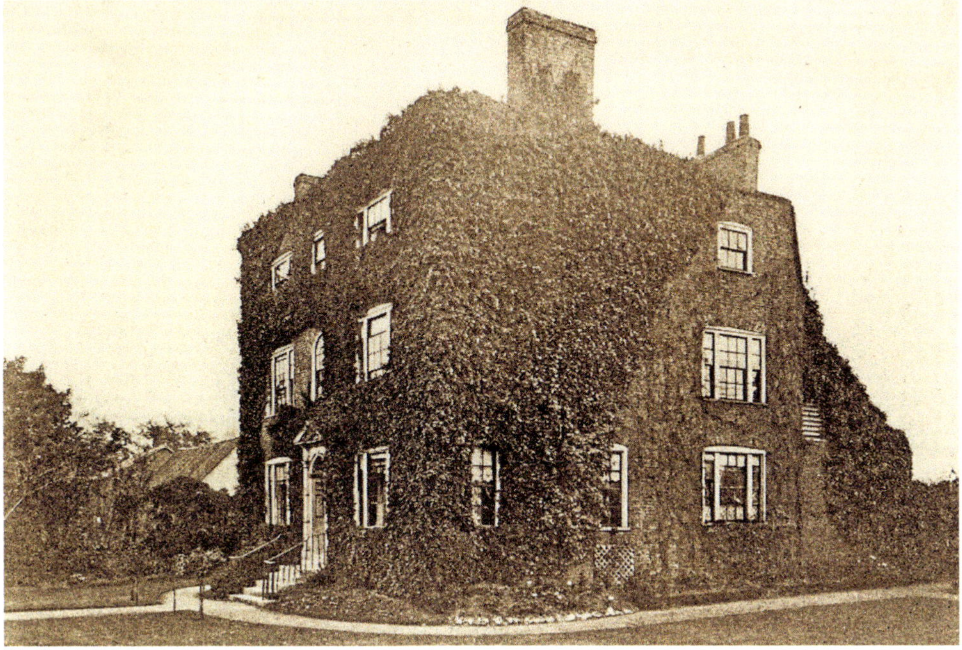

Hunts

Hunts was a farmhouse which dated from the early eighteenth century. It was once the home of James Noakes who built the windmill. The farmland covered the area where the Springfield Gardens estate now stands. The house stood to the left of Springfield Road where the shops now stand. The Springfield estate was the centre of national news in 1935 when the daughters of the American Consul in Naples fell to their death from an aircraft and were discovered there. It was later found that they committed suicide. (With thanks to John Drury)

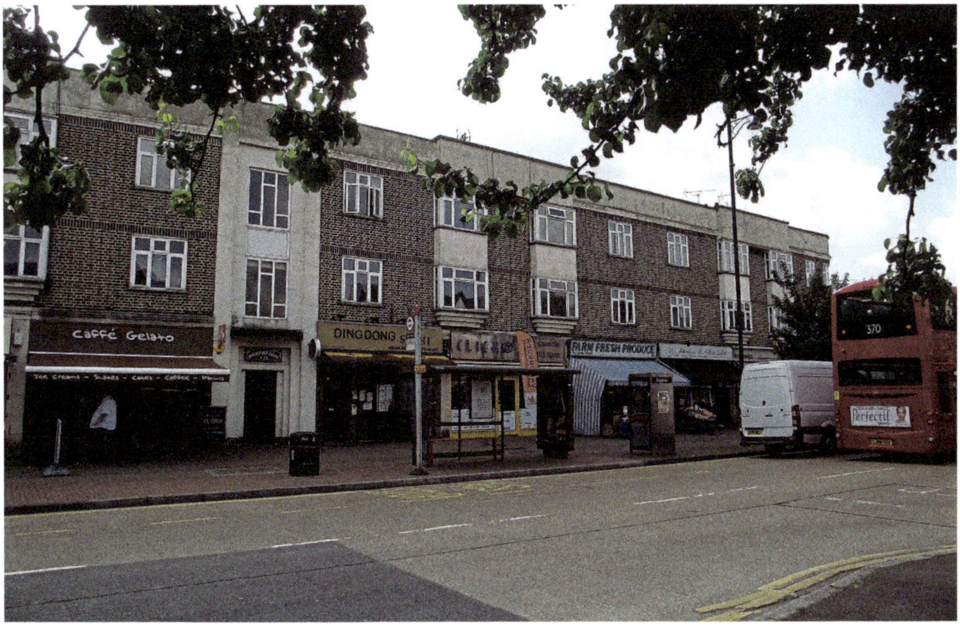

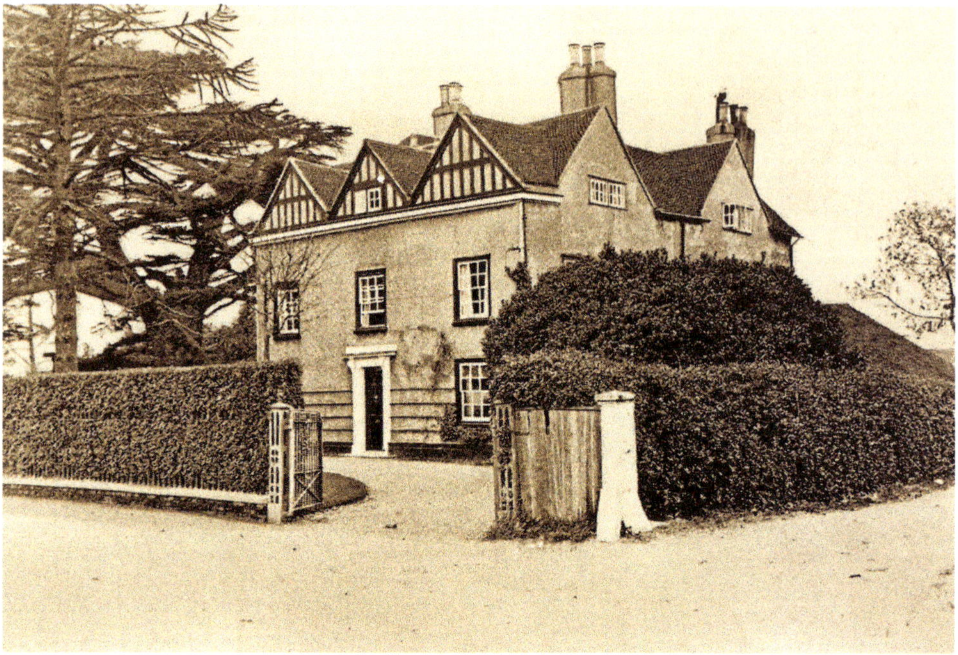

Hoppy Hall

There is some debate over the spelling of Hoppy Hall. Some spell it 'Hoppey' but I have it on good authority that the former name is the correct one. The house stood where the petrol station, car park and sorting office now stands in Corbets Tey Road. It dated from the early eighteenth century and, like other buildings in the area, was demolished in the mid-1930s. (With thanks to John Drury)

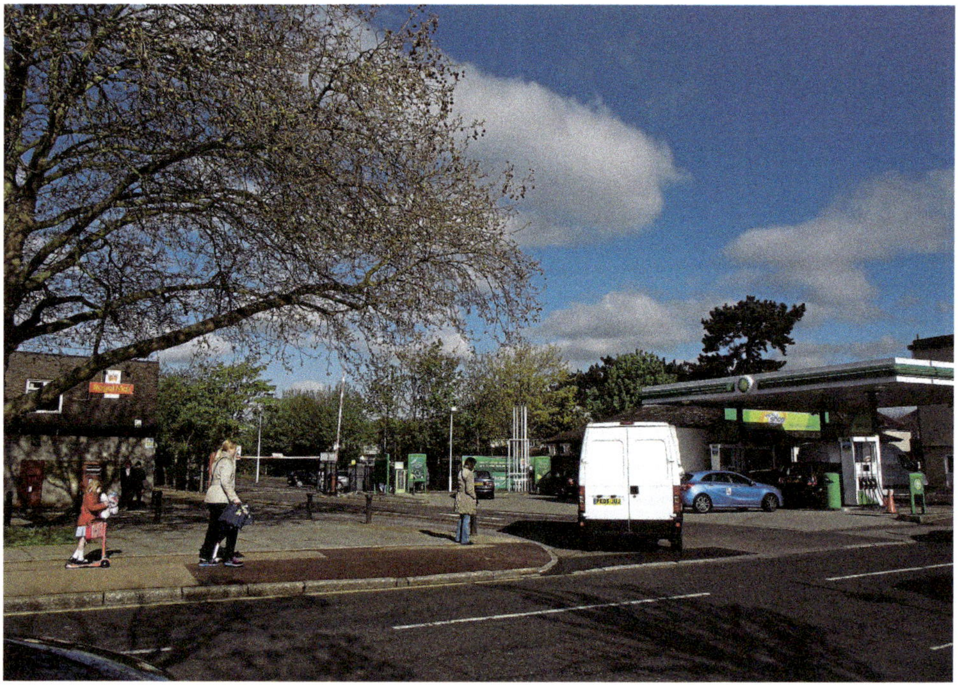

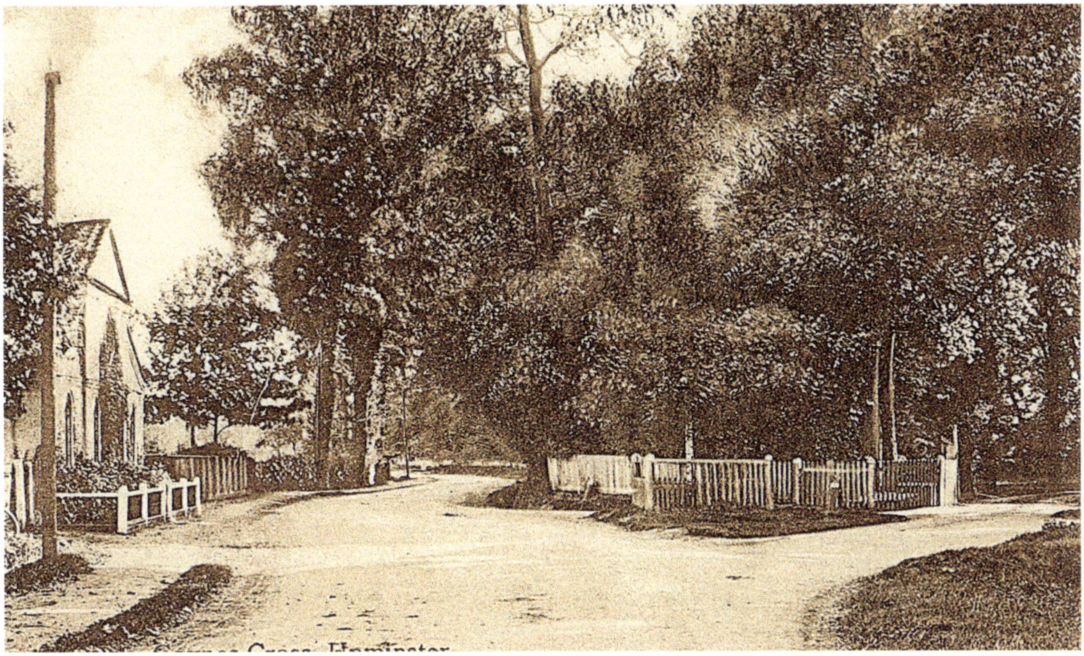

Gaynes Cross

The old building shown was a lodge or estate cottage for Great Gaynes Manor House that stood nearby. Little Gaynes Lane was the start of the land forming Gaynes Manor. The lane was once known as Hacton Lane as it led to Hacton House. Crime may seem a modern phenomenon, but in August 1933 it came to Corbets Tey when James Bateman, the father of the owner of a store and post office, which, according to *The Times*, was at Gaynes Cross, fought off three men who tried to rob the store. One of the men was armed with a gun. The old cottage still survives among the modern houses.

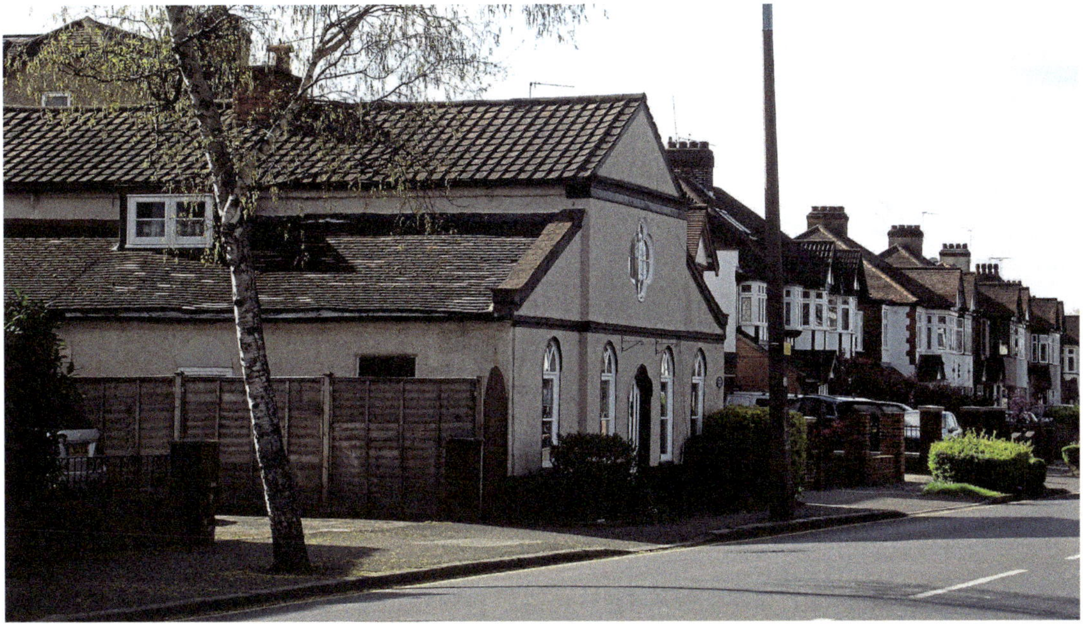

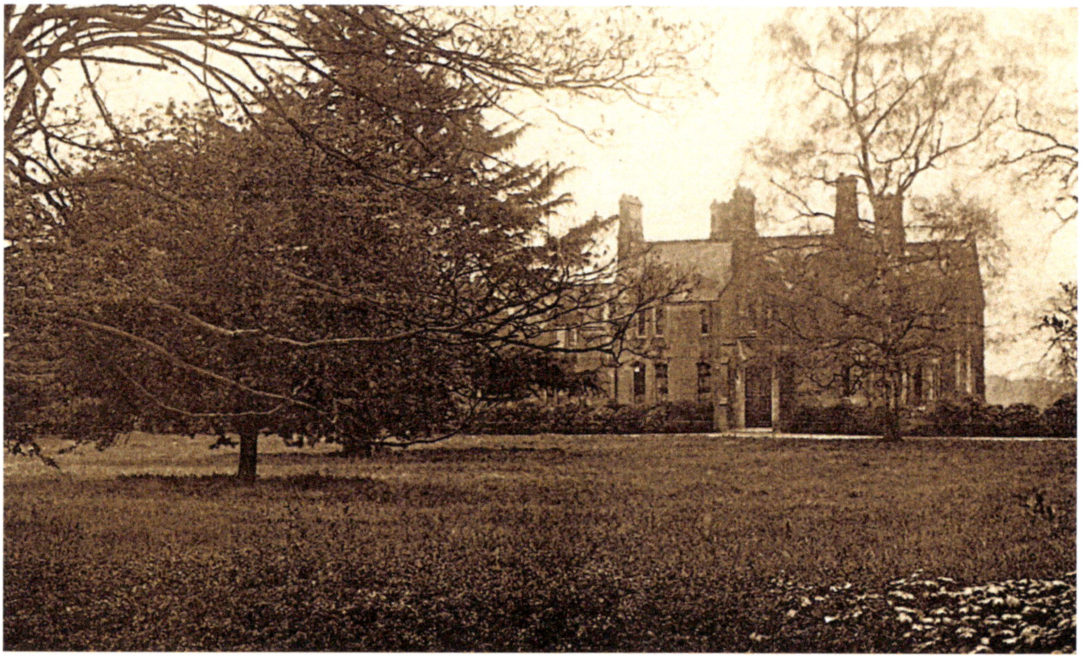

Gaynes

Travelling back in history, there had been house on the site of Gaynes for many years. It was bought and rebuilt in the late eighteenth century by Sir James Esdaile who also built many of the other large houses in the area. This house only lasted until 1820 when much of it was demolished and a new house was built by the reverend, John Clayton. This survived until the area was developed in the 1920s. The modern image shows a bridge that was built over the lake in the park that surrounded Gaynes. It now stands in what is known as Parklands and is Grade II listed. (With thanks to Swan Books)

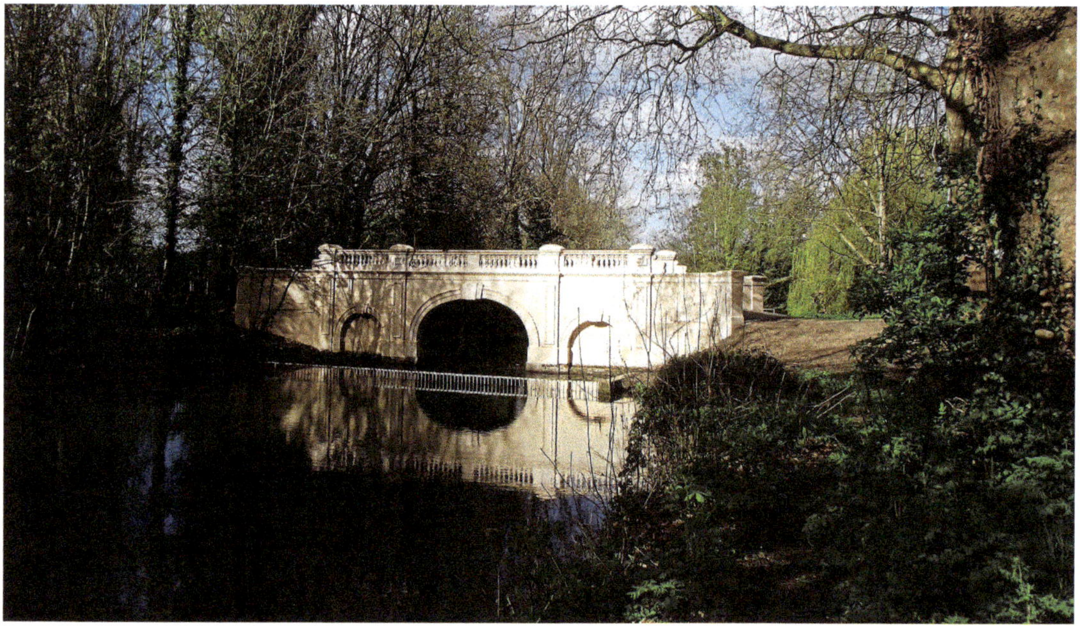

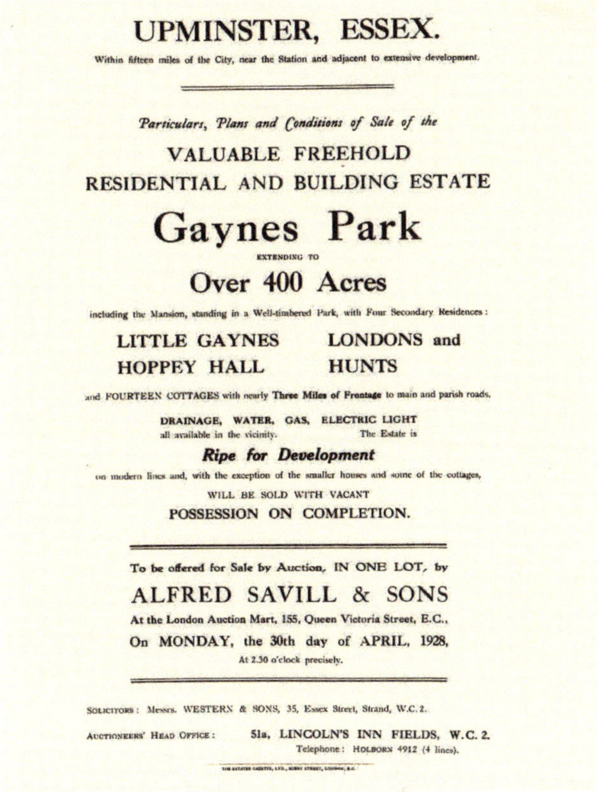

UPMINSTER, ESSEX.

Within fifteen miles of the City, near the Station and adjacent to extensive development.

Particulars, Plans and Conditions of Sale of the

VALUABLE FREEHOLD
RESIDENTIAL AND BUILDING ESTATE

Gaynes Park

EXTENDING TO

Over 400 Acres

including the Mansion, standing in a Well-timbered Park, with Four Secondary Residences:

LITTLE GAYNES LONDONS and
HOPPEY HALL HUNTS

and FOURTEEN COTTAGES with nearly **Three Miles of Frontage** to main and parish roads.

DRAINAGE, WATER, GAS, ELECTRIC LIGHT
all available in the vicinity. The Estate is

Ripe for Development

on modern lines and, with the exception of the smaller houses and some of the cottages,

WILL BE SOLD WITH VACANT
POSSESSION ON COMPLETION.

To be offered for Sale by Auction, IN ONE LOT, by

ALFRED SAVILL & SONS

At the London Auction Mart, 155, Queen Victoria Street, E.C.,

On MONDAY, the 30th day of APRIL, 1928,

At 2.30 o'clock precisely.

SOLICITORS: Messrs. WESTERN & SONS, 35, Essex Street, Strand, W.C. 2.

AUCTIONEERS' HEAD OFFICE: 51a, LINCOLN'S INN FIELDS, W.C. 2.
Telephone: HOLBORN 4912 (4 lines).

The Sale of Gaynes

The Gaynes estate went up for sale in the late 1930s along with some of the large houses still owned or previously owned by the estate which stood in the area, such as Hoppy Hall, Hunts and London's. Little Gaynes Lane, shown in the modern image, was the entrance to the estate.

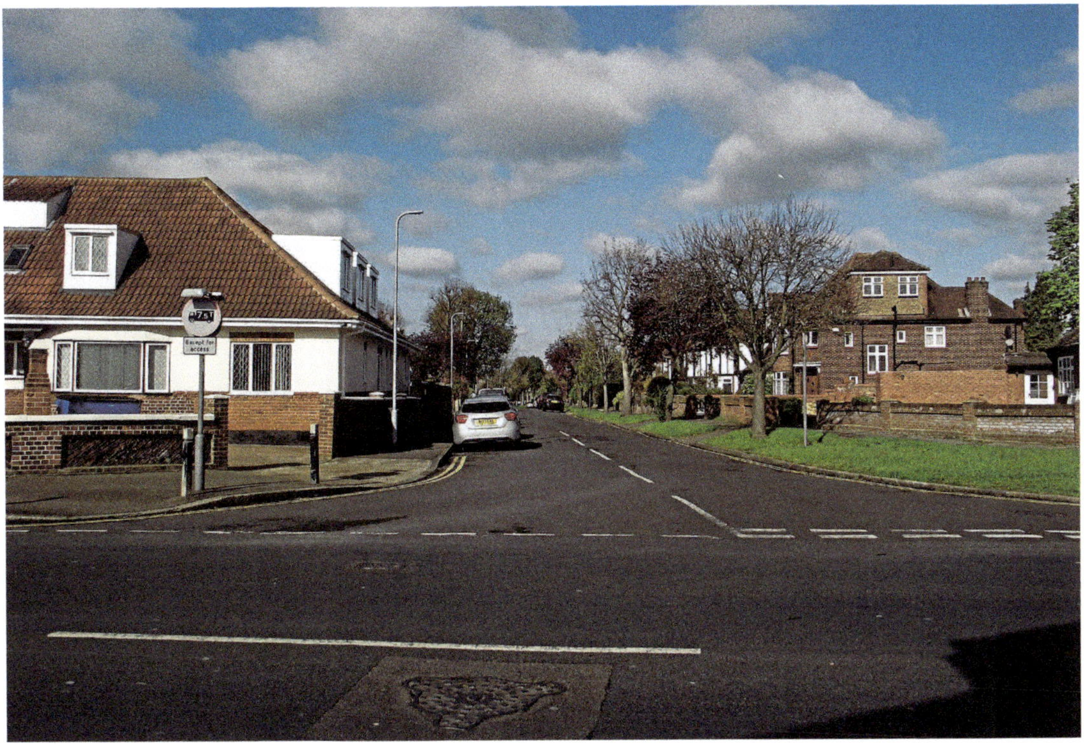

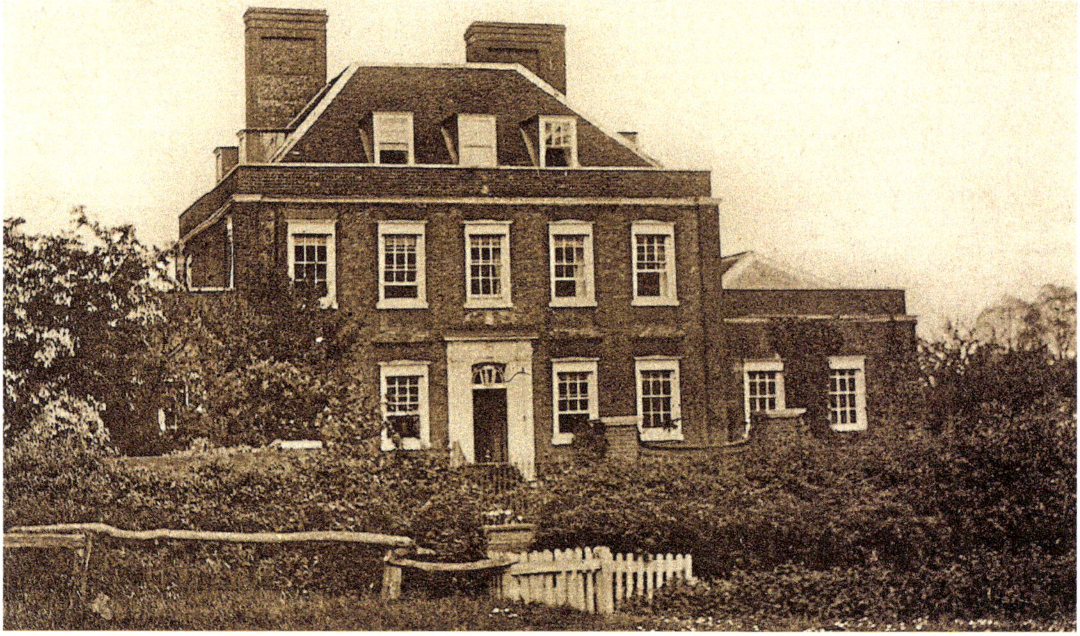

Fox Hall

Fox Hall was one of the large houses in Corbets Tey Road that has since vanished. It was originally known as Osbourne's (after its first inhabitants) when it was built in the early eighteenth century. It then became Fox Hunter's Hall before becoming Fox Hall. One of its residents was a man named Jamsetjee Gazdar. Gazdar was a barrister and was the first Indian to practice at the English Bar. He had chambers at Lincolns Inn and died at Fox Hall in 1922. The hall is remembered in the name Fox Hall Road, shown in the modern image. (With thanks to Havering Libraries Local Studies Dept)

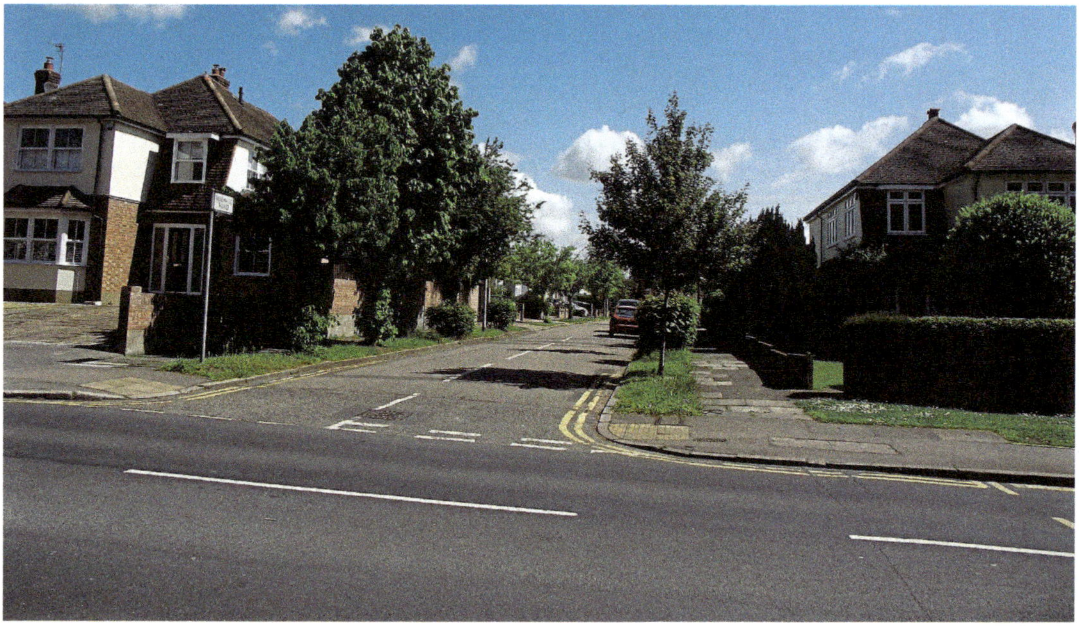

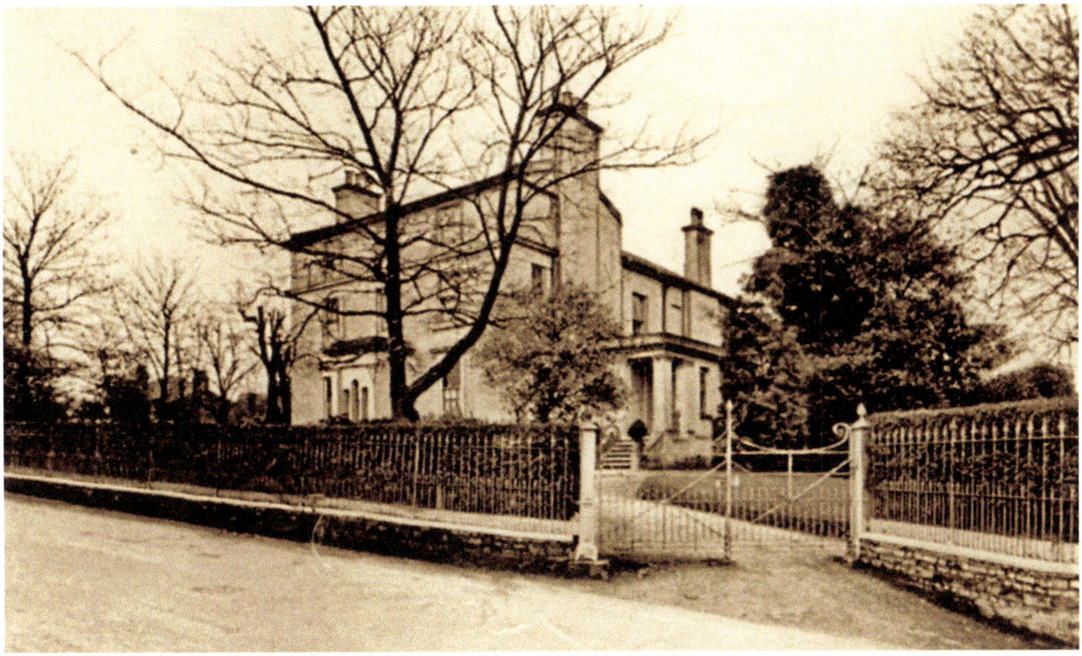

London's

London's was once part of a 50-acre farm. It was built in the late eighteenth century, as were many local houses by Sir James Esdaile, and was part of the Gaynes estate. It got its name from Dr London who lived there. It was sold in the early nineteenth century but some years later it was bought back by the owner of Gaynes, who at that time was H. Gilliiat. It is remembered in the name London's Close, which stands on the site. (With thanks to Havering Libraries Local Studies Dept)

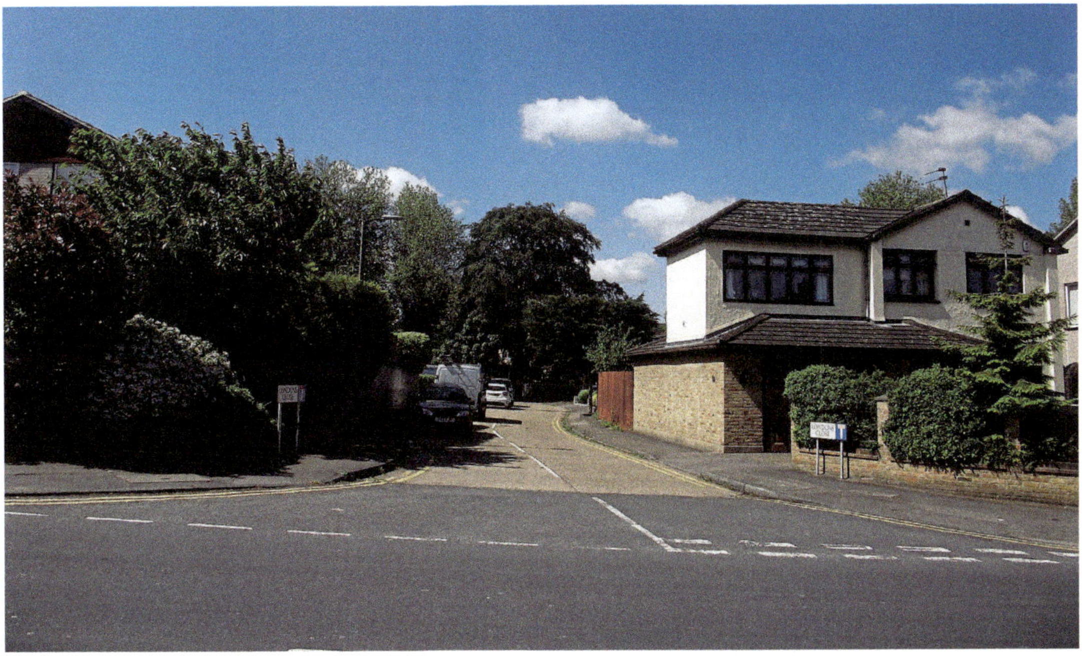

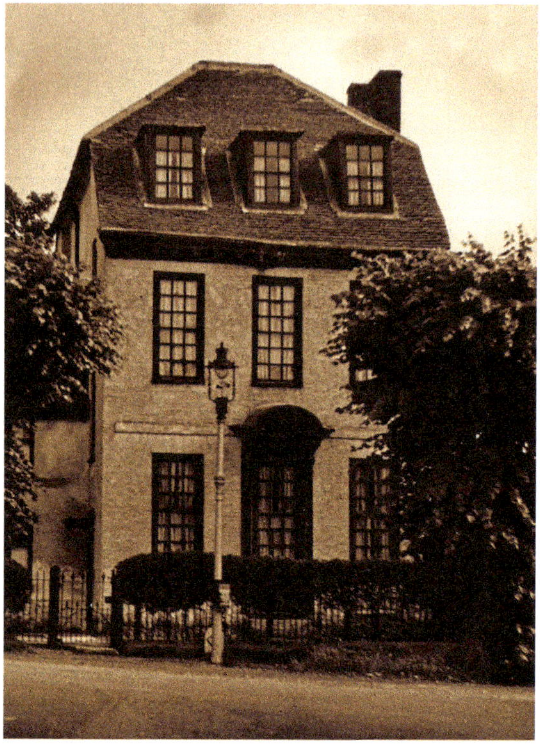

High House

High House, which stands in the village of Corbet's Tey, has no connections with the High House that also stood in Corbet's Tey Road, close to the centre of Upminster and opposite the Church of St Laurence. The name High House would seem to be self-explanatory as it is higher than the other old buildings in the village. It is around 300 years old and was once a farm. At the turn of the nineteenth century, it was used as a school. It has had a number of well-known local residents, such as Dr London and the widow Pontyz. It is now the site of High House Garden Centre. (With thanks to Havering Libraries Local Studies Dept)

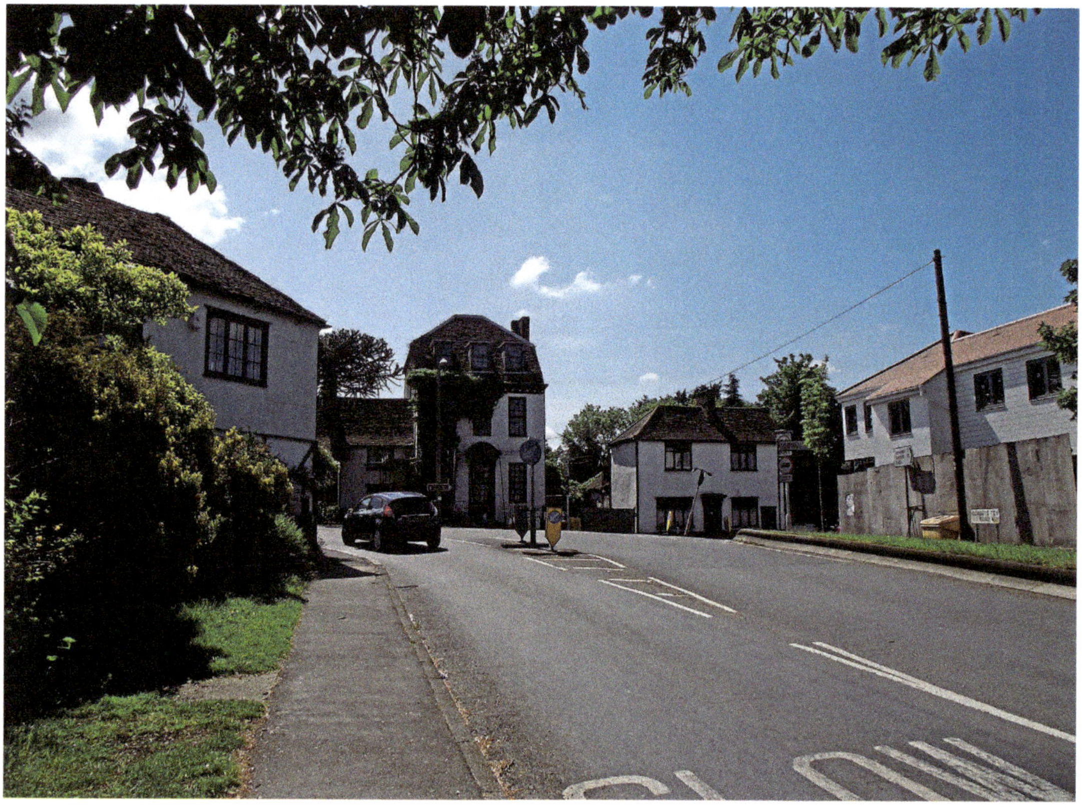

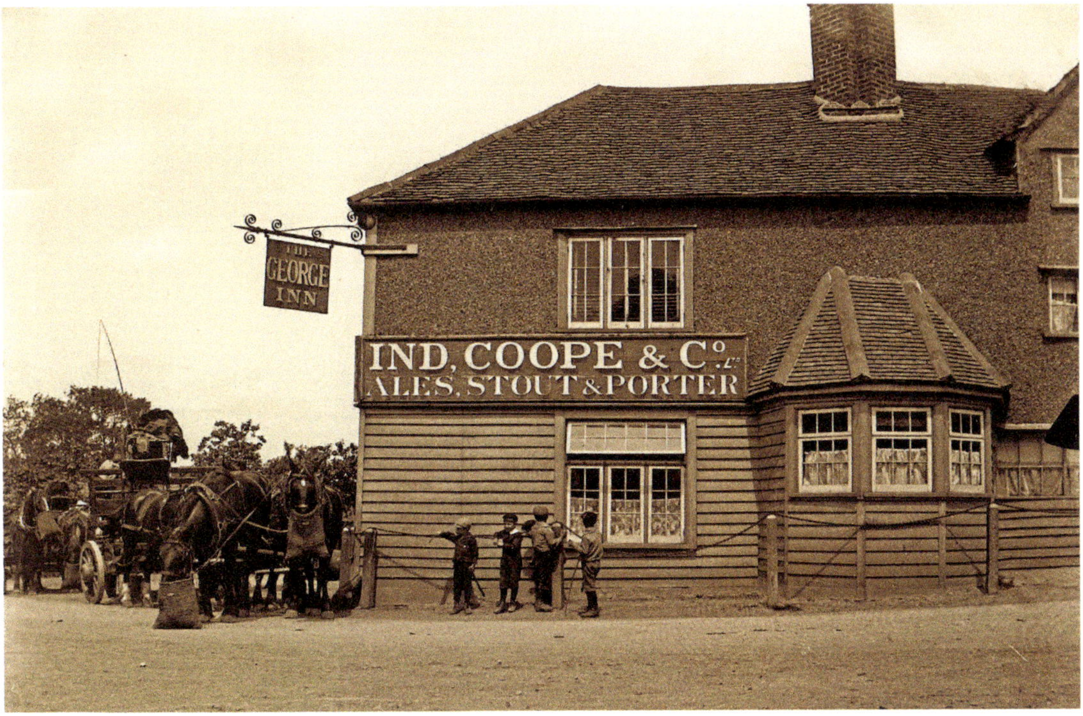

George Inn

The George Inn was once based in what is now known as the Old Cottage. The building is around 400 years old and, as well as being known as the George, it was also, for a time, the George and Dragon. It closed for business at the turn of the twentieth century when the owners, Ind Coope & Co., transferred the licence to Romford. The Old Cottage still stands on the corner where Corbets Tey Road meets Ockendon Road. (With thanks to Havering Libraries Local Studies Dept)

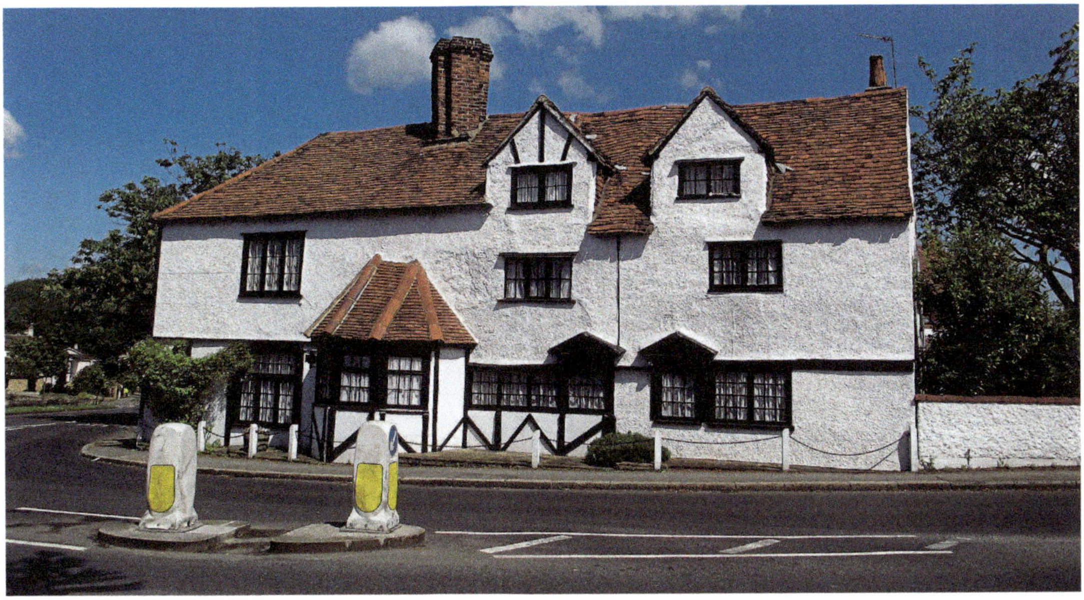

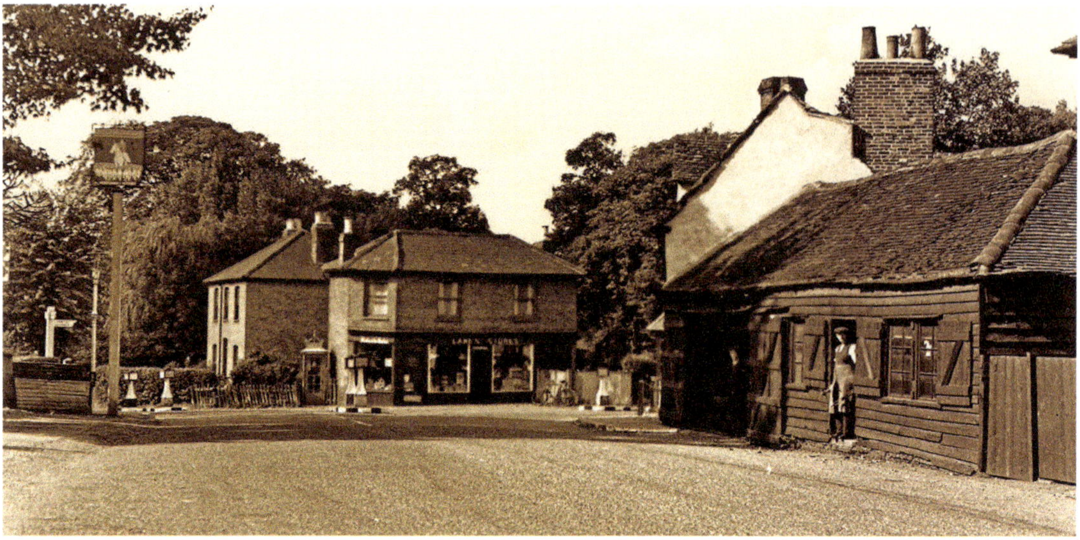

The Old Forge

It was difficult to place the site of the old forge from the old image but it seems to have stood between two old cottages that have survived in the modern times. The one on the left of the site is shown in the modern image and used to be the George Inn from the previous image. The forge was still in operation, working on local farm horses up until the Second World War.

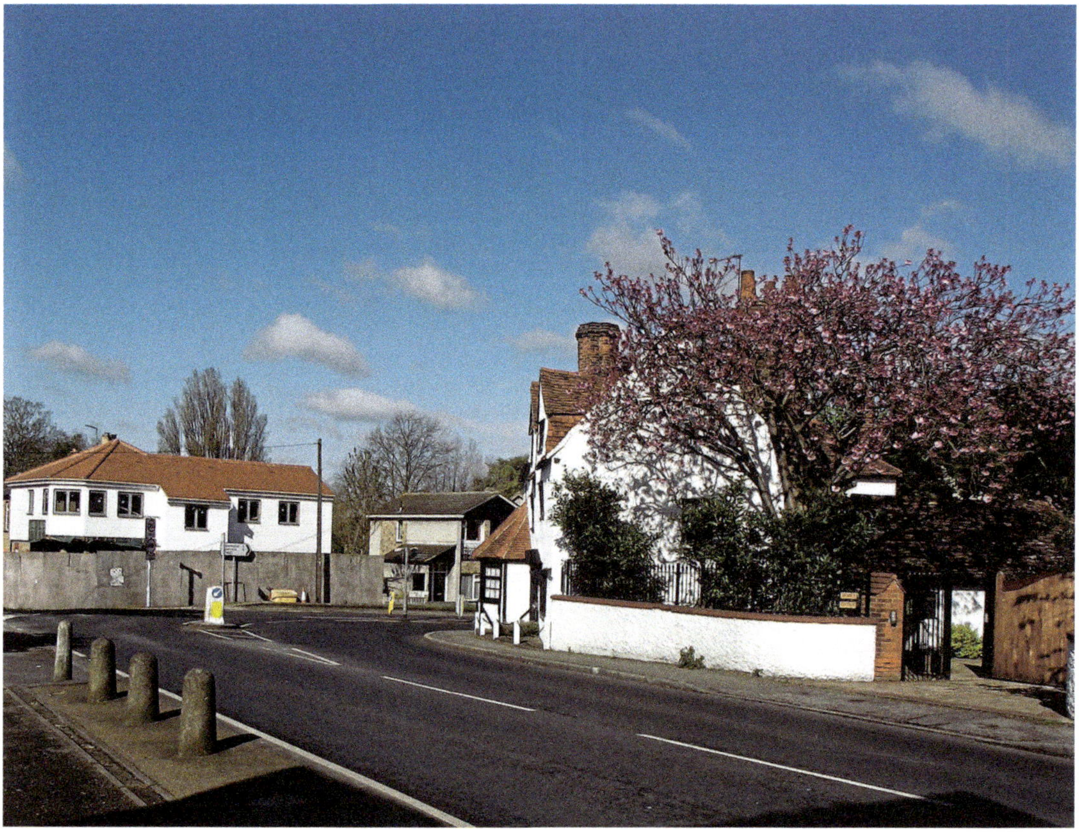

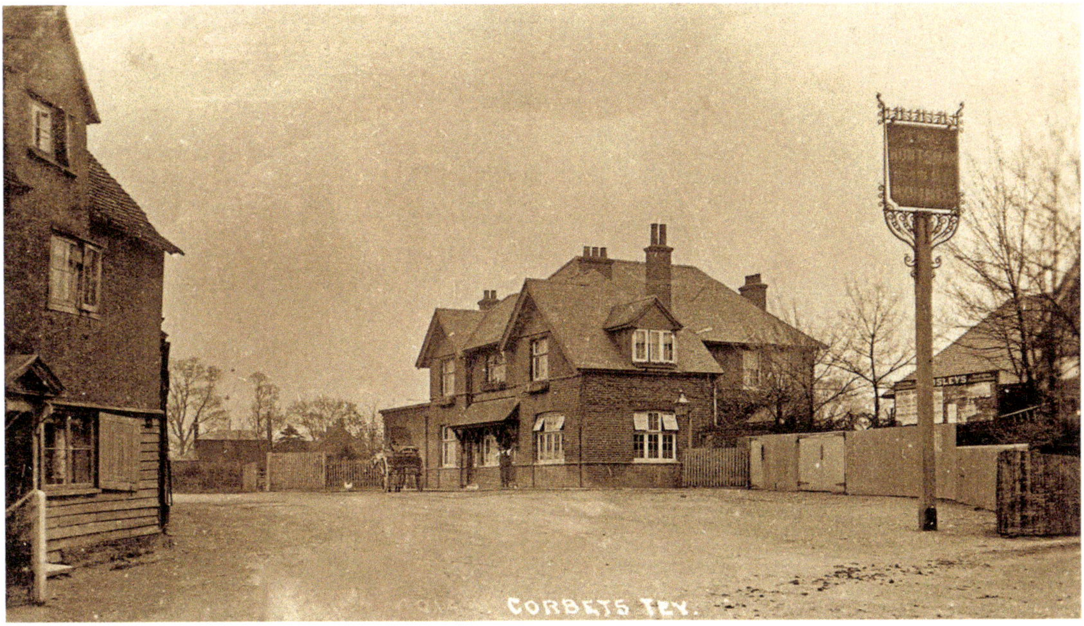

Huntsman and Hounds

The present building stands on the site of a former inn of the same name. This was demolished in 1895 and the new one built. The licensee at this time was Frank Rowe, who also was the landlord at the White Hart Hacton before this. The business is often used by those returning from services at the nearby crematorium.

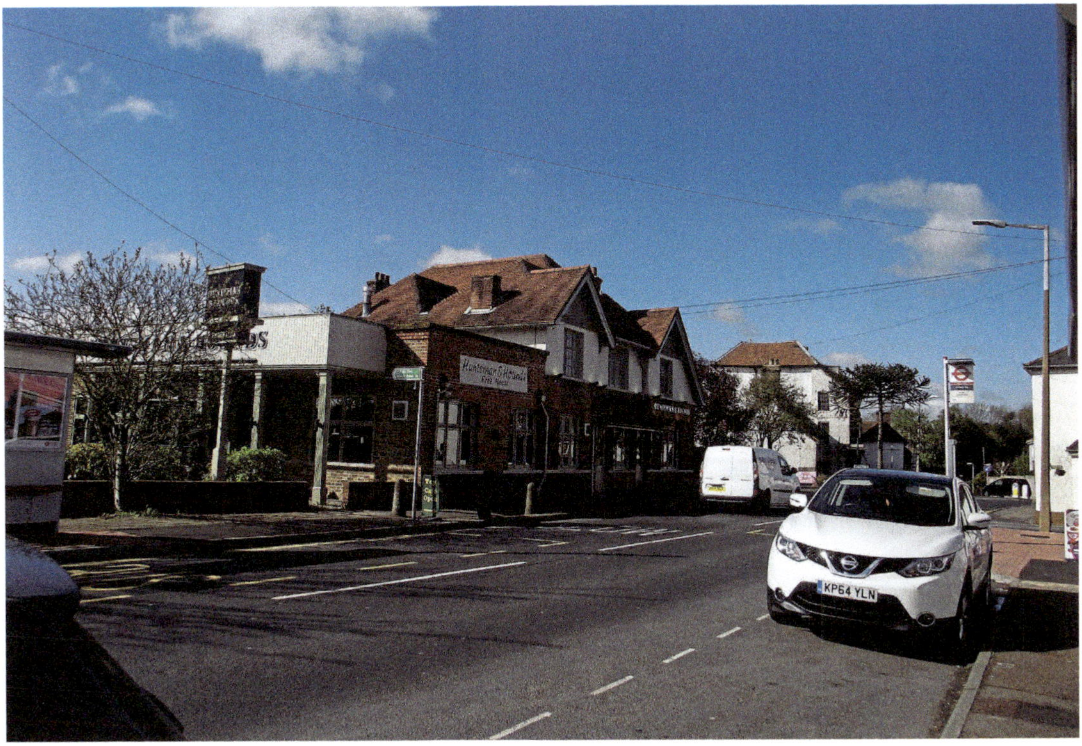

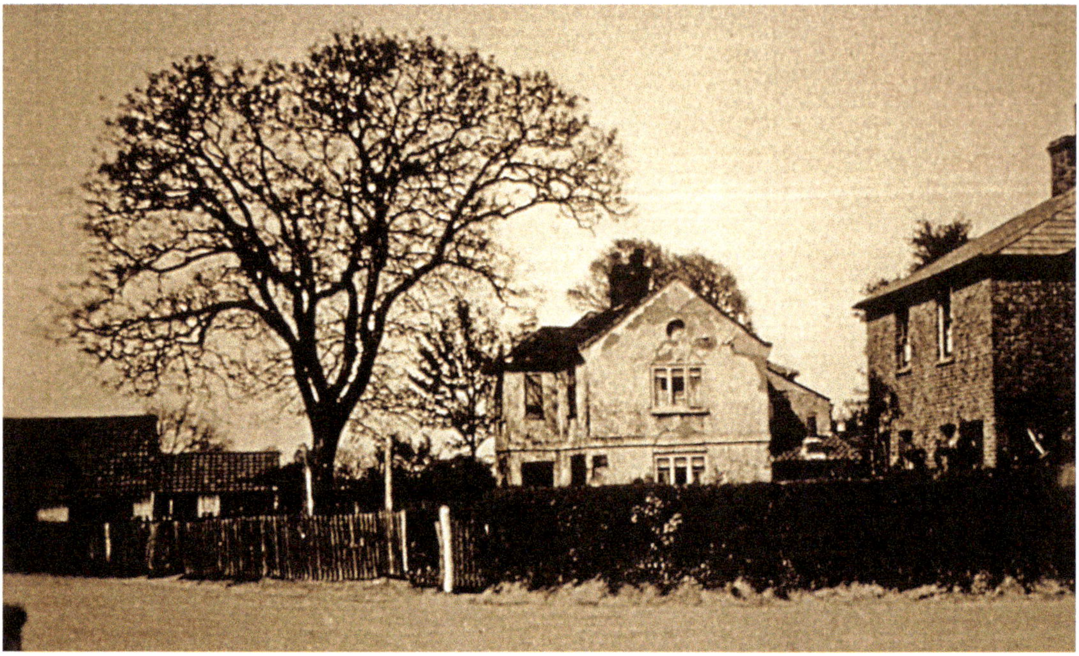

Cabbage Corner

I could not find out anything about Cabbage Corner (shown on the old image) except that it was in Ockendon Road. It could have been any of the corners in the road and I have matched it with a modern view of the corner with Sunning's Lane. As the area was known for market garden-type crops, it could have been the site as there are buildings there that are not as numerous further along Ockendon Road. I later had this confirmed by someone who recognised the old cottages. (With thanks to Havering Libraries Local Studies Dept)

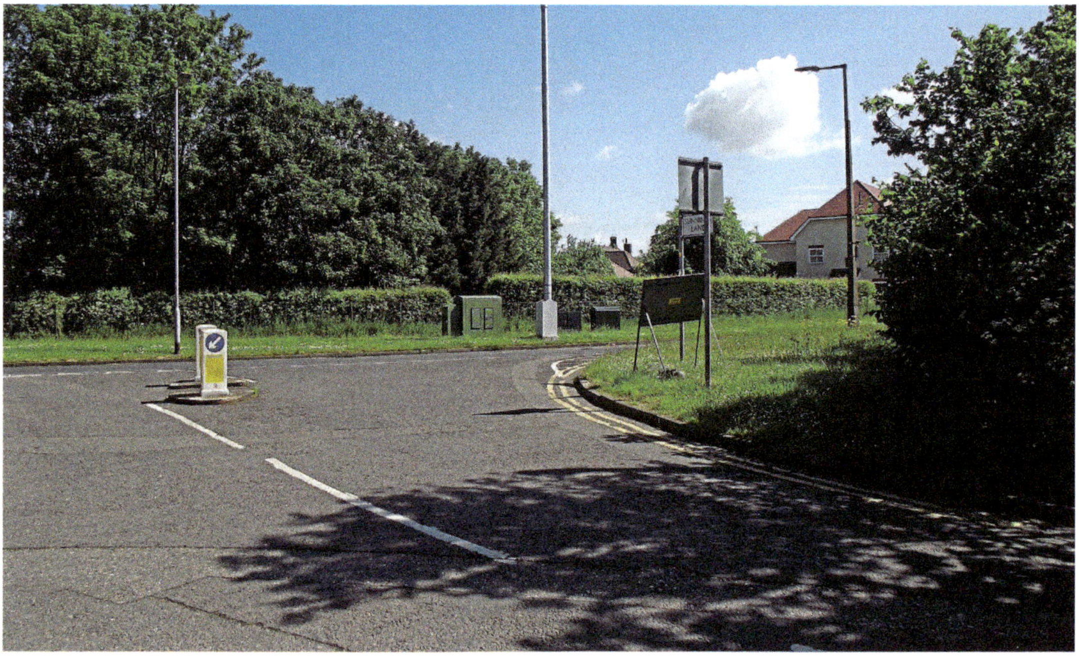

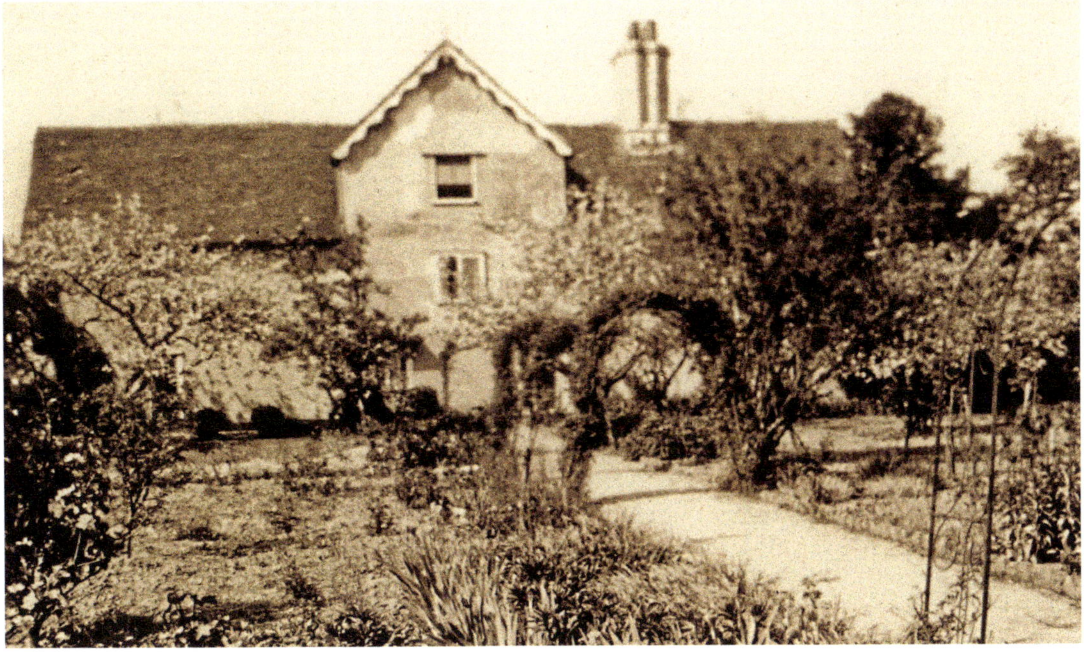

Great Sunning's

Great Sunning's and Little Sunning's, better known as Sullens Farm, are perhaps the oldest houses still standing in Upminster. Much of the old interior fittings of Great Sunning's, which may date back to the 1600s, have been removed. The house was old enough for the owner once to have paid the king so many wolves per year, as a way to rid the land of the animals – it is hard to imagine wolves roaming the countryside of Upminster today. The exterior of the building seems to have changed little. (With thanks to Havering Libraries Local Studies Dept)

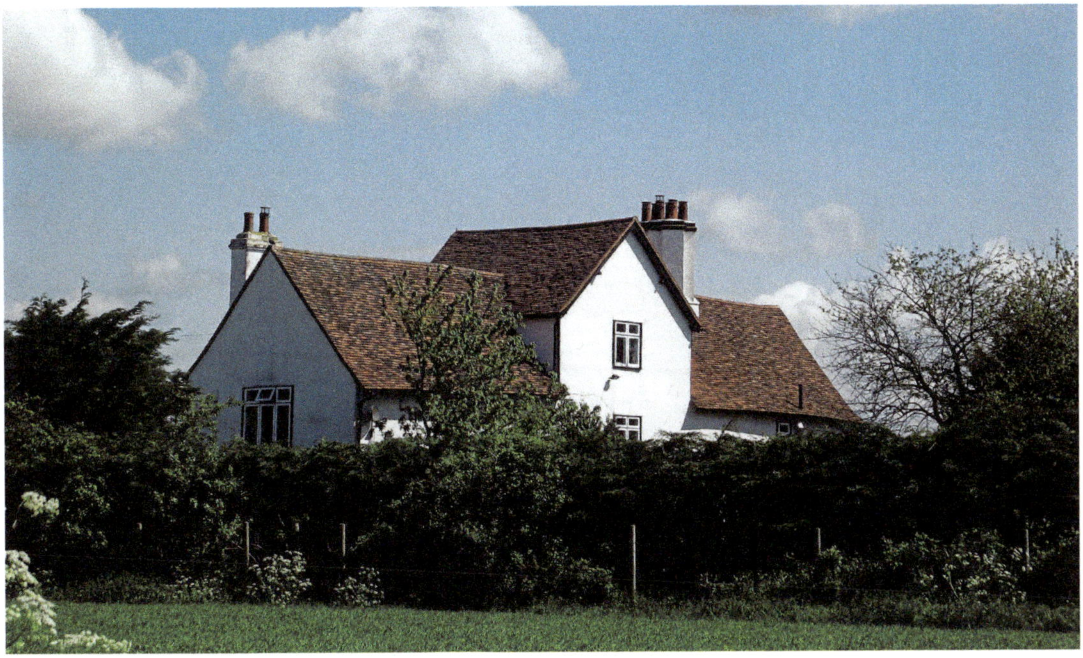

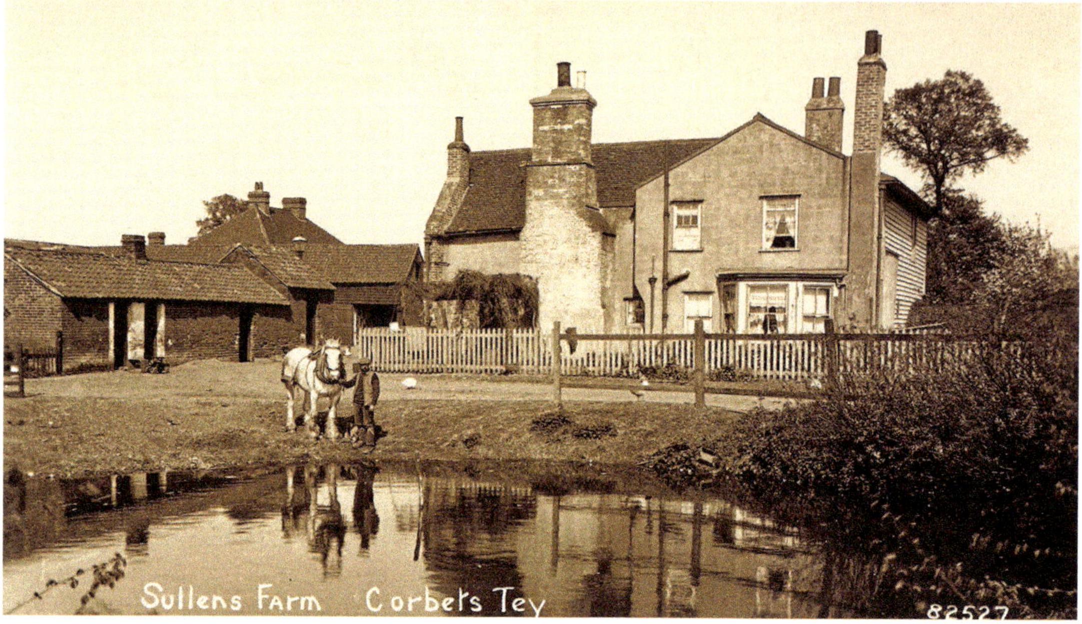

Sullens Farm

Much of the land around Corbets Tey was once farmland and was used for market garden crops. The old image shows a horse being watered at the pond – it was horses that did much of the work on farms. Sullens was one that moved with the times and, just after the First World War, they had a Foden steam tractor. The farm used to stand in what was once known as Green Lanes but this is now Sunning's Lane, once an important route to North Ockendon and now a quiet country lane with houses on one side overlooking farm fields.

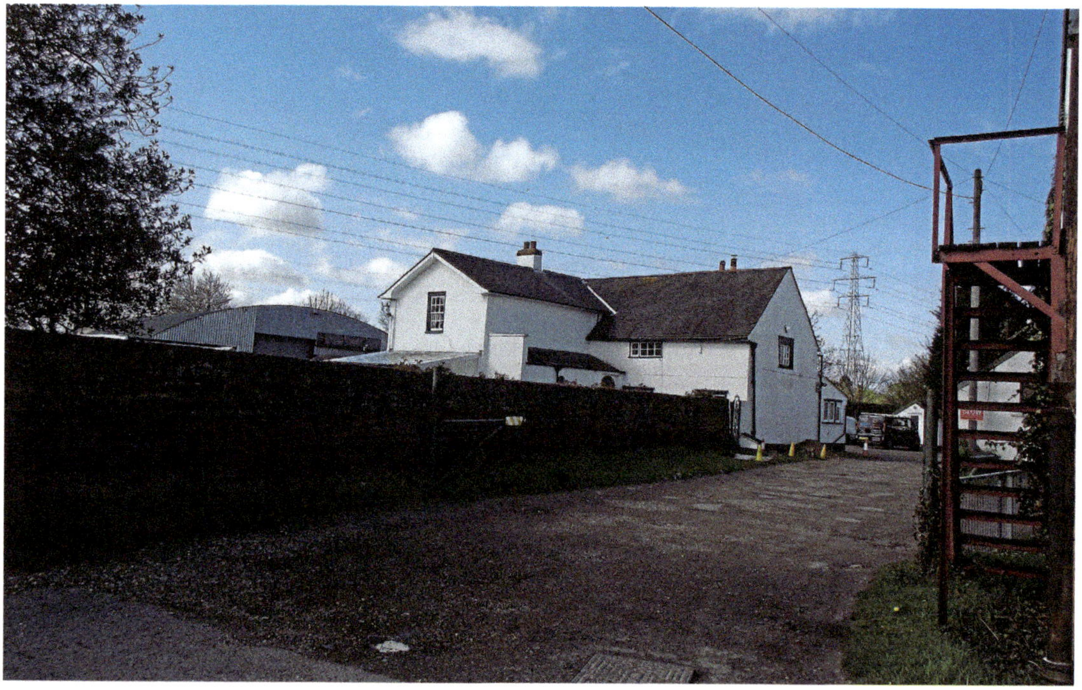

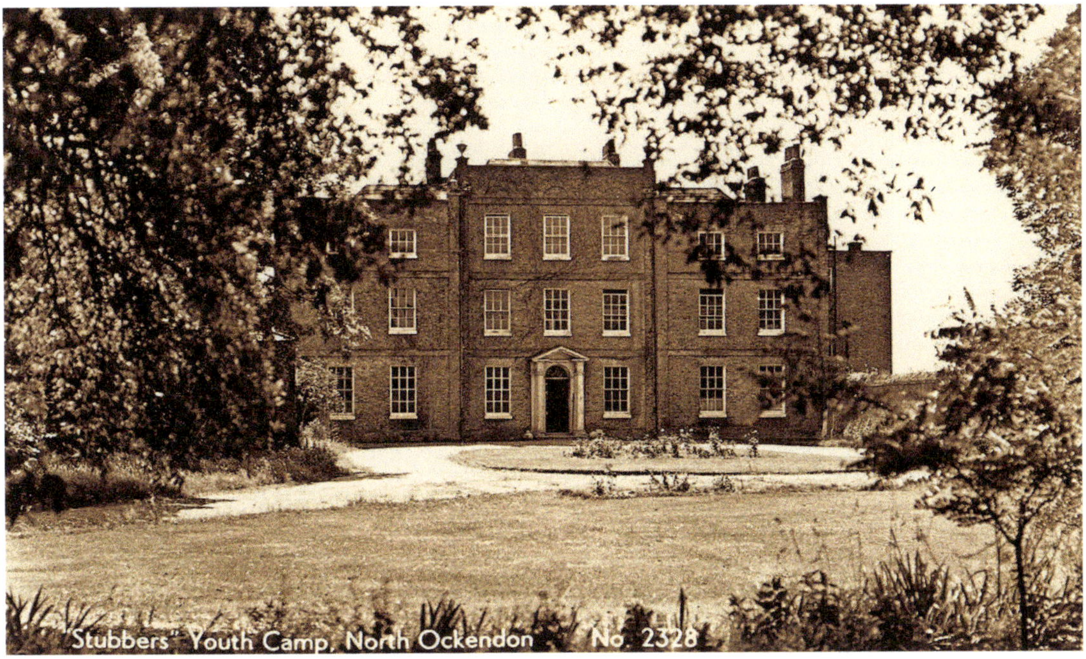

Stubbers

Stubbers is situated close to the boundary between Corbets Tey and North Ockendon. The building dated back to the fifteenth century. The Russell family owned the house for much of its history. It was sold to the Essex Education Committee in 1947 for use as a youth centre. The house was demolished in 1960 and the land is now used as an outdoor pursuits centre, as can be seen from the large number of tents in the modern image.

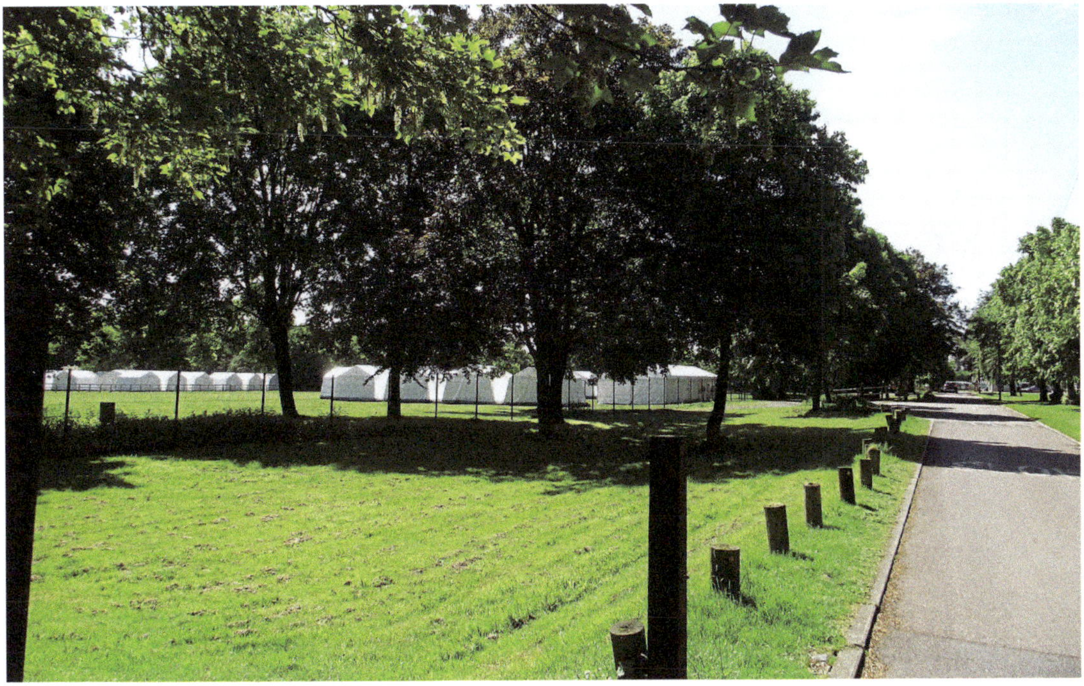

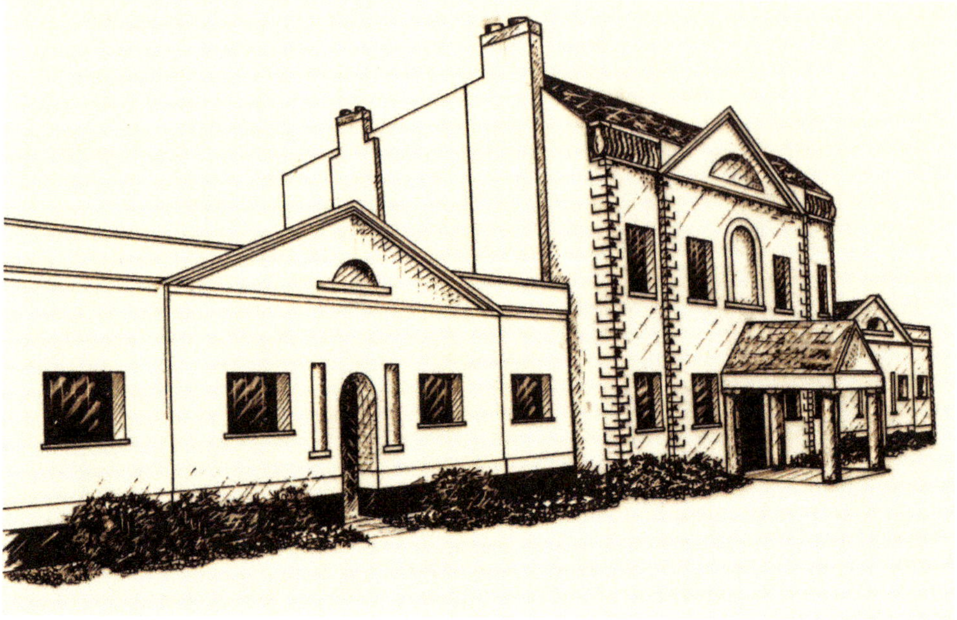

Hacton House

Hacton House stands close to the junction of Little Gaynes Lane and Hacton Lane. It dates from around 1770, was built by William Braund and was one of the major houses in Upminster at the time. There was some dispute between Braund and Sir James Esdaile, who owned Gaynes, over a fence he put up on land in front of the house. There have been a number of alterations to the house that have altered its appearance. The building is now flats but is set back off the road so as to be out of sight and I suspect the presence of such a large house will come as a surprise to many local residents. (With thanks to John Drury)

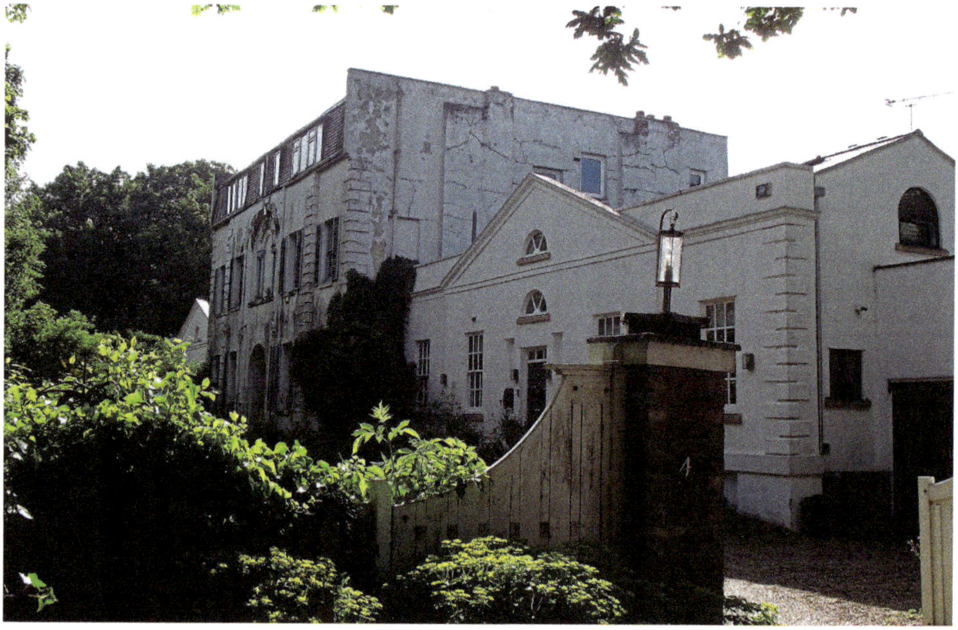

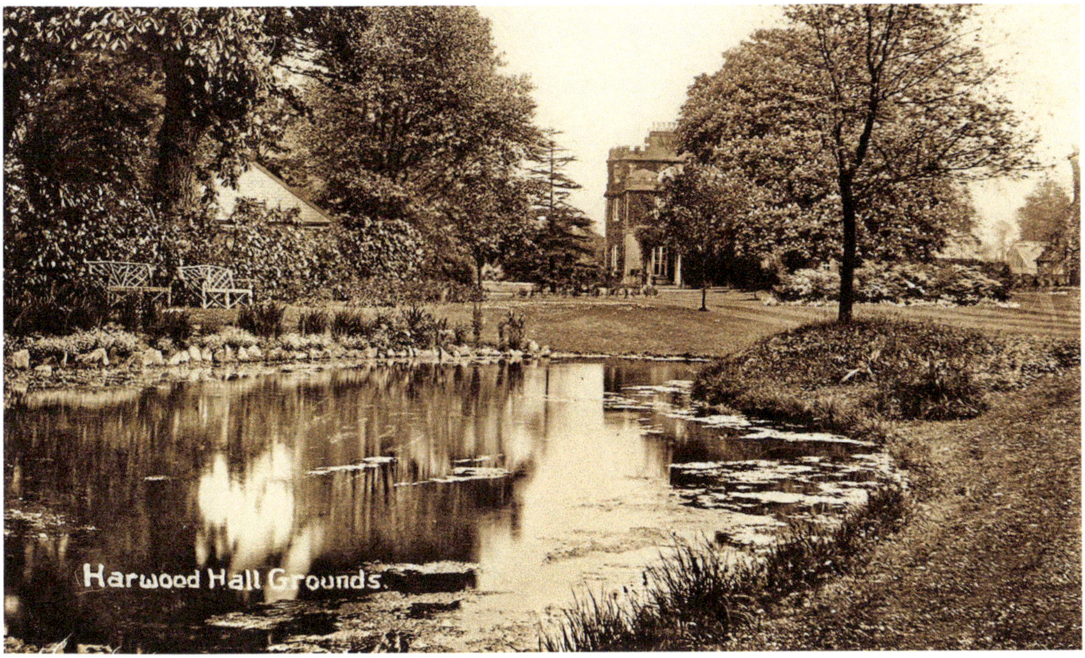

Harwood Hall I

Harwood Hall was built by Sir James Esdaile in 1782. It was once the home of a well-known local figure and the house obviously had an effect on him. Henry Holmes lived at Harwood Hall until the late nineteenth century. He then bought part of the Langton's estate in Hornchurch from his father-in-law John Waggener. He then built Grey Towers House, which was very similar in design to his previous home. Holmes had raised a battery of local volunteer artillery and was later Deputy Lieutenant of Essex. He was known as 'the Colonel' and although he died before the First World War, his home became the base of the Sportsman's Battalion when the war began.

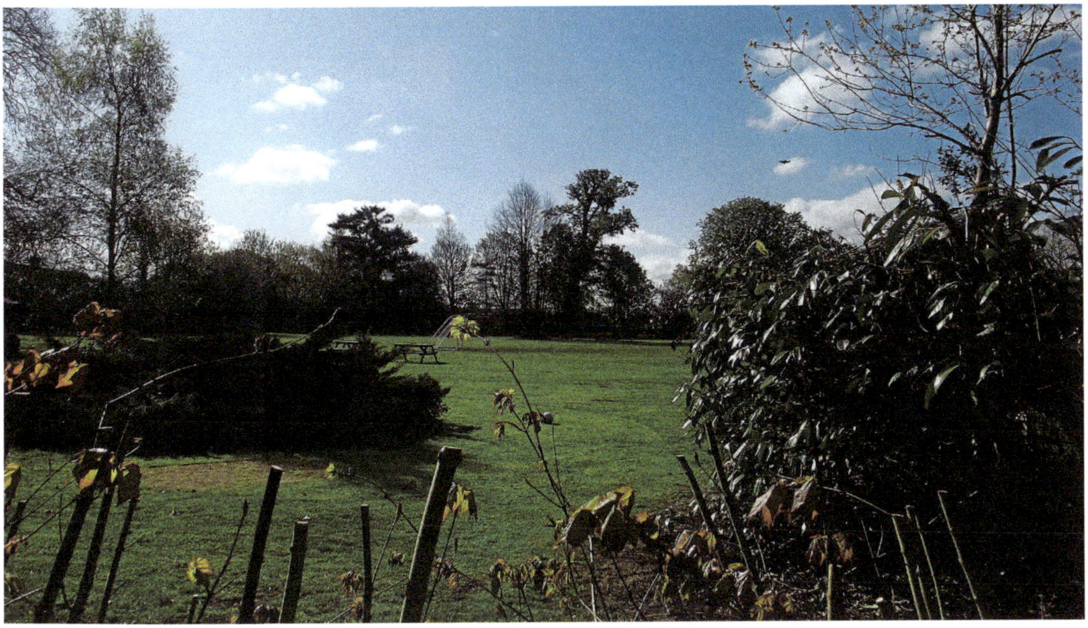

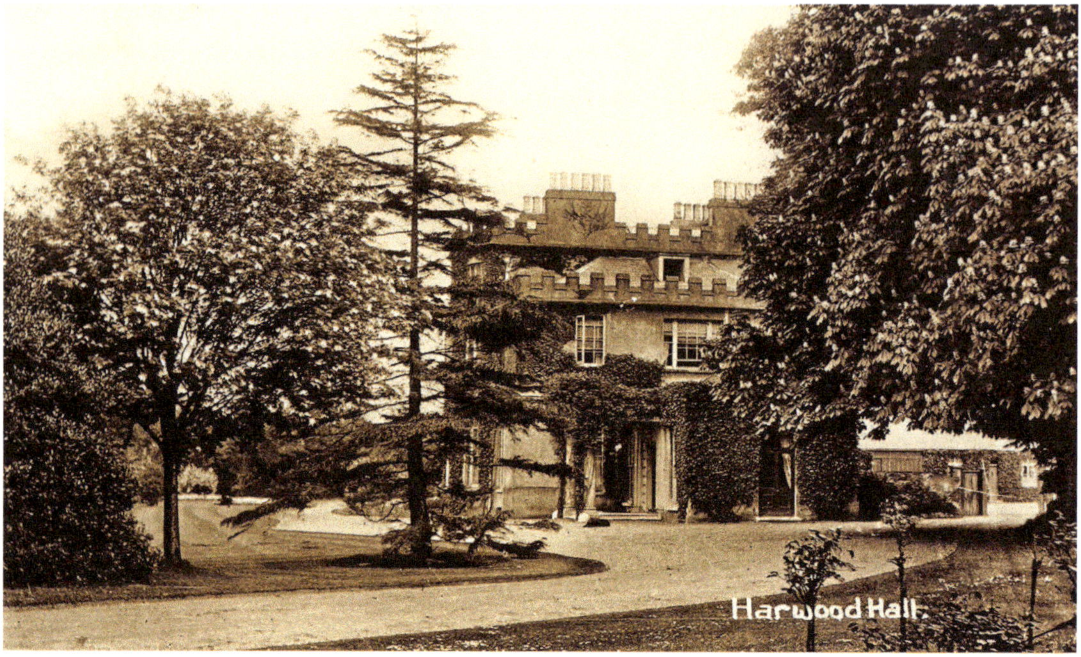

Harwood Hall II

The hall was advertised for auction in the *The Times* in September 1924. It was described as suitable for a city gentleman. The hall is still standing and is now a Montessori school.

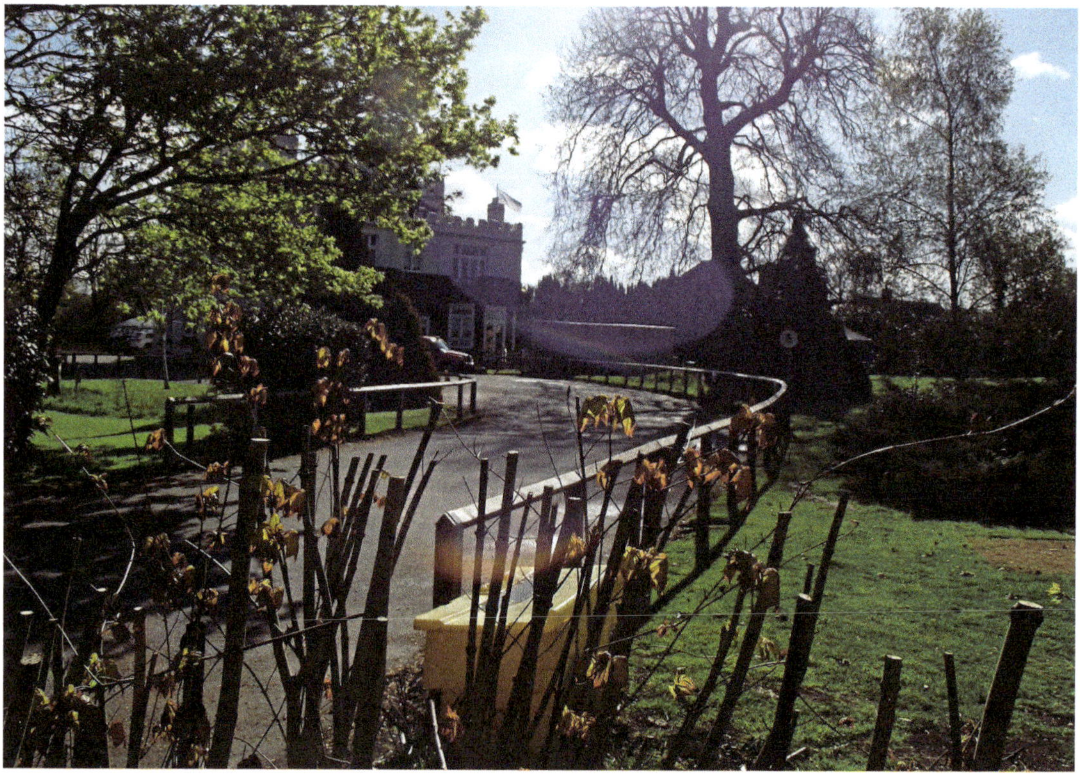